The Oxford Russian
Grammar and Verbs

Terence Wade

Oxford   New York
Oxford University Press
2002

OXFORD
UNIVERSITY PRESS

Great Clarendon Street, Oxford OX2 6DP

Oxford University Press is a department of the University of Oxford.
It furthers the University's objective of excellence in research, scholarship,
and education by publishing worldwide in

Oxford New York

Auckland Bangkok Buenos Aires Cape Town Chennai Dar es Salaam Delhi
Hong Kong Istanbul Karachi Kolkata Kuala Lumpur Madrid Melbourne Mexico City
Mumbai Nairobi São Paulo Shanghai Singapore Taipei Tokyo Toronto

and an associated company in Berlin

Oxford is a registered trade mark of Oxford University Press
in the UK and in certain other countries

Published in the United States
by Oxford University Press Inc., New York

British Library Cataloguing in Publication Data

Data available

Library of Congress Cataloging in Publication Data

Data available

ISBN 0-19-860380-0

10 9 8 7 6 5 4 3 2 1

Typeset in Slimbach and Trade Gothic
by Read Setter
Printed in Great Britain by
Clays Ltd, Bungay, Suffolk

Contents

Preface

The *Oxford Russian Grammar and Verbs* is part of a series of Oxford grammars of modern languages. It is designed for beginners and intermediate level learners at school or university as well as the adult studying the language on his/her own or at evening classes. It contains everything that is essential up to A level standard.

The text is divided into chapters dealing with the individual parts of speech, with particular emphasis given to the verb. There are also chapters on word order and punctuation. A separate glossary explains the grammatical terms used in the book and two indexes allow the user to look up individual points of grammar and individual Russian words.

The explanatory style of the book has been kept as simple as possible and numerous examples illustrate points of grammar as they arise. The design and layout of the text is arranged predominantly in single- and double-page spreads to aid ease of use. The verb list and the glossary of grammatical terms have a grey tint to the outside edge of the pages to enable quick reference.

Terence Wade

Acknowledgements

The author would like to thank in particular Albina Ozieva who gave advice on Russian usage and the Russian examples, and Dr Della Thompson of OUP who oversaw the project and made many useful and helpful suggestions. Thanks are also due to Dr Richard Ingham, Series Adviser, for his valuable comments on the text.

Proprietary terms

List of abbreviations

acc.	accusative
dat.	dative
fem.	feminine
gen.	genitive
impf.	imperfective
instr.	instrumental
intrans.	intransitive
masc.	masculine
MD	multidirectional
nom.	nominative
pf.	perfective
prep.	prepositional
trans.	transitive
UD	unidirectional

The noun

A noun names a person, animal, thing, natural phenomenon, quality, substance, fact, event, abstract notion, etc.:

ма́льчик boy
соба́ка dog
стул chair
доброта́ kindness

I Gender (masculine, feminine, or neuter)

(a) Nouns that denote male persons or animals are masculine:

брат brother
мужчи́на man
бара́н ram

(b) Those that denote female persons or animals are feminine:

сестра́ sister
мать mother
тигри́ца tigress

(c) The gender of nouns that denote things, phenomena, qualities, etc. depends on the ending of the noun.

Masculine nouns

(a) All nouns ending in a **consonant** or **-й** are masculine, as are some ending in a **soft sign** (**ь**):

заво́д factory
музе́й museum
дождь rain

(b) Masculine nouns ending in a soft sign include 'natural' masculines, animate and inanimate agent nouns in **-тель**, the names of months ending in a soft sign, and others whose gender has to be learnt individually:

па́рень lad   ию́ль July
писа́тель writer   слова́рь dictionary
дви́гатель engine   день day

Feminine nouns

All nouns ending in **-а/-я** are feminine (except for 'natural' masculines and neuter nouns in **-мя**), as are nouns in **-ия**:

кни́га book
бу́ря storm
ста́нция station

Also, very many **nouns ending in a soft sign**, including:
nouns that denote **females**;

nouns in **-жь, -чь, -шь, -щь, -знь**;

nouns in **-сть** (except **гость** 'guest' and **тесть** 'father-in-law');

nouns derived from adjectives and verbs:

мать mother   рожь rye
ночь night   мышь mouse
вещь thing   жизнь life
честь honour   зе́лень greenery
за́пись recording

There are also many others whose gender has to be learnt individually.

Neuter nouns

Most nouns ending in **-o** or **-e** and all nouns in **-ие, -ье, -ьё**, or **-мя** are neuter:

слово   word
море   sea
здание   building
счастье   happiness
ружьё   shot-gun
время   time

Common gender nouns in -a/-я

These nouns are masculine or feminine, depending on the sex of the person involved:

коллега   colleague (masculine or feminine)

Indeclinable names of **animals** are also of common gender:

кенгуру   kangaroo
шимпанзе   chimpanzee

The names of many **professions** are grammatically masculine, but take a feminine short-form adjective or past tense when the practitioner is a woman: **Врач довольна. Врач писала** 'The (female) doctor is pleased. The (female) doctor was writing'.

Indeclinable foreign nouns

Indeclinable foreign nouns (loanwords) end in **-ао, -ау, -е, -и, -о, -оа, -у, -уа, -ю**, or **-э** and are mainly neuter (an exception is masculine **кофе** 'coffee'), e.g.:

какао   cocoa
ноу-хау   know-how
кафе   cafe
такси   taxi
бистро   bistro
шоу   show
интервью   interview

I Number (singular and plural)

(a) Nouns are either singular, denoting one object or person (**стол** 'table', **же́нщина** 'woman'), or plural, denoting more than one (**столы́** 'tables', **же́нщины** 'women').

(b) The **masculine plural** is formed by the addition of a vowel, usually **-ы**, to nouns ending in a consonant (**-и** after **г, к, х, ж, ч, ш, щ** [*see page 6*]):

автóбус bus	**автóбус-ы** buses
урóк lesson	**урóк-и** lessons
пляж beach	**пля́ж-и** beaches

or by the *replacement* of final **-й** or **-ь** by **-и**:

герó-й hero	**герó-и** heroes
гóлуб-ь dove	**гóлуб-и** doves

(c) The **feminine plural** is formed by the *replacement* of final **-а** by **-ы** (**-и** after **г, к, х, ж, ч, ш, щ**):

лáмп-а lamp	**лáмп-ы** lamps
кни́г-а book	**кни́г-и** books

and of final **-я** or **-ь** by **-и**:

тёт-я aunt	**тёт-и** aunts
вещ-ь thing	**вéщ-и** things

(d) The **neuter plural** is formed by *replacing* **-о** by **-а**, **-е/-ё** by **-я**:

чýвств-о feeling	**чýвств-а** feelings
плáть-е dress	**плáть-я** dresses
ружь-ё shot-gun	**рýжь-я** shot-guns

I Declension

There are six **cases**, each showing the function of a noun in the clause (only the most basic meanings or functions are given here):

Nominative
the subject of the clause

Отéц пьёт
Father is drinking

Accusative
the object of the verb

Он пьёт **винó**
He drinks **wine**

Genitive
possession, ownership

Дом **сы́на**
My son's house

Dative
indirect object, recipient

Он дал кни́гу **мáльчику**
He gave the book **to the boy**

Instrumental
with, by means of

Я пишу́ **мéлом**
I write **with chalk**

Prepositional/Locative
location

Я живу́ **в гóроде**
I live **in town**

> **!** **Note:** (a) relics of the **vocative** case in: Бóже мой! 'my God!', Гóсподи! 'Good Lord!'.
> (b) some truncated forms are used with vocative meaning in colloquial Russian: мам! 'Mum!', Нин! 'Nina!', etc.
> (c) the prepositional/locative case is always used with a preposition.

I The declensions

There are three declensions:

The first declension: all masculine nouns (except those ending in **a/я**, and путь 'way') and all neuter nouns (except those ending in **-мя**)

The second declension: nouns in **a/я** (mainly feminine, with a few 'natural' masculines, e.g. юноша 'youth', дядя 'uncle', and nouns of common gender e.g. сирота 'orphan')

The third declension: feminine soft-sign nouns, neuter nouns in **-мя**, and masculine путь 'way'

The first declension (masculine and neuter nouns)

The first declension subdivides into masculine nouns ending in **a consonant**, **-й**, or **-ь**, and neuter nouns ending in **-о**, **-е** (including **-ие/-ье/-ьё**).

Masculine hard-ending nouns (nouns ending in a hard consonant)

Most masculine nouns follow the standard pattern (types 1 and 2 below). Others display variations conditioned by the spelling rules:

Spelling rule one: **ы** is replaced by **и** after the letters **г, к, х** and **ж, ч, ш, щ**

Spelling rule two: **о** can appear after the letters **ж, ч, ш, щ,** and **ц** only if stressed, otherwise it is replaced by **е**.

> **!** **Note:** the accusative singular and plural of all masculine **animate** nouns is the same as the genitive.

Types of masculine first-declension nouns ending in a hard consonant:

Type 1: **зал** 'hall' (inanimate nouns)

Type 2: **капитáн** 'captain' (animate nouns)

Type 3: **парк** 'park' (nouns in -г, -к, -х)

Type 4: **рынок** 'market' (nouns in -ок/-ек/-ёк)

Type 5: **конéц** 'end', **тáнец** 'dance' (nouns in -ц)

Type 6: **нож** 'knife' (nouns in -ж, -ч, -ш, -щ)

Type 1: Inanimate nouns, e.g. зал 'hall'

	Singular	Plural
Nom.	зал	зал-ы
Acc.	зал	зал-ы
Gen.	зáл-а	зáл-ов
Dat.	зáл-у	зáл-ам
Instr.	зáл-ом	зáл-ами
Prep.	зáл-е	зáл-ах

Nouns changing their stress in declension include **гриб** 'mushroom' (genitive **грибá**), **двор** 'yard', **куст** 'bush', **лист** 'sheet of paper', **стол** 'table', **суд** 'law court', **труд** 'labour', **ум** 'mind', **хвост** 'tail', etc. Note also **Днепр** 'Dnieper' and **Пётр** (genitive **Петрá**) 'Peter'.

Nominative/accusative plural in stressed -á

Some masculine hard-ending nouns take stressed **-á** in the nominative/accusative plural: **áдрес** 'address', **адресá** 'addresses'; **бéрег** 'shore', **берегá** 'shores'; **бок** 'side', **бокá** 'sides'; **век** 'century', **векá** 'centuries'; **вéчер** 'evening', **вечерá** 'evenings'; **глаз** 'eye', **глазá** 'eyes'; **гóлос** 'voice', **голосá** 'voices'; **дом** 'house', **домá** 'houses'; **лес** 'forest', **лесá** 'forests'; **óстров** 'island', **островá** 'islands'; **пáспорт** 'passport', **паспортá** 'passports'; **пóезд** 'train', **поездá** 'trains', etc.

Prepositional/locative case in -ý

The following nouns take prepositional/locative stressed -ý after the prepositions **в** 'in' and **на** 'on' (*never* after **о** 'about, concerning': **о ле́се** 'about the forest', or **при** 'in the presence of, attached to': **при отце́** 'in father's presence', **при заво́де** 'attached to the factory'):

бе́рег 'bank':	Они́ отдыха́ли **на берегу́ мо́ря**
	They were relaxing **at the seaside**
Дон 'the Don':	Росто́в нахо́дится **на Дону́**
	Rostov is situated **on the Don**
лёд 'ice':	Они́ танцева́ли **на льду**
	They were dancing **on the ice**
лес 'forest':	Грибы́ расту́т **в лесу́**
	Mushrooms grow **in the forest**
мост 'bridge':	Мы стоя́ли **на мосту́**
	We were standing **on the bridge**
о́тпуск 'holiday':	Мы бы́ли **в отпуску́** (colloquial variant of **в о́тпуске**) We were **on holiday**
пол 'floor':	Соба́ка спала́ **на полу́**
	The dog was sleeping **on the floor**
порт 'port':	Он рабо́тает **в порту́**
	He works **in the port**
ряд 'row':	Мы сиде́ли **в пя́том ряду́**
	We were sitting **in row five**
сад 'garden':	**В саду́** расту́т ро́зы
	Roses grow **in the garden**
шкаф 'cupboard':	Ва́ше пальто́ виси́т **в шкафу́**
	Your coat is hanging **in the cupboard**

Other nouns with stressed prepositional/locative in -ý (many of them monosyllabic) include бал 'ball', Крым 'the Crimea', лоб 'forehead' (на лбу 'on the forehead'), нос 'nose, prow of ship', полк 'regiment', пост 'post', пруд 'pond', рот 'mouth' (во рту 'in the mouth'), снег 'snow', у́гол 'corner' (в углу́ 'in the corner', на углу́ 'on, at the corner'). For the 'fleeting vowel' in declension, *see pages 10–11, 17.*

Type 2: Animate nouns, e.g. капита́н 'captain'

Note that the accusative singular and plural of masculine animate nouns is **the same as the genitive:**

	Singular	*Plural*
Nom.	капита́н	капита́н-ы
Acc.	капита́н-а	капита́н-ов
Gen.	капита́н-а	капита́н-ов
Dat.	капита́н-у	капита́н-ам
Instr.	капита́н-ом	капита́н-ами
Prep.	капита́н-е	капита́н-ах

Similarly all animate masculine nouns, e.g. делега́т 'delegate', дирижёр 'conductor', инжене́р 'engineer', кандида́т 'candidate', мини́стр 'minister', офице́р 'officer', поэ́т 'poet', тури́ст 'tourist', чемпио́н 'champion', etc. (and, with stress change in declension, кит 'whale', accusative/genitive кита́, слон accusative/genitive слона́ 'elephant').

> ! **Note:** Some masculine animate nouns have nominative plural -á, e.g. дире́ктор 'director', plural директора́ 'directors' (accusative/genitive plural директоро́в).

Type 3: Masculine nouns in г, к, х

Note that **-ы** is replaced by **-и** in the nominative/accusative plural in accordance with the spelling rule, e.g. **парк** 'park'.

	Singular	*Plural*
Nom.	парк	па́рк-**и**
Acc.	парк	па́рк-**и**
Gen.	па́рк-а	па́рк-**ов**
Dat.	па́рк-у	па́рк-**ам**
Instr.	па́рк-ом	па́рк-**ами**
Prep.	па́рк-е	па́рк-**ах**

Similarly банк 'bank', plural ба́нк-**и**, флаг 'flag', plural фла́г-**и**, слух 'rumour', plural слу́х-**и**, etc.

The **accusative** singular/plural of all masculine animate nouns (*see also page 9*) is the same as the **genitive**: ма́льчик 'boy', accusative/genitive singular ма́льчик-**а**, accusative/genitive plural ма́льчик-**ов**.

Stress changes from stem to endings in грузови́к, genitive грузовика́ 'lorry', учени́к 'pupil', язы́к 'language', etc.

Type 4: Masculine nouns in -ок/-ек/-ёк

The fleeting vowel *-o/-e/-ё* is lost in declension, e.g. **ры́нок** 'market'.

Nom.	ры́нок	ры́нк-**и**
Acc.	ры́нок	ры́нк-**и**
Gen.	ры́нк-а	ры́нк-**ов**
Dat.	ры́нк-у	ры́нк-**ам**
Instr.	ры́нк-ом	ры́нк-**ами**
Prep.	ры́нк-е	ры́нк-**ах**

Similarly звоно́к 'bell', значо́к 'badge', като́к 'rink', конёк 'skate', genitive конька́, кусо́к 'piece', мешо́к 'sack', оре́шек 'nut', песо́к 'sand', плато́к 'headscarf', пода́рок 'present', порошо́к 'powder', etc. Уро́к 'lesson', genitive уро́ка, знато́к 'connoisseur', genitive знатока́, and игро́к 'player', genitive игрока́ *retain* **-o-** throughout declension.

The **accusative** singular/plural of animate nouns (*see also page 9*) is the same as the **genitive**: знато́к 'connoisseur', accusative/genitive singular знатока́, accusative/genitive plural знатоко́в.

Type 5: Masculine nouns in -ц

Virtually all of these nouns end in **-ец**, with fleeting vowel **-е-** lost in declension, e.g. **конéц** 'end', genitive **концá**. Stem-stressed nouns have **-ем** in the instrumental singular and **-ев** in the genitive plural, since **о** may appear after **ц** only in *stressed* position, e.g. **тáнец** 'dance', instrumental singular **тáнцем**, genitive plural **тáнцев**.

	Singular	Plural	Singular	Plural
Nom.	конéц	конц-ы́	тáнец	тáнц-ы
Acc.	конéц	конц-ы́	тáнец	тáнц-ы
Gen.	конц-á	конц-óв	тáнц-а	тáнц-ев
Dat.	конц-ý	конц-áм	тáнц-у	тáнц-ам
Instr.	конц-óм	конц-áми	тáнц-ем	тáнц-ами
Prep.	конц-é	конц-áх	тáнц-е	тáнц-ах

Similarly (end stress): **дворéц** 'palace', **огурéц** 'cucumber', **отéц** 'father', **продавéц** 'sales assistant'; (stem stress): **пéрец** 'pepper', **инострáнец** 'foreigner' (and many nationalities: **америкáнец** 'American', **нéмец** 'German', **шотлáндец** 'Scot', etc.).

Note: (a) the second of two adjacent vowels is replaced by -й- in declension: **бельѓец** 'Belgian', genitive **бельѓйца**, **китáец** 'Chinese', genitive **китáйца** (also **зáяц** 'hare', genitive **зáйца**). The combination -ле- is replaced by -ль-: **пáлец** 'finger', genitive **пáльца**.

(b) the vowel **е** is *retained* in declension where -ец is preceded by two or more consonants: **близнéц** 'twin', genitive **близнецá**, **кузнéц** 'blacksmith', genitive **кузнецá**, **мертвéц** 'dead person', genitive **мертвецá**.

(c) the accusative singular/plural of *animate* nouns in -ец (see also page 9) is the same as the genitive singular/plural, thus **певéц** 'singer': Я слýшаю **певцá**/**певцóв** 'I listen to the singer/singers'.

(d) **Мéсяц** 'month' declines like тáнец 'dance', but with no fleeting vowel, e.g. **дéвять мéсяцев** 'nine months'.

Type 6: Masculine nouns in ж, ч, ш, щ

! **Note:** Nouns ending in the soft consonants ч and щ are included here since their declension is identical to that of nouns ending in the hard consonants ж and ш.

The plural form **-ы** is replaced by **-и** in accordance with the spelling rule (*see page 6*). Genitive plural is **-ей**, e.g. **нож** 'knife':

	Singular	*Plural*
Nom.	нож	нож-и́
Acc.	нож	нож-и́
Gen.	нож-а́	нож-е́й
Dat.	нож-у́	нож-а́м
Instr.	нож-о́м	нож-а́ми
Prep.	нож-е́	нож-а́х

! **Note:** Like **нож** 'knife', many of the nouns have end stress in declension, thus: каранда́ш 'pencil', genitive каранда́ш-а́, likewise ключ 'key', плащ 'raincoat', эта́ж 'storey', etc. The instrumental singular ending of nouns with *stem* stress throughout declension is **-ем** (since -о can appear after -ж, -ч, -ш, and -щ only in *stressed* position), thus пляж 'beach' instrumental singular пля́ж-ем, това́рищ 'comrade', instrumental singular това́рищ-ем. Compare stem-stressed patronymic Серге́евич 'Sergeevich', instrumental Серге́евич-ем and end-stressed patronymic Ильи́ч 'Il'ich', instrumental Ильич-о́м.

The **accusative** singular/plural of masculine animate nouns (*see also page 9*) is the same as the **genitive**: врач 'doctor' accusative/genitive singular врач-а́, accusative/genitive plural врач-е́й.

Some special features of the masculine hard-ending declension

(a) The partitive genitive in -y

A number of nouns that denote substances have a partitive genitive (indicating that only part of a substance is involved) in **-y**: лук 'onions' (partitive genitive лу́к-у), са́хар 'sugar' (partitive genitive са́хар-у), суп 'soup' (partitive genitive су́п-у), сыр 'cheese' (partitive genitive сы́р-у), таба́к 'tobacco' (partitive genitive табак-у́), and others (including наро́д 'people' (partitive genitive наро́д-у)). For partitive usage, *see page 29.*

(b) Nouns in which the genitive plural is identical with the nominative singular

The genitive plural of a number of nouns is the same as the nominative singular. The nouns fall into the following categories:

(i) certain items of footwear: **ботинок** '(ankle-high) boot' (пара ботинок 'a pair of (ankle-high) boots'), **сапог** 'boot', **чулок** 'stocking'

(ii) certain measurements: **грамм** 'gram' (сто грамм '100 grams', but сто граммов in written Russian)

(iii) certain nationalities: **грузин** 'Georgian', **румын** 'Romanian', **турок** 'Turk'. Since these are animate nouns, the genitive plural is also the *accusative* plural: Я вижу **грузин, румын, турок** 'I see the Georgians, the Romanians, the Turks'

(iv) certain military terms: **солдат** 'soldier', **партизан** 'guerrilla' (the genitive plural of these animate nouns is also the *accusative* plural)

(v) others: **раз** 'time' (5 **раз** 'five times'), **человек** 'person' after cardinal and some indefinite numerals: 5 **человек** 'five people', **несколько человек** 'a few people' (but много людей 'a lot of people').

(c) Summary of genitive plural endings in hard-ending masculine nouns

Hard-ending nouns may have genitive plural endings -**ов**, -**ев**, or -**ей**.

-**ов**: the genitive plural of all hard-ending nouns (e.g. зал, 'hall' genitive plural **залов**), except for those ending in -**ж, -ч, -ш, -щ**, and stem-stressed nouns in -**ц**

-**ев**: stem-stressed nouns in -**ц**: месяц 'month', genitive plural **месяцев**

-**ей**: nouns in -**ж, -ч, -ш, -щ**: гараж 'garage', genitive plural **гаражей**

> **!** **Note:** (a) some nouns have 'zero' ending in the genitive plural (e.g. **раз** 'time', see above).
>
> (b) the genitive plural of all masculine animate nouns (*see also page 9*) is also the accusative plural: Я знаю **мальчиков/испанцев/врачей** 'I know the boys/the Spaniards/the doctors'.

Masculine hard-ending nouns with irregular plural forms

Nominative plural -ья, genitive plural -ьев

	брат 'brother' Plural	лист 'leaf' Plural	стул 'chair' Plural
Nom.	брáт-ья	лúст-ья	стýл-ья
Acc.	брáт-ьев	лúст-ья	стýл-ья
Gen.	брáт-ьев	лúст-ьев	стýл-ьев
Dat.	брáт-ьям	лúст-ьям	стýл-ьям
Instr.	брáт-ьями	лúст-ьями	стýл-ьями
Prep.	брáт-ьях	лúст-ьях	стýл-ьях

Лист meaning 'sheet of paper' (as opposed to 'leaf'), genitive листá, declines like зал 'hall'.

Nominative plural -ья, genitive plural -ей

	муж 'husband' Plural	сын 'son' Plural	друг 'friend' Plural
Nom.	муж-ья́	сынов-ья́	друз-ья́
Acc.	муж-éй	сынов-éй	друз-éй
Gen.	муж-éй	сынов-éй	друз-éй
Dat.	муж-ья́м	сынов-ья́м	друз-ья́м
Instr.	муж-ья́ми	сынов-ья́ми	друз-ья́ми
Prep.	муж-ья́х	сынов-ья́х	друз-ья́х

! **Note:** The accusative plural (and singular) of animate брат, друг, муж, and сын is the same as the genitive: Я вúжу свои́х брáтьев 'I see my brothers', Я встречáю друзéй 'I meet my friends', Они́ лю́бят свои́х мужéй/свои́х сыновéй 'They love their husbands/their sons'.

Nouns in -анин/-янин: англича́нин 'Englishman'/славяни́н 'Slav'

	Plural	Plural
Nom.	англича́н-е	славя́н-е
Acc.	англича́н	славя́н
Gen.	англича́н	славя́н
Dat.	англича́н-ам	славя́н-ам
Instr.	англича́н-ами	славя́н-ами
Prep.	англича́н-ах	славя́н-ах

❗ **Note:** stress change in the plural of **гражданин** 'citizen': **гра́ждане**, accusative/genitive **гра́ждан**.

Господи́н 'gentleman', коте́нок 'kitten' (nouns in -ёнок denoting the young of animals and birds, -о́нок after -ж, -ч, -ш)

	Plural	Plural
Nom.	господ-а́	кот-я́та
Acc.	госпо́д	кот-я́т
Gen.	госпо́д	кот-я́т
Dat.	господ-а́м	кот-я́там
Instr.	господ-а́ми	кот-я́тами
Prep.	господ-а́х	кот-я́тах

❗ **Note:** (a) **ребя́та**, plural of **ребёнок** 'child' is a colloquial variant of **де́ти** 'children'.

(b) **щено́к** 'puppy' has plural **щеня́та** or **щенки́**.

(c) nouns in -о́нок have plurals in -а́та: **волчо́нок** 'wolf-cub', plural **волча́та**.

	сосе́д 'neighbour'	хозя́ин 'owner'
	Plural	Plural
Nom.	сосе́д-и	хозя́ев-а
Acc	сосе́д-ей	хозя́ев
Gen.	сосе́д-ей	хозя́ев
Dat.	сосе́д-ям	хозя́ев-ам
Instr.	сосе́д-ями	хозя́ев-ами
Prep.	сосе́д-ях	хозя́ев-ах

Soft-ending masculine nouns (nouns in -й and -ь)

Masculine nouns in -й

The case endings of masculine nouns in -й are the 'soft'
equivalents of the endings of the 'hard' declension, cf. зал 'hall'
and музе́й 'museum':

Singular

hard nominative	зал	soft nominative	музе́-й
hard accusative	зал	soft accusative	музе́-й
hard genitive	за́л-а	soft genitive	музе́-я
hard dative	за́л-у	soft dative	музе́-ю
hard instrumental	за́л-ом	soft instrumental	музе́-ем
hard prepositional	за́л-е	soft prepositional	музе́-е

Plural

hard nominative	за́л-ы	soft nominative	музе́-и
hard accusative	за́л-ы	soft accusative	музе́-и
hard genitive	за́л-ов	soft genitive	музе́-ев
hard dative	за́л-ам	soft dative	музе́-ям
hard instrumental	за́л-ами	soft instrumental	музе́-ями
hard prepositional	за́л-ах	soft prepositional	музе́-ях

! **Note:** (a) the prepositional singular ending is **-е** in hard *and* soft declensions.
(b) some nouns in **-й** have prepositional locative endings in stressed **-ю** (*see
page 8* for hard-ending prepositional locative in stressed **-у**): **бой** 'battle', **в
бою́** 'in battle' (nominative plural **бои́**, genitive plural **боёв**), **край** 'edge', **на
краю́** 'on the edge' (nominative plural **края́**, genitive plural **краёв**).
(c) nouns in **-ий** decline like **музе́й** except for prepositional **-ии**: **ге́ний** 'genius',
о ге́ни-и 'about a genius'.
(d) as elsewhere, the accusative of animate nouns (*see also page 9*) is the same
as the genitive: **геро́й** 'hero', accusative/genitive singular **геро́я**, accusative/
genitive plural **геро́ев**.

Masculine nouns in –ь

These have the same endings as nouns in **-й**, except for genitive plural **-ей**:

	Singular	*Plural*
Nom.	спекта́кль	спекта́кл-и
Acc.	спекта́кль	спекта́кл-и
Gen.	спекта́кл-я	спекта́кл-ей
Dat.	спекта́кл-ю	спекта́кл-ям
Instr.	спекта́кл-ем	спекта́кл-ями
Prep.	спекта́кл-е	спекта́кл-ях

! **Note:** (a) учи́тель 'teacher', nominative plural учителя́, ла́герь 'camp', nominative plural лагеря́.

(b) some of the nouns have a fleeting vowel that is lost in declension: день 'day', genitive дня, ка́мень 'stone', genitive ка́мня, ко́рень 'root', genitive ко́рня, etc.

(c) some nouns take end stress in declension, with instrumental singular -ём, e.g. дождь 'rain', genitive дождя́ (под дождём 'in the rain').

(d) third-declension путь 'way' is of masculine gender, but declines partly like a feminine noun in the singular: genitive/dative/prepositional пути́, instrumental путём

Declension of лю́ди 'people' and де́ти 'children'

Nom.	лю́д-и	де́т-и
Acc.	люд-е́й	дет-е́й
Gen.	люд-е́й	дет-е́й
Dat.	лю́д-ям	де́т-ям
Instr.	люд-ьми́	дет-ьми́
Prep.	лю́д-ях	де́т-ях

Neuter nouns in -o

Neuter nouns in **-o** have the same endings as hard-ending masculine nouns (e.g. **зал** 'hall', *see page 7*) except for nominative/accusative singular **-o**, nominative/accusative plural **-a**, and zero genitive plural, e.g. **блю́до** 'dish':

	Singular	*Plural*
Nom.	блю́д-о	блю́д-а
Acc.	блю́д-о	блю́д-а
Gen.	блю́д-а	блюд
Dat.	блю́д-у	блю́д-ам
Instr.	блю́д-ом	блю́д-ами
Prep.	блю́д-е	блю́д-ах

Stress change in the plural

This occurs in many nouns, either from stem onto ending: сло́во 'word', nominative plural слова́, genitive plural слов, dative plural слова́м; or from ending onto stem: лицо́ 'face', nominative plural ли́ца, genitive plural лиц, dative plural ли́цам.

> **!** **Note:** (a) -e- to -ё- in: колесо́ 'wheel' nominative plural колёса, genitive plural колёс, dative plural колёсам.
> (b) if two consonants precede -o, a vowel usually appears between them in the genitive plural, -o- if adjacent to к: окно́ 'window', nominative plural о́кна, genitive plural о́кон, otherwise -e-: письмо́ 'letter', nominative plural пи́сьма, genitive plural пи́сем.
> (c) яйцо́ 'egg', nominative plural я́йца, genitive plural яи́ц.

Irregular plurals in -ья/ьев

де́рево 'tree', nominative plural дере́вья, genitive plural дере́вьев

крыло́ 'wing', nominative plural кры́лья, genitive plural кры́льев

перо́ 'feather, pen' nominative plural пе́рья, genitive plural
пе́рьев

Irregular plurals in -и

коле́но 'knee', nominative plural коле́ни, genitive plural коле́ней
(коле́н after prepositions: встать с коле́н 'to rise from one's
knees')

плечо́ 'shoulder', nominative plural пле́чи, genitive plural плеч

у́хо 'ear', nominative plural у́ши, genitive plural уше́й

я́блоко 'apple', nominative plural я́блоки, genitive plural я́блок

> **!** **Note:** The genitive plural of ле́то 'summer' is used as the genitive plural of год
> 'year' (пять лет наза́д 'five years ago').

Neuter nouns in -e, e.g. мо́ре 'sea'

	Singular	*Plural*
Nom.	мо́р-е	мор-я́
Acc.	мо́р-е	мор-я́
Gen.	мо́р-я	мор-е́й
Dat.	мо́р-ю	мор-я́м
Instr.	мо́р-ем	мор-я́ми
Prep.	мо́р-е	мор-я́х

Likewise по́ле 'field' and nouns in -ье (singular only):
воскресе́нье 'Sunday', здоро́вье 'health', (не)сча́стье
'(un)happiness', and (singular only) end-stressed бельё 'linen,
underwear' (в белье́ 'in one's underwear').

> **!** **Note:** (a) пла́тье 'dress', nominative plural пла́тья, genitive plural пла́тьев.
> (b) я is replaced by a after ц, thus: се́рдце 'heart', genitive singular се́рдца,
> nominative plural сердца́.
> (c) a number of loanwords in -e- (and in -и etc., *see page 3*) do not decline.

Neuter nouns in -ие

Nouns in **-ие** decline like **мо́ре** 'sea' except for the prepositional singular in **-и** and genitive plural in **-й**, e.g. **собы́тие** 'event'

	Singular	Plural
Nom.	собы́ти-е	собы́ти-я
Acc.	собы́ти-е	собы́ти-я
Gen.	собы́ти-я	собы́ти-й
Dat.	собы́ти-ю	собы́ти-ям
Instr.	собы́ти-ем	собы́ти-ями
Prep.	собы́ти-и	собы́ти-ях

Many of the nouns are abstract and singular only, others have plurals: влия́ние 'influence', впечатле́ние 'impression', поколе́ние 'generation', etc.

Neuter (third-declension) nouns in -мя, e.g. и́мя 'first name'

	Singular	Plural
Nom.	и́м-я	имен-а́
Acc.	и́м-я	имен-а́
Gen.	имен-и	имён
Dat.	имен-и	имен-а́м
Instr.	имен-ем	имен-а́ми
Prep.	имен-и	имен-а́х

Likewise вре́мя 'time', зна́мя 'banner' (nominative plural знамёна genitive plural знамён), and a number of less commonly-used nouns.

The second declension (nouns in -а/я)

Feminine nouns in -a

Type 1: feminine inanimate nouns, e.g. ла́мпа 'lamp'

	Singular	Plural
Nom.	ла́мп-а	ла́мп-ы
Acc.	ла́мп-у	ла́мп-ы
Gen.	ла́мп-ы	ламп
Dat.	ла́мп-е	ла́мп-ам
Instr.	ла́мп-ой	ла́мп-ами
Prep.	ла́мп-е	ла́мп-ах

! **Note:** (a) most feminine nouns in -a decline like ла́мпа 'lamp'.
(b) nouns in unstressed -ца, -жа, -ча, -ша, -ща take -ей in the instrumental singular (-o- can appear after these consonants only in stressed position): грани́ца 'boundary', instrumental singular грани́цей, likewise кры́ша 'roof', столи́ца 'capital city', etc.
(c) nouns in -жа, -ча, -ша, -ща take -и in the genitive singular and nominative/accusative plural.

Stress change

Many nouns in -а́ switch stress to the stem in the plural: страна́ 'country', plural стра́ны, стран, стра́нам, стра́нами, стра́нах (likewise война́ 'war', игра́ 'game', глава́ 'chapter', etc. (-e- may change to -ё- under stress: звезда́ 'star', plural звёзды, звёзд, звёздам, звёздами, звёздах).

Type 2: Feminine animate nouns in -a, e.g. же́нщина 'woman':

	Singular	Plural
Nom.	же́нщин-а	же́нщин-ы
Acc.	же́нщин-у	же́нщин
Gen.	же́нщин-ы	же́нщин
Dat.	же́нщин-е	же́нщин-ам
Instr.	же́нщин-ой	же́нщин-ами
Prep.	же́нщин-е	же́нщин-ах

! **Note:** (a) the accusative **plural** of animate feminine nouns is identical with the genitive plural: Он ви́дит **коро́в** 'He sees the cows'.
(b) many end-stressed nouns switch to stem stress in the plural: сирота́ 'orphan' plural сиро́ты, with -e- to -ё- under stress: жена́ 'wife' plural жёны, жён, жёнам, жёнами, жёнах. Likewise пчела́ 'bee'.
(c) a few 'natural' masculines (retaining masculine agreement: мой па́па 'my Dad'), and common-gender nouns in -a, e.g. обжо́ра 'glutton' decline like же́нщина.

Type 3: Nouns in -га, -ка, -ха

Note that the vowel **-ы** is replaced by **-и** after **-г-, -к-, -х-** in the genitive singular and nominative/accusative plural, e.g. **книга** 'book':

	Singular	Plural
Nom.	кни́г-а	кни́г-и
Acc.	кни́г-у	кни́г-и
Gen.	кни́г-и	книг
Dat.	кни́г-е	кни́г-ам
Instr.	кни́г-ой	кни́г-ами
Prep.	кни́г-е	кни́г-ах

Type 4: Nouns that take –о- or –е- between consonants in the genitive plural, e.g. ба́нка 'jar'

	Singular	Plural
Nom.	ба́нк-а	ба́нк-и
Acc.	ба́нк-у	ба́нк-и
Gen.	ба́нк-и	ба́нок
Dat.	ба́нк-е	ба́нк-ам
Instr.	ба́нк-ой	ба́нк-ами
Prep.	ба́нк-е	ба́нк-ах

Likewise бу́лка 'roll' (genitive plural бу́лок), буты́лка 'bottle' (буты́лок), ви́лка 'fork' (ви́лок), ма́рка 'stamp' (ма́рок), оши́бка 'mistake' (оши́бок), перча́тка 'glove' (перча́ток), пласти́нка 'record' (пласти́нок), таре́лка 'plate' (таре́лок).

! **Note:** (a) **-е-** appears in the genitive plural between ж, ч, ш, and к: игру́шка 'toy' (игр'ушек), кни́жка 'notebook' (кни́жек), ло́жка 'spoon' (ло́жек), па́чка 'packet' (па́чек), руба́шка 'shirt' (руба́шек), спи́чка 'match' (спи́чек), ча́шка 'cup' (ча́шек), or replaces й before к: копе́йка 'kopeck' (копе́ек).
(b) the accusative plural of animate nouns is the same as the genitive plural: де́вушка 'girl' (де́вушек), ко́шка 'cat' (ко́шек). *See also page 9.*
(c) some other combinations of consonants have inter-consonantal vowel **-е-** in the genitive plural: сва́дьба 'wedding' (сва́деб), сосна́ 'pine-tree' (со́сен), тюрьма́ 'prison' (тю́рем).
(d) others have no inter-consonantal vowel in the genitive plural: бу́ква 'letter of the alphabet' (букв), игра́ 'game', про́сьба 'request', фо́рма 'form', ци́фра 'figure', ша́хта 'mine', etc.

Feminine nouns in -я

In the declension of nouns in -я, the vowel endings of the hard declension **a**, **y**, **ы**, **о** are replaced by their soft equivalents: **я**, **ю**, **и**, **e**.

Бу́ря 'storm' (note that **-ь** in the genitive plural preserves the softness of the final consonant):

	Singular	Plural
Nom.	бу́р-я	бу́р-и
Acc.	бу́р-ю	бу́р-и
Gen.	бу́р-и	бурь
Dat.	бу́р-е	бу́р-ям
Instr.	бу́р-ей	бу́р-ями
Prep.	бу́р-е	бу́р-ях

> **!** **Note:** (a) instrumental singular **-ёй** under stress: земля́ 'land', instrumental singular землёй.
> (b) some nouns have inter-consonantal vowel **-e-** in the genitive plural (some with, some without a final soft sign): ба́шня 'tower' (genitive plural ба́шен), ви́шня 'cherry' (ви́шен), дере́вня 'village' (дереве́нь), спа́льня 'bedroom' (спа́лен), ту́фля 'shoe' (ту́фель).
> (c) ку́хня 'kitchen' takes **-o-** in the genitive plural: ку́хонь.

Feminine nouns in -ья: статья́ 'article'

	Singular	Plural
Nom.	стать-я́	стать-и́
Acc.	стать-ю́	стать-и́
Gen.	стать-и́	стат-е́й
Dat.	стать-е́	стать-я́м
Instr.	стать-ёй	стать-я́ми
Prep.	стать-е́	стать-я́х

Similarly nouns in unstressed **-ья**, except for instrumental singular **-ьей** and genitive plural **-ий**, e.g. го́стья 'female guest', instr. singular го́стьей, genitive plural го́стий.

Feminine nouns in -ия: а́рмия 'army'

	Singular	Plural
Nom.	а́рми-я	а́рми-и
Acc.	а́рми-ю	а́рми-и
Gen.	а́рми-и	а́рми-й
Dat.	а́рми-и	а́рми-ям
Instr.	а́рми-ей	а́рми-ями
Prep.	а́рми-и	а́рми-ях

Most of the nouns are loanwords: демонстра́ция 'demonstration'
ста́нция 'station' фами́лия 'surname' экску́рсия 'excursion', etc.

Feminine nouns in -ая, -ея: иде́я 'idea'

	Singular	Plural
Nom.	иде́-я	иде́-и
Acc.	иде́-ю	иде́-и
Gen.	иде́-и	иде́-й
Dat.	иде́-е	иде́-ям
Instr.	иде́-ей	иде́-ями
Prep.	иде́-е	иде́-ях

Similarly ста́я 'pack (of wolves), flock (of birds), shoal (of fish)',
etc.

Summary of genitive plural endings in the second declension

Nouns in -a: zero ending: ла́мпа 'lamp' (**ламп**) ви́лка 'fork'
(**ви́лок**), ло́жка 'spoon' (**ло́жек**)

Nouns in -я: zero ending: бу́ря 'storm' (**бурь**), ка́пля 'drop'
(**ка́пель**), ба́шня 'tower' (**ба́шен**)

Nouns in -ья: -ей: статья́ 'article' (**стат-е́й**)

Nouns in -ья: -ий: го́стья 'female guest' (**го́ст-ий**)

Nouns in -ея/-ая: -й: ста́я 'pack' (**ста-й**)

Nouns in -ия: -й: ста́нция 'station' (**ста́нци-й**)

The third declension (soft-sign feminine nouns: крова́ть 'bed')

	Singular	*Plural*
Nom.	крова́ть	крова́т-и
Acc.	крова́ть	крова́т-и
Gen.	крова́т-и	крова́т-ей
Dat.	крова́т-и	крова́т-ям
Instr.	крова́ть-ю	крова́т-ями
Prep.	крова́т-и	крова́т-ях

Note: (a) some nouns have stressed **-и́** in the prepositional/locative case (after the prepositions **в** 'in' and **на** 'on'): **на груди́** 'on the chest', **в грязи́** 'in the mud, covered in mud', **на двери́** 'on the door', **в связи́ с** 'in connection with', **в глоба́льной сети́** 'on the world-wide web', **в тени́** 'in the shade'.

(b) the letter я is replaced by а after ж, ч, ш, щ, thus вещь 'thing', dative/instrumental/prepositional plural вещ-а́м, вещ-а́ми, вещ-а́х, likewise мышь 'mouse', ночь 'night', речь 'speech', etc.

(c) some nouns lose **-o-** in the genitive/dative/prepositional singular: ложь 'lie, falsehood', лжи (instr. ло́жью), likewise любо́вь 'love', любви́ (instr. любо́вью), etc.

(d) дочь 'daughter' declines дочь, до́чери, до́чери, до́черью, до́чери, plural до́чери, дочере́й, дочеря́м, дочерьми́, дочеря́х. Likewise мать 'mother', except for instrumental plural матеря́ми.

(e) the plural animate accusative/genitive rule applies to feminine soft-sign nouns: Я люблю́ свои́х дочере́й 'I love my daughters'. *See also pages 21, 22.*

(f) путь 'way' and neuter nouns in **-мя** also belong to the third declension (*see also pages 6, 17, and 20*).

Declension of surnames

Those in **-ев, -ёв, -ов, -ин, -ын** decline partly as nouns, partly as adjectives, e.g. Бу́нин, Бу́нина, Бу́нины:

	Masculine	*Feminine*	*Plural*
Nom.	Бу́нин	Бу́нин-а	Бу́нин-ы
Acc.	Бу́нин-а	Бу́нин-у	Бу́нин-ых
Gen.	Бу́нин-а	Бу́нин-ой	Бу́нин-ых
Dat.	Бу́нин-у	Бу́нин-ой	Бу́нин-ым
Instr.	Бу́нин-ым	Бу́нин-ой	Бу́нин-ыми
Prep.	Бу́нин-е	Бу́нин-ой	Бу́нин-ых

Note: (a) surnames in -ский and -о́й (e.g. Ма́йский, Толсто́й) decline like adjectives.

(b) those in -о (Бондаре́нко, Хитрово́) do not decline.

(c) male foreign surnames ending in a consonant decline (e.g., а́дрес Фри́дриха Ши́ллера 'Friedrich Schiller's address'), but not female (а́дрес А́нны Ши́ллер 'Anna Schiller's address').

(d) foreign surnames in -е, -и, -о, -у, and stressed -а́ and -я́ (Гёте, Тати́, Моро́, Шо́у, Дюма́) do not decline.

I Use of the cases

The nominative case

The nominative case denotes the subject of an action or state:

Моя́ сестра́ пи́шет письмо́   **My sister** is writing a letter
Маши́на останови́лась   **The car** stopped

It is also used:
(a) to identify:

Э́то на́ша **да́ча**   That is our **country cottage**
Э́то на́ши **роди́тели**   These are our **parents**

(b) to point out:

Вот **ма́ма**   There is **Mum**

(c) in definitions:

Росси́я – больша́я страна́   **Russia** is a big country

(d) in constructions involving possession, **ну́жный** 'necessary' and **нра́виться/по-** 'to please':

У ученика́ есть **лине́йка**   The pupil has **a ruler**
Не́мцу нужна́ **ка́рта**   The German needs **a map**
Де́тям понра́вится **пье́са**   The children will like **the play**

(e) in comparisons after **чем** 'than':

Москва́ бо́льше, **чем Ки́ев**   Moscow is bigger **than Kiev**

(f) in titles when the genre ('novel', 'newspaper', etc.) is also given:

Он чита́л газе́ту <<**Неде́ля**>>   He was reading the newspaper **"Nedelya"**

but

Он чита́л <<**Неде́лю**>>   He was reading **"Nedelya"**

The accusative case

The accusative case denotes:

(a) the object of a transitive verb:

> Я купи́л **карти́ну**   I bought **a painting**
> Мать лю́бит **сынове́й**   The mother loves **her sons**
> Она́ откры́ла **дверь**   She opened **the door**

(b) duration:

> Он ждал **всю весну́**   He waited **all spring**
> Он **всё вре́мя** шу́тит   He jokes **the whole time**

(c) repetition:

> Я э́то говори́л **ты́сячу раз**   I have said that **1,000 times**
> Я рабо́таю **ка́ждый день**   I work **every day**

(d) distance, weight, price:

> Он бежа́л **киломе́тр**   He ran **a kilometre**
> Она́ пла́кала **всю доро́гу**   She cried **all the way**
> Кни́га сто́ит **со́рок рубле́й**   The book costs **forty roubles**
> Чемода́н ве́сит **20 килогра́ммов**   The case weighs **20 kilos**

(e) the object of **жаль** 'sorry for':

> Ему́ жаль **жену́**   He is sorry for **his wife**

The genitive case

The genitive case denotes:

(a) possession:

маши́на **отца́**   father's car

(b) authorship:

рома́н **Толсто́го**   a novel **by Tolstoy**

(c) the object of a verbal noun:

обрабо́тка **информа́ции**   the processing **of information**

(d) the whole in relation to a part:

спи́нка **сту́ла**   a **chair**-back

(e) descriptive detail:

де́ло **первостепе́нной ва́жности**   a matter **of prime importance**

(f) quantity (with indefinite numerals and the verb **хвата́ть/ хвати́ть** 'to be enough'):

мно́го/немно́го **люде́й**   many/not many **people**
ма́ло/нема́ло **де́нег**   not much/quite a lot of **money**
не́сколько **лет**   a few **years**
доста́точно/недоста́точно **хле́ба**   enough/not enough **bread**
Ско́лько **челове́к?**   How many **people?**
Хва́тит **вре́мени**   There will be enough **time**

The genitive also combines in quantitative meaning with the names of groups and collectives, measurements, and receptacles:

толпа́ **люде́й**   a crowd **of people**
то́нна **угля́**   a ton **of coal**
бока́л **вина́**   a glass **of wine**

The partitive genitive

(a) The partitive genitive is used with verbs that denote requesting/consuming/providing *part* of a substance or liquid, or a number of like objects:

Я хочу/прошу **молока**   I want/ask for **some milk**
Он принёс **спичек**   He brought **some matches**

(b) Except for **хотеть/за-** 'to want' and **просить/по-** 'to request', verbs involved tend to be perfective only:

Он выпил **воды**   He drank **some water**
Она съела **хлеба**   She ate **some bread**

> **!** **Note:** imperfective пить and есть take the accusative case: он пил **воду** 'he was drinking **water**', она ела **хлеб** 'she was eating **bread**'. Use of the accusative case with a perfective verb implies 'all':
> Он выпил **воду**   He drank **(all) the water**
> Она съела **хлеб**   She ate **(all) the bread**

(c) Examples of the partitive genitive:

Я налил ему **водки**   I poured him **some vodka**
Он заказал **икры**   He ordered **some caviar**
Она нарвала **цветов**   She picked **some flowers**

(d) Some nouns denoting substances have a partitive genitive in **-y/-ю**, used with verbs, receptacles, and indefinite numerals (*see also page 12*):

чашка **чаю**   a cup **of tea**
Дайте мне **сахару**   Give me **some sugar**
кусок **сыру**   a piece **of cheese**
тарелка **супу**   a plate **of soup**

The **-a/-я** genitive forms of these nouns are also possible in these contexts and *must* be used when quantity is not implied: запах **чая** 'the smell **of tea**' цена **сахара** 'the price of sugar', or when the noun is qualified by an adjective: чашка **жидкого чая** 'a cup of weak tea'.

The use of the genitive to denote non-existence or non-availability

Нет (past **не было**, future **не будет** + genitive singular/plural) is used to denote non-existence or non-availability:

Нет **ключа/ключей**   There's no **key**/there're no **keys**
Не было **озера/озёр**   There wasn't **a lake**/there weren't any **lakes**
Не будет **фильма/фильмов**   There won't be **a film**/any **films**

The construction is also used with persons:

Его нет/не было/не будет дома   **He** isn't/wasn't/won't be in

However, the nominative is used to denote identification, compare:

Это была не **моя машина**   That wasn't **my car**

and

Не было машины   There wasn't **a car**

The construction can denote absence of possession/availability:

У меня нет времени   I **don't have** the time
У него не было детей   He **didn't have any** children
У них не будет телефона   They **won't have** a telephone

Analogous constructions involve other negated forms:

У нас **не имеется** сведений   We have **no information**
К утру **не осталось** еды   By morning **there was no food left**
Машин **не было видно**   **There were no cars to be seen**

Genitive or accusative after a negated transitive verb

(a) The genitive is often used after a negated transitive verb (one that normally takes the accusative; the rule does not affect negated verbs that take the dative or instrumental):

Она ведёт **дневник** (accusative)   She keeps a **diary**
Она не ведёт **дневника** (genitive)   She doesn't keep a **diary**

(b) The genitive is particularly common after a negated verb when **не** is reinforced by other negative forms: **никако́й, ни оди́н, ни**, etc.:

> Он **не** сде́лал **ни одно́й оши́бки**   He **didn't** make a **single** mistake
> Э́то **не** име́ет **никако́го значе́ния**   That has **no significance at all**
> **Не** слы́шу **ни сло́ва**   I can't hear **a (single) word**

(c) It is also common when **не** combines with abstract nouns:

> **Не** обраща́й **внима́ния** на него́   Pay no **attention** to him
> Я не при́нял **уча́стия** в спо́ре   I took no **part** in the argument

However, the *accusative* case is used after a negated verb:

(a) to distinguish specific objects (accusative) from objects in general (genitive):

> Я не получи́л **письма́** (genitive)   I didn't receive **a letter**
> Я не получи́л **письмо́** (accusative)   I didn't receive **the letter**

(b) when a person is the object of the verb:

> Я не зна́ю **твою́ мать**   I don't know **your mother**

(c) when some other part of the sentence, not the verb, is negated:

> **Не она́** пропусти́л по́езд   **She wasn't the one** who missed the train ('She' is negated)
> Он свари́л суп **не как сле́дует**   He **didn't** make the soup properly ('properly' is negated)
> Я не счита́ю э́ту кни́гу **поле́зной**   I don't consider this book **useful** ('useful' is negated)

(d) after **чуть не/едва́ не** 'almost'; **я не могу́ не** 'I can't help':

> Я **чуть не** разби́л ва́зу   I **almost** broke the vase
> Я **не могу́ не** люби́ть их иску́сство   I **can't help** liking their art

If in doubt, however, use the *genitive* after a negated transitive verb.

Adjectives that take the genitive

These (both long *and* short forms, *see page 43*) include
достойный 'worthy of', лишённый 'lacking in', and полный 'full
of':

Он достоин похвалы́   He is worthy **of praise**
Он лишён чу́вства ю́мора   He lacks **a sense of humour**
Авто́бус по́лон наро́ду   The bus is full **of people**

Verbs that take the genitive

(a) Some verbs invariably take the genitive: добива́ться/доби́ться
'to achieve, to obtain', достига́ть/дости́чь or дости́гнуть 'to
achieve', жела́ть/по- 'to desire', заслу́живать 'to deserve',
каса́ться/косну́ться 'to touch, touch on':

Она́ доби́лась успе́ха   She achieved **success**
Он дости́г свое́й це́ли   He achieved **his aim**
Я жела́ю тебе́ сча́стья   I wish you **happiness**
Э́то заслу́живает её внима́ния   That deserves **her attention**
Он косну́лся её плеча́   He touched **her shoulder**
Я каса́юсь ва́жной те́мы   I touch on **an important subject**

(b) Others take the genitive of nouns denoting generalized or
abstract ideas and the accusative of those denoting persons and
specific objects:

(i) verbs of waiting: ждать 'to wait for', ожида́ть 'to expect' :

Я ждал по́езда/по́езд   I was waiting for **a/the train**
Ива́н ждёт Ма́шу   Ivan is waiting for **Mary**
Мы ожида́ли свое́й о́череди   We were awaiting **our turn**

(ii) Verbs of seeking, asking, wanting:

иска́ть 'to seek, try to obtain' (+ genitive), 'to look for, try to find' (+ accusative):

> Мы и́щем **защи́ты**   We are seeking **protection**
>
> Я ищу́ **ну́жную мне кни́гу**   I am looking for a **book I need**
>
> Она́ и́щет **рабо́ту**   She is trying to find **work**

проси́ть/по- 'to request' + genitive of abstract nouns and substances (partitive genitive), accusative of objects and persons:

> Я прошу́ **проще́ния**   I ask forgiveness
>
> Она́ про́сит **хле́ба**   She asks for **some bread**
>
> Ма́льчик про́сит **самока́т**   The boy asks for **a scooter**
>
> Она́ про́сит **ма́му** помо́чь   He asks **Mum** to help

тре́бовать/по- 'to demand' + genitive of abstract nouns, accusative of objects:

> Она́ потре́бовала **объясне́ния**   She demanded **an explanation**
>
> Он тре́бует **квита́нцию**   He demands **a receipt**

хоте́ть 'to want' + genitive of abstract nouns and substances (partitive genitive), accusative of objects:

> Бо́льше всего́ мы хоти́м **ми́ра**   Most of all we want **peace**
>
> Хо́чешь **ча́ю?**   Would you like **some tea?**
>
> Я хочу́ **моби́льный телефо́н**   I want a **mobile phone**

(iii) Verbs of fearing, avoiding: **боя́ться** 'to be afraid of', **избега́ть/избежа́ть** 'to avoid' + genitive of abstract nouns, accusative of persons:

> Он бои́тся **темноты́**   He is afraid of **the dark**
>
> Он бои́тся **жену́**   He is afraid of **his wife**
>
> Я избега́ю **неприя́тностей**   I avoid **trouble**
>
> Она́ избега́ет **свою́ сестру́**   She avoids **her sister**

For the genitive with numerals, *see pages 82–95, passim.*

The dative case

The dative as indirect object of a verb

(a) A main function of the dative case is to act as the **indirect object** of a verb, that is to say, it denotes the recipient, addressee, or beneficiary of an action. The object received appears in the accusative case:

> Она́ дала́ кни́гу ма́льчику   She gave **the boy** a book or She gave a book **to the boy**

> ❗ **Note:** The English versions are synonymous, but only the second version contains a clear indication ('**to the boy**') that the boy is the recipient. In the first version this is inferred. In Russian the dative case (ма́льчику 'to the boy') is used in rendering either version.

(b) Other verbs involved in the construction include **дари́ть/по-** 'to give', **задава́ть/зада́ть** 'to ask (a question)', **говори́ть/сказа́ть** 'to tell', **покупа́ть/купи́ть** 'to buy', **пока́зывать/показа́ть** 'to show', **писа́ть/на-** 'to write', **посыла́ть/посла́ть** 'to send', **предлага́ть/ предложи́ть** 'to offer', **продава́ть/прода́ть** 'to sell', **звони́ть/по-** 'to ring, telephone', **шить/с-** 'to sew, make', **плати́ть/за-** 'to pay':

> Он подари́л **неве́сте** кольцо́   He gave **his fiancée** a ring
> Он за́дал **ученику́** вопро́с   He asked **the pupil** a question
> Она́ сказа́ла **судье́** пра́вду   She told **the judge** the truth
> Она́ купи́ла **сы́ну** велосипе́д   She bought **her son** a bicycle
> Он написа́л **ма́тери** письмо́   He wrote a letter **to his mother**
> Он показа́л **сестре́** пода́рок   He showed **his sister** the present
> Он предложи́л **бра́ту** конфе́ту   He offered **his brother** a sweet
> Он про́дал свою́ маши́ну **дру́гу**   He sold his car **to a friend**
> Рабо́чий позвони́л **инжене́ру**   The worker rang **the engineer**
> Она́ сши́ла **подру́ге** пла́тье   She made a dress **for her friend**
> Я плачу́ **касси́ру**   I pay **the cashier**   (In this example, **де́ньги** 'money' is understood.)
> Он посла́л чек **сы́ну**   He sent a cheque **to his son**

> ❗ **Note:** if a **person** is sent, the preposition к is used:
> Они́ отпра́вили ма́льчика **к тёте**   They sent the boy **to his aunt**

Impersonal constructions with the dative case

(a) English nominative phrases denoting physical state ('I am/feel hot, cold, warm, comfortable', etc.) are the equivalent of phrases with the **dative case** in Russian:

Де́тям хо́лодно   **The children** feel cold
Сестре́ тепло́   **My sister** feels warm
Тури́стам жа́рко   **The tourists** feel hot
Ба́бушке удо́бно   **Grandma** is comfortable

(b) The construction is also used to express state of mind, inclination, impression, and state of health:

Ученика́м ску́чно   **The pupils** are bored
Фе́рмеру гру́стно   **The farmer** is sad
Как Ма́ше не сты́дно!   **Masha** should be ashamed!
Ива́ну надое́ло смотре́ть телеви́зор   **Ivan** is/was bored
  watching TV
Спортсме́ну хо́чется спать   **The athlete** feels drowsy
Мне ка́жется, что она́ права́   It seems **to me** that she is right
Больно́му сего́дня лу́чше   **The patient** feels better today

Adjectives that take the dative

Most of these correspond to English equivalents with 'to':
благода́рный 'grateful to', **ве́рный** 'faithful, loyal to', **знако́мый** 'familiar to', **изве́стный** 'known to', **подо́бный** 'similar to', **послу́шный** 'obedient to', **рад** 'glad' (to see) (short form only):

Я благода́рен **дру́гу**   I am grateful **to my friend**
Он бу́дет ве́рен **жене́**   He will be faithful **to his wife**
Э́та мело́дия знако́ма **де́тям**   This tune is familiar **to children**
Его́ и́мя изве́стно **всем фи́ннам**   His name is known **to all Finns**
Его́ стихи́ подо́бны **пу́шкинским**   His verse is similar **to Pushkin's**
Ребёнок послу́шен **роди́телям**   The child is obedient **to its parents**
Я всегда́ рад **Ве́ре**   I am always glad **to see Vera**

Verbs that take the dative

(a) Many verbs that take the dative describe rendering a service or complying: **помогáть/помóчь** 'to help', **служи́ть/по-** 'to serve', **совéтовать/по-** 'to advise', **соотвéтствовать** 'to correspond (to)':

Дéвочка помоглá **мáтери**   The little girl helped **her mother**
ОÓН слýжит **дéлу** ми́ра   The UNO serves the **cause** of peace
Áрмия слýжит **нарóду**   The army serves **the people**
Он совéтует **женé** согласи́ться   He advises **his wife** to agree
Э́то **соотвéтствует** и́стине   That **corresponds** to the truth

(b) Others imply hindrance or harm: **вреди́ть/по-** 'to harm', **грози́ть/при-** 'to threaten', **изменя́ть/измени́ть** 'to betray' **мешáть/по-** 'to hinder, prevent', **запрещáть/запрети́ть** 'to forbid':

Курéние вреди́т **здорóвью**   Smoking damages **the health**
Они́ грозя́т **залóжникам**   They threaten **the hostages**
Я запрети́л **дéтям** кури́ть   I forbade **the children** to smoke
Шпиóн измени́л **рóдине**   The spy betrayed **his country**
Шум мешáл **отцý** рабóтать   The noise prevented **father** from working

(c) Others still denote attitude or reaction: **вéрить/по-** 'to believe', **доверя́ть/довéрить** 'to trust', **зави́довать/по-** 'to envy', **рáдоваться/об-** 'to rejoice', **удивля́ться/удиви́ться** 'to be surprised':

Никтó не вéрит **поли́тикам**   No one believes **politicians**
Больнóй доверя́ет **врачý**   The patient trusts **the doctor**
Онá зави́дует **своéй подрýге**   She envies **her friend**
Он обрáдовался её **успéхам**   He rejoiced at her **progress**
Я удиви́лся **егó словáм**   I was surprised at **his words**

> **!** Note: **Учи́ть** 'to teach' takes the accusative of the person taught and the dative of the subject taught: Онá учи́ла **детéй фи́зике** 'She taught **the children physics**'.

The instrumental case

Functional meaning of the instrumental case

(a) The instrumental case denotes that the object in the
instrumental is being used to perform a function: Он открыл
дверь ключо́м 'He opened the door **with a key**'. Likewise:

> Он ре́жет хлеб ножо́м   He cuts the bread **with a knife**
>
> Она́ пи́шет карандашо́м   She writes **with a pencil**
>
> Он копа́ет лопа́той   He digs **with a spade**
>
> Я плачу́ рубля́ми   I pay in ('with') **roubles**
>
> Она́ ко́рмит ребёнка гру́дью   She **breast**-feeds the child

> **!** **Note:** If 'with' = 'characterized by, carrying', it is rendered by **c** + instrumental:
> 'He speaks **with an accent**' Он говори́т с акце́нтом; 'He stands **with an axe** in
> his hand' Он стои́т с топоро́м в руке́.

(b) The construction also involves parts of the body: Он дви́гает
руко́й 'He moves his hand', кача́ть/по- голово́й 'to shake one's
head', кива́ть/кивну́ть голово́й 'to nod one's head', маха́ть/
махну́ть руко́й 'to wave the hand', пожима́ть/пожа́ть плеча́ми 'to
shrug the shoulders'. Objects held in the hand can also appear in
the instrumental: Он хло́пнул две́рью 'He slammed the door'.

The instrumental as agent in passive constructions

In a passive construction, the natural *object* of an action becomes
the *grammatical* subject. In other words, the object of an action
in an *active* construction becomes the grammatical *subject* in a
passive construction:

> Нача́льник уво́лил его́   The boss dismissed **him**
>
> Он был уво́лен нача́льником   He was dismissed **by the boss**

> **!** **Note:** The agent of the action (the boss) appears in the **instrumental**.

Adjectives that take the instrumental case

(a) Adjectives that take the instrumental case often appear in the short form. The instrumental 'delimits' the meaning of the adjective, specifying the sphere it relates to (e.g. rich **in coal**, etc.).

богáтый 'rich':

Финля́ндия бога́та **озёрами**   Finland is rich in **lakes**

больнóй 'sick':

Он бóлен **туберкулёзом**   He has got **tuberculosis**

довóльный 'pleased':

Мы довóльны **результа́тами**   We are pleased with **the results**

обя́занный 'indebted':

Я обя́зан емý **свои́м успéхом**   I am indebted to him for **my success**

(b) A number of other adjectives are used with the instrumental in the meaning '**by virtue of**': Доли́на замеча́тельна **свое́й красотóй** 'The valley is remarkable **for its beauty**', **Хара́ктером** он похóж на отца́ '**In temperament** he is like his father'.

The use of the instrumental in giving dimensions

Unlike English ('30 metres **high**', '3 miles **wide**', etc.), Russian uses nouns instead of adjectives to indicate dimension (the construction is close to English 'in height', 'in depth', etc.):

зда́ние **высотóй** (в) 20 этажéй   a building 20 storeys **high**
óзеро **глубинóй** (в) 40 мéтров   a lake 40 metres **deep**
стол **длинóй** (в) три мéтра   a table three metres **long**
пóле **плóщадью** (в) 2.000 кв.м.   a field 2, 000 sq. m. **in area**
доска́ **толщинóй** (в) два см.   a plank two centimetres **thick**
у́лица **ширинóй** (в) 30 мéтров   a street 30 metres **wide**

! **Note:** (a) the preposition (**в**) can usually be omitted, especially in conversation and in specialist literature.

(b) dimension words in questions about dimension appear in the **genitive** case: Какóй **ширины́** доли́на? 'How **wide** is the valley?', Какóго он **рóста**? 'How **tall** is he?', etc.

Verbs that take the instrumental case

These include verbs that denote:

(a) use, control, ownership: **владе́ть** 'to own', **заве́довать** 'to manage, be in charge of', **кома́ндовать** 'to command', **по́льзоваться/вос-** 'to use', **располага́ть** 'to have at one's disposal', **руководи́ть** 'to be in charge of, supervise', **управля́ть** 'to manage, run':

Она́ владе́ет **больши́м до́мом**   She owns **a large house**
Он заве́дует **городски́м тра́нспортом**   He is in charge of **city transport**
Он кома́ндует **диви́зией**   He commands **a division**
Я не по́льзуюсь **ли́фтом**   I don't use **the lift**
Он руководи́т **мое́й рабо́той**   He supervises **my work**
Я располага́ю **свобо́дным вре́менем**   I have **some spare time**
Президе́нт управля́ет **страно́й**   The president runs **the country**

(b) attitude: **горди́ться** 'to be proud of', **дорожи́ть** 'to value', **интересова́ться** 'to be interested in', **любова́ться/по-** 'to admire', **увлека́ться/увле́чься** 'to be keen on':

Он горди́тся **свои́ми детьми́**   He is proud of **his children**
Она́ дорожи́т **на́шей дру́жбой**   She values **our friendship**
Он интересу́ется **языка́ми**   He is interested in **languages**
Она́ любу́ется **пейза́жем**   She admires **the landscape**
Он увлека́ется **ша́хматами**   He is keen on **chess**

(c) various other meanings: **боле́ть** 'to be sick with', **дыша́ть** 'to breathe', **же́ртвовать/по-** 'to sacrifice', **занима́ться/заня́ться** 'to be occupied with', **па́хнуть** 'to smell of', **рискова́ть/рискну́ть** 'to risk', **страда́ть** 'to suffer from':

Она́ боле́ет **бронхи́том**   She has got **bronchitis**
Он ды́шит **све́жим во́здухом**   He breathes **fresh air**
Она́ же́ртвует **свое́й карье́рой**   She sacrifices **her career**
Он занима́ется **спо́ртом**   He goes in **for sport**
Па́хло **овоща́ми**   There was a smell **of vegetables**
Она́ рискова́ла **свое́й жи́знью**   She was risking **her life**
Он страда́ет **бессо́нницей**   He suffers **from insomnia**

Adverbial expressions in the instrumental case

These comprise:
(a) parts of the day:

у́тром in the morning
днём in the daytime, in the afternoon
ве́чером in the evening
но́чью at night

These can be expanded:

сего́дня у́тром this morning
одна́жды но́чью one night

(b) seasons of the year:

весно́й in spring **о́сенью** in autumn
ле́том in summer **зимо́й** in winter

These can also be expanded:

ра́нней зимо́й in **early** winter
весно́й **про́шлого го́да** **last** spring
э́тим ле́том **this** summer

(c) modes of transport:

по́ездом by train
самолётом by air
авто́бусом by bus

Я вы́летел **пе́рвым ре́йсом** I went out **on the first flight**

(d) manner:

други́ми слова́ми in other words
шёпотом in a whisper
каки́м о́бразом? in what way?
таки́м о́бразом thus, in that way
любо́й цено́й at all costs

The instrumental case after the verb 'to be'

(a) The instrumental is mandatory after all forms of the verb **быть** 'to be' (the future, the infinitive, the conditional, the gerund, the imperative), *except* the past tense (*see also page 49*):

Я бу́ду **инжене́ром**   I will be an **engineer**

Он хо́чет **быть врачо́м**   He wants to be **a doctor**

Е́сли бы я был **худо́жником**,   If I were **an artist** I would paint
  я написа́л бы её портре́т   her portrait

Бу́дучи **учи́телем**, он не бога́т   Being **a teacher**, he is not
  wealthy

Хо́чешь быть поэ́том? Будь **поэ́том!**   You want to be a poet?
  Be a **poet!**

(b) After the *past* tense of **быть** 'to be', a distinction is made
between the nominative case of a noun, which may denote
permanent status:

По профе́ссии он был **хи́мик**   By profession he was **a chemist**

and the instrumental case, which may denote *temporary* status:

В то вре́мя он был **ма́льчиком**   At that time he was **a boy**

(c) However, it is also quite normal now for the *instrumental* to
denote permanent status as well:

Ди́ма был **хоро́шим челове́ком**   Dima was **a good man**

Она́ была́ **сестро́й** моего́ дру́га   She was my friend's **sister**

(d) If two nouns are linked by a form of the verb **быть**, the noun
with the more general meaning appears in the instrumental, while
that with the more specific meaning appears in the nominative:

На́шей гла́вной пробле́мой был **бюрократи́зм**   Our main
  problem was **red tape**

(e) The instrumental is also used with the verbs рабо́тать 'to
work', служи́ть 'to serve', etc.:

Он рабо́тал **меха́ником**   He worked **as a mechanic**

Он служи́л **солда́том**   He served **as a soldier**

and in constructions with an in-built meaning of time:

Он жил там **подро́стком**   He lived there as (= when he was) **an
  adolescent**

The instrumental case after other verbs

Other verbs that take the instrumental case include **оказываться/ оказаться** 'to turn out to be', **оставаться/остаться** 'to remain', **становиться/стать** 'to become', **считаться** 'to be considered', **чувствовать себя** 'to feel', **являться/явиться** 'to be':

Он оказался **ложным другом**   He turned out to be **a false friend**

Он остался **жертвой** войны   He remained **a victim** of the war

Он стал **учителем**   He became **a teacher**

Она считается **гением**   She is considered to be **a genius**

Основным средством транспорта является поезд   **The basic means** of transport is the train

Verb + accusative + instrumental case

The verbs **назначать/назначить** 'to appoint', **называть/назвать** 'to name', **считать/счесть** 'to consider' take the accusative of a person or object and the instrumental of their name, function, or status:

Я считаю его **хорошим другом**   I consider him **a good friend**

Они назвали ребёнка **Васей (or Вася)**   They named the child **Vasya**

Его назначили **директором**   They appointed him **director**

Meanings of similarity and function

кепка **блином**   **flat** cap (lit. 'like a pancake')

Птица летит **стрелой**   The bird flies **like an arrow**

Он вернулся **героем**   He returned **a hero**

Он вырос **славным парнем**   He grew up to be **a fine young man**

For the prepositional/locative case, *see pages 184–193.*

The adjective

An adjective is a part of speech that describes a noun or pronoun. Most Russian adjectives have two forms: a **long form** (also known as the **attributive** form), that ends in two vowels and precedes the noun:

до́брый челове́к   **a kind** man

and a **short form** (also known as the **predicative** form), the masculine of which ends in a consonant, the feminine, neuter, and plural in a vowel. The short form usually follows the subject:

Он **добр** к ней   He **is kind** to her
Она́ **добра́** к нему́   She **is kind** to him

The long form declines in all six cases and **agrees** with the noun it qualifies in case, gender, and number. The short form has four forms only (masculine, feminine, and neuter singular, and plural), and does not decline.

I Long form of the adjective

Declension

There are four major categories of adjectival declension:
Hard declension: **бе́лый** 'white', **густо́й** 'thick'.
Soft declension: **пре́жний** 'former'.
'Mixed' declension I. Adjectives in **-гий, -кий, -хий/-го́й, -ко́й, -хо́й**: **до́лгий** 'long', **ру́сский** 'Russian', **ти́хий** 'quiet', **дорого́й** 'dear', **тако́й** 'such', **глухо́й** 'deaf'.
'Mixed' declension II. Adjectives in **-жий, -чий, -ший, -щий/-жо́й, -шо́й**: **похо́жий** 'similar', **горя́чий** 'hot', **хоро́ший** 'good', **о́бщий** 'common', **чужо́й** 'alien', **большо́й** 'big'.

The endings of the 'mixed' declension are determined by the spelling rules (*see page 6*).

> **Note:** All long-form adjectives are subject to the animate accusative/genitive rule (*see pages 9, 21*).

Declension of the hard-ending adjective

Type 1: adjectives with the stress on the stem (бе́лый 'white')

	Masculine	Feminine	Neuter	Plural
Nom.	бе́л-ый	бе́л-ая	бе́л-ое	бе́л-ые
Acc.	бе́л-ый	бе́л-ую	бе́л-ое	бе́л-ые
Gen.	бе́л-ого	бе́л-ой	бе́л-ого	бе́л-ых
Dat.	бе́л-ому	бе́л-ой	бе́л-ому	бе́л-ым
Instr.	бе́л-ым	бе́л-ой	бе́л-ым	бе́л-ыми
Prep.	бе́л-ом	бе́л-ой	бе́л-ом	бе́л-ых

Most adjectives in Russian follow the same pattern as **бе́лый** 'white'.

Type 2: adjectives with end stress (густо́й 'thick')

	Masculine	Feminine	Neuter	Plural
Nom.	густ-о́й	густ-а́я	густ-о́е	густ-ы́е
Acc.	густ-о́й	густ-у́ю	густ-о́е	густ-ы́е
Gen.	густ-о́го	густ-о́й	густ-о́го	густ-ы́х
Dat.	густ-о́му	густ-о́й	густ-о́му	густ-ы́м
Instr.	густ-ы́м	густ-о́й	густ-ы́м	густ-ы́ми
Prep.	густ-о́м	густ-о́й	густ-о́м	густ-ы́х

> **Note:** (a) A smaller number of adjectives follow the pattern of **густо́й** 'thick': больно́й 'sick', голубо́й 'light-blue', злой 'wicked', золото́й 'golden', круто́й 'steep', мирово́й 'world', молодо́й 'young', основно́й 'basic', пожило́й 'elderly', просто́й 'simple', прямо́й 'direct', родно́й 'native' слепо́й 'blind', сыро́й 'damp', худо́й 'thin', and some others.
> (b) Their declension differs from that of stem-stressed **бе́лый** 'white', apart from stress, only in the masculine nominative and accusative cases (**-о́й** instead of **-ый**).

Declension of the soft-ending adjective

In the declension of the soft-ending adjective, the initial vowels of the hard endings (**ы, о, а, у**) are replaced by their soft equivalents (**и, е, я, ю**). Пре́жний 'former':

	Masculine	*Feminine*	*Neuter*	*Plural*
Nom.	пре́жн-ий	пре́жн-яя	пре́жн-ее	пре́жн-ие
Acc.	пре́жн-ий	пре́жн-юю	пре́жн-ее	пре́жн-ие
Gen.	пре́жн-его	пре́жн-ей	пре́жн-его	пре́жн-их
Dat.	пре́жн-ему	пре́жн-ей	пре́жн-ему	пре́жн-им
Instr.	пре́жн-им	пре́жн-ей	пре́жн-им	пре́жн-ими
Prep.	пре́жн-ем	пре́жн-ей	пре́жн-ем	пре́жн-их

Apart from ка́рий 'hazel-coloured', adjectives in this group have the suffix **-н-**; many express meanings of time or space. These can be divided into groups in accordance with meaning:

(a) *Seasons of the year:*

весе́нний	spring	**ле́тний**	summer
осе́нний	autumn	**зи́мний**	winter

Morning and evening:

у́тренний	morning
вече́рний	evening

Yesterday, today, tomorrow:

вчера́шний	yesterday's	**сего́дняшний**	today's
за́втрашний	tomorrow's		

(b) *Opposites in time and space:*

ра́нний	early	**по́здний**	late
неда́вний	recent	**да́вний**	of long standing
бли́жний	near	**да́льний**	far
ве́рхний	upper	**ни́жний**	lower
вну́тренний	internal	**вне́шний**	external
за́дний	back	**пере́дний**	front

(c) *Others:* **и́скренний** 'sincere', **кра́йний** 'extreme', **ли́шний** 'superfluous', **после́дний** 'last', **си́ний** 'dark blue', **сре́дний** 'middle'.

Mixed declension Type I: nouns in -гий, -кий, -хий/-гой, -кой, -хой (ру́сский 'Russian', плохо́й 'bad')

	Masculine	Feminine	Neuter	Plural
Nom.	ру́сск-ий	ру́сск-ая	ру́сск-ое	ру́сск-ие
Acc.	ру́сск-ий	ру́сск-ую	ру́сск-ое	ру́сск-ие
Gen.	ру́сск-ого	ру́сск-ой	ру́сск-ого	ру́сск-их
Dat.	ру́сск-ому	ру́сск-ой	ру́сск-ому	ру́сск-им
Instr.	ру́сск-им	ру́сск-ой	ру́сск-им	ру́сск-ими
Prep.	ру́сск-ом	ру́сск-ой	ру́сск-ом	ру́сск-их

The mixed nature of the endings is accounted for by the spelling rule which requires ы to be replaced by и after г, к, or х. This affects the masculine singular nominative, accusative, and instrumental, the neuter singular instrumental, and the whole of the plural.

Nom.	плох-о́й	плох-а́я	плох-о́е	плох-и́е
Acc.	плох-о́й	плох-у́ю	плох-о́е	плох-и́е
Gen.	плох-о́го	плох-о́й	плох-о́го	плох-и́х
Dat.	плох-о́му	плох-о́й	плох-о́му	плох-и́м
Instr.	плох-и́м	плох-о́й	плох-и́м	плох-и́ми
Prep.	плох-о́м	плох-о́й	плох-о́м	плох-и́х

! **Note:** (a) apart from stress, the declensions of ру́сский and плохо́й differ only in the masculine nominative and accusative singular.
(b) the spelling rule (ы is replaced by и after г, к, х) affects the masculine and neuter instrumental of плохо́й, and the whole of the plural.

There are a limited number of adjectives in -гий (e.g. до́лгий 'long', стро́гий 'strict'), -хий (e.g. ве́тхий 'ancient', ти́хий 'quiet'), -гой (e.g. дорого́й 'dear', друго́й 'other'), and -хой (e.g. глухо́й 'deaf', сухо́й 'dry'). Suffix -ск- is very widely represented in adjectives of nationality (испа́нский 'Spanish', шве́дский 'Swedish', etc.), town and river names (моско́вский 'Moscow', донско́й 'of the Don'), names of humans (мужско́й 'male', де́тский 'children's') and organizations (парла́ментский 'parliamentary').

Mixed declension Type 2: adjectives in -жий, -чий, -ший, -щий/-жóй, -шóй (горя́чий 'hot', большóй 'big')

	Masculine	*Feminine*	*Neuter*	*Plural*
Nom	горя́ч-ий	горя́ч-ая	горя́ч-ее	горя́ч-ие
Acc.	горя́ч-ий	горя́ч-ую	горя́ч-ее	горя́ч-ие
Gen.	горя́ч-его	горя́ч-ей	горя́ч-его	горя́ч-их
Dat.	горя́ч-ему	горя́ч-ей	горя́ч-ему	горя́ч-им
Instr.	горя́ч-им	горя́ч-ей	горя́ч-им	горя́ч-ими
Prep.	горя́ч-ем	горя́ч-ей	горя́ч-ем	горя́ч-их

Likewise похóжий 'similar', прохóжий 'passing', свежий 'fresh', шипу́чий 'fizzy', мла́дший 'junior', ста́рший 'senior', хорóший 'good', блестя́щий 'shining, brilliant', бу́дущий 'future', óбщий 'common, general', etc.

The mixed nature of the above endings is accounted for by the spelling rules: и (never ы) appears after ж, ч, ш, щ. After ж, ч, ш, and щ, о can appear only in *stressed* position.

Nom	больш-óй	больш-а́я	больш-óе	больш-и́е
Acc.	больш-óй	больш-у́ю	больш-óе	больш-и́е
Gen.	больш-óго	больш-óй	больш-óго	больш-и́х
Dat.	больш-óму	больш-óй	больш-óму	больш-и́м
Instr.	больш-и́м	больш-óй	больш-и́м	больш-и́ми
Prep.	больш-óм	больш-óй	больш-óм	больш-и́х

This time only one spelling rule applies: и (never ы) after ж, ч, ш, and щ (о *can* appear after ш because it is *stressed*).

Чужóй 'alien, someone else's' and compounds of большóй 'big' (e.g. небольшóй 'small') are the only other commonly-used adjectives represented by this declension (there are *no* adjectives in -чой or -щой).

Uses of the long form of the adjective

(a) the long form of the adjective agrees with the noun in gender, number, and case. In attributive function, it usually precedes the noun:

	Masculine singular	*Feminine singular*
Nom.	**Реакти́вный самолёт** лети́т	**Бу́рная река́** течёт
	The jet aircraft is flying	The turbulent river flows
Acc.	Я слы́шу **гро́мкий** го́лос	Я чита́ю **хоро́шую** кни́гу
	I hear a loud voice	I am reading a good book
Gen.	дом его́ **мла́дшего** сы́на	Нет **горя́чей** воды́
	his younger son's house	There is no hot water
Dat.	Я звоню́ **гла́вному** врачу́	Я помога́ю **бе́дной** же́нщине
	I ring the senior doctor	I help the poor woman
Instr.	Я пишу́ **кра́сным** карандашо́м	Я прие́хал **ра́нней** весно́й
	I write with a red pencil	I arrived in early spring
Prep.	Я живу́ в **большо́м** го́роде	Я ду́маю о **ру́сской** во́дке
	I live in a large town	I think about Russian vodka

Plural: больши́е заво́ды 'large factories':

Nom.	больш-**и́е** заво́д-ы
Acc.	больш-**и́е** заво́д-ы
Gen.	больш-**и́х** заво́д-ов
Dat.	больш-**и́м** заво́д-ам
Instr.	больш-**и́ми** заво́д-ами
Prep.	больш-**и́х** заво́д-ах

(b) it may also follow the noun, if there are dependent words (e.g. от сне́га in the following example), separated from the noun by a *comma* and with 'who' or 'which' understood. The rules of agreement apply:

Мы любу́емся **гора́ми, бе́лыми от сне́га**   We admire **the hills, which are white** with snow

(c) in predicative function, it follows immediately after the noun, as its predicate:

Ребёнок **послу́шный**   The child **is obedient**
Утро **све́жее**   The morning **is fresh**
Ве́тер **си́льный**   The wind **is strong**

(d) in the past or future tenses the *instrumental* is preferred in *written* Russian when the verb 'to be' is involved:

Ребёнок был **послу́шным**   The child was **obedient**
Ко́жа у неё была́ **бе́лой**   Her skin was **white**
Фотогра́фия бу́дет **уда́чной**   The photograph will be **successful**

> **! Note:** The nominative is preferred in *colloquial* speech (for the **short form** of the adjective as a predicate, *see pages 53–55*).

(e) it is also used in the *instrumental* case after **каза́ться/по-** 'to seem' and some other verbs:

Брасле́т каза́лся **недороги́м**   The bracelet seemed **inexpensive**
Дверь оказа́лась **за́пертой**   The door turned out to be **locked**
Чу́вство го́лода ста́ло **привы́чным**   The feeling of hunger became **habitual**
Шко́ла счита́лась **отли́чной**   The school was considered **excellent**
Э́то реше́ние явля́ется **оконча́тельным**   This decision is **final**

(f) it also answers the questions 'in what order?', 'in what state?':

Он пришёл **пе́рвым**   He arrived **first**
Она́ оста́вила кни́гу **раскры́той**   She left the book **open**
Дай больно́му молоко́ **горя́чим**   Give the invalid his milk **hot**

Additional comments on the long form of the adjective

(a) Consonant change in adjectival formation

The letters **г**, **к**, **х**, **ц**, and **л** change, respectively, to **ж**, **ч**, **ш**, **ч**, and **ль** before suffix **-н-** in adjectives derived from nouns:

г-ж доро́га 'road' **доро́жный** знак road sign

к-ч восто́к 'east' **восто́чная** грани́ца eastern border

х-ш во́здух 'air' **возду́шный** шар balloon

ц-ч у́лица 'street' **у́личный** фона́рь street lamp

л-ль футбо́л 'football' **футбо́льное** по́ле football pitch

(b) Special types of adjective

Type ма́мин 'Mum's', **отцо́в** 'Dad's', and a number of others derived from the names of family members and some others.

Type -енький. Denotes smallness (e.g. ма́ленький 'small'), sometimes with an emotive nuance (e.g. све́женький, from све́жий 'fresh').

Type -оватый/-еватый '-ish' (denoting a small degree of some quality): сладкова́тый 'sweetish', синева́тый 'bluish'.

Type -ивый. Denotes inclination or characteristic: лжи́вый 'deceitful, lying', заду́мчивый 'pensive'.

Type -истый. Denotes abundance: камени́стый 'stony'.

(c) Adjectival nouns

(i) Some words have the form of an adjective but the meaning of a noun (rather like the 'reds' in English, of a football team, or 'the good, the bad, and the ugly'). In many cases, an absent noun is 'understood'.

(ii) Animates distinguish gender: **рабо́чий, рабо́чая** 'worker', **слу́жащий, слу́жащая** 'white-collar worker' (however, **часово́й** 'sentry' and **учёный** 'academic' are masculine only). Inanimates take their gender and number from the noun which is implied:

крива́я (ли́ния 'line' understood) '*curve*'
столо́вая (ко́мната 'room' understood) '*dining room*'
живо́тное (существо́ 'being' understood) '*animal*'
моро́женое (блю́до 'dish' understood) '*ice-cream*'
бу́дущее (вре́мя 'time' understood) '*the future*'
чаевы́е (де́ньги 'money' understood) '*a tip*'

! Note: also гла́вное 'the main thing', са́мое ва́жное 'the most important thing'.

(iii) Many of the adjectival nouns continue to function as adjectives: **столо́вая** ло́жка 'table spoon', **выходно́й** or **выходно́й** день 'day off'.
(iv) All decline like adjectives: Нет **моро́женого** 'There is no ice-cream'.
(v) the animate-accusative = genitive rule applies to animate masculine adjectival nouns in the singular (Я ви́жу **рабо́чего** 'I see **the worker**') and all animate adjectival nouns in the plural (Я ви́жу **рабо́чих** 'I see **the workers**', Я кормлю́ **живо́тных** 'I feed **the animals**').

(d) Loan adjectives of the type бе́ж 'beige'

Some of these adjectives relate to fashion, others to food and other topics. They are indeclinable and usually *follow* the noun:

ю́бка **ми́ни**   **mini** skirt
карто́фель **фри**   chips, French **fries**
часы́ **пик**   **rush** hour
вес **бру́тто**   **gross** weight

| The short form of the adjective

Formation

(a) The short form of an adjective is made by removing the whole of the masculine long-form ending and the final vowels of the feminine, neuter, and plural: *Long form* бога́тый 'rich', *Short forms* бога́т (masculine), бога́та (feminine), бога́то (neuter), бога́ты (plural).

(b) Stress may be fixed, as in the above, or mobile, with a tendency to stem stress in the masculine, neuter, and plural, and end stress in the feminine:

Long form	Short form
молодо́й 'young':	мо́лод, молода́, мо́лодо, мо́лоды
до́брый 'kind':	добр, добра́, добро́, до́бры́

The fleeting vowel

(a) A fleeting vowel, usually -e-, appears between two consonants or replaces -й- in many *masculine* short forms:

бе́дный 'poor':	бе́ден, бедна́, бе́дно, бе́дны́
споко́йный 'calm':	споко́ен, споко́йна, споко́йно, споко́йны

(b) The fleeting vowel -o- is used:

  (i) before к or г:

бли́зкий 'close':	бли́зок, близка́, бли́зко, бли́зки́
до́лгий 'long':	до́лог, долга́, до́лго, до́лги

! Note: -e- is used instead of -o- after ж, ч, ш: тя́жек from тя́жкий 'severe'.

  (ii) in по́лон (from по́лный 'full'), зол (from злой 'evil'), and смешо́н (from смешно́й 'funny')

(c) A few short-form masculine adjectives have fleeting vowel -ё-: умён from у́мный 'clever', хитёр from хи́трый 'cunning', силён from си́льный 'strong'.

Irregular short forms

Long form	Short forms
большо́й 'big':	вели́к, велика́, велико́, велики́
ма́ленький 'small':	мал, мала́, мало́, малы́
досто́йный 'worthy':	досто́ин, досто́йна, досто́йно, досто́йны

Functions of the short form of the adjective

(a) The short form of the adjective appears only in predicative position, i.e. it usually follows the noun and is linked to it by a form of the verb 'to be'. In cases where long and short forms are synonymous, either can be used in predicative position:

Приро́да там **прекра́сная/прекра́сна**   The scenery there is **wonderful**

(b) The long and short forms of some adjectives differ in meaning and are not interchangeable:

Э́тот стари́к **плохо́й**   This old man is **wicked**
Стари́к совсе́м **плох**   The old man is pretty **poorly**
Она́ **хоро́шая**   She is **good**
Она́ **хороша́** собо́й   She is **good-looking**

(c) In the case of some short forms, a distinction is made between *temporary* state (short form) and *permanent* state (long form):

Он **бо́лен**/Она́ **больна́**   He/She is ill
Он **больно́й**/Она́ **больна́я**   He/She is **chronically ill**

Short-form adjectives commonly used to denote a temporary state or relating to particular circumstances:

Он **го́лоден**	He is hungry	Она́ **голодна́**	She is hungry
Он **гото́в**	He is ready	Она́ **гото́ва**	She is ready
Он **дово́лен**	He is pleased	Она́ **дово́льна**	She is pleased
Он **жив**	He **is alive**	Она́ **жива́**	She is alive
Он **за́нят**	He **is busy**	Она́ **занята́**	She is busy
Он **здоро́в**	He **is healthy**	Она́ **здоро́ва**	She is healthy
Он **непра́в**	He is wrong	Она́ **неправа́**	She is wrong
Он **несча́стен**	He is unhappy	Она́ **несча́стна**	She is unhappy
Он **прав**	He is right	Она́ **права́**	She is right
Он **сча́стлив**	He is happy	Она́ **сча́стлива**	She is happy
Он **сыт**	He is full	Она́ **сыта́**	She is full
Он **уве́рен**	He **is sure**	Она́ **уве́рена**	She is sure

Delimitation of meaning

(a) The short form is *mandatory* in predicative position when the adjective and noun identify with each other only in certain aspects. For example, 'This country is rich' can be rendered as **Э́та страна́ бога́тая** (long form) or **Э́та страна́ бога́та** (short form), but the short form is *compulsory* in rendering 'This country is rich **in oil**' (**Э́та страна́ бога́та не́фтью**), since 'rich' is limited to *one* area only: oil.

(b) Likewise, 'The child is obedient' can be rendered as **Ребёнок послу́шный** (long form) or **Ребёнок послу́шен** (short form), but if, for example, the dative of роди́тели 'parents' is added, the short form *must* be used: **Ребёнок послу́шен роди́телям** 'The child is obedient to its parents' (because the meaning is delimited by **роди́телям**).

(c) Delimitation (i.e., restriction to a particular context) can be effected in the following ways:

 (i) By a noun in an oblique case

Корзи́на полна́ я́год   The basket is **full of berries**
Речь досто́йна внима́ния   The speech is **worthy of attention**
Она́ верна́ своему́ му́жу   She is **faithful to her husband**
Край бе́ден ре́ками   The area is **poor in rivers**.

 (ii) By a prepositional phrase

Он равноду́шен к му́зыке   He is **indifferent to music**
Она́ добра́ по нату́ре   She is **kind by nature**
Биле́т действи́телен по май   The ticket is **valid up to and including May**
Он глух на пра́вое у́хо   He is **deaf in the right ear**
Пестици́ды вредны́ для жуко́в   Pesticides are **harmful to beetles**

 (iii) By a clause or infinitive

Я согла́сен, что на́до де́йствовать   I **agree we must act**
Я гото́в помо́чь   I am **ready to help**
Он сли́шком мо́лод, что́бы по́мнить войну́   He is **too young to remember the war**

Adjectives (long and short) following the noun

A distinction must be made between a 'delimited' short adjective in predicative position (following the noun and linked to it by the verb 'to be'):

Он **равноду́шен** к му́зыке   He is **indifferent** to music

and a long adjective that also follows the noun but is separated from it by a comma and agrees with it in case, gender, and number, with 'who is', 'which is' etc. understood:

Я встре́тил челове́ка, **равноду́шного** к му́зыке   I met a man (who was) **indifferent** to music

The short form of adjectives of dimension

While the long forms of adjectives of dimension imply complete identity with the nouns they qualify: Дом **большо́й/ма́ленький** 'The house is big/small' (i.e. by normal standards), the short form relates the dimension to particular circumstances; Дом **вели́к** 'The house is too big' (e.g. for a small family), Дом **мал** 'The house (possibly the *same* house) is too small' (e.g. for a large family). The construction is often used with clothing:

Брю́ки **узки́**   The trousers are too tight
Ю́бка **длинна́**   The skirt is **too long**
Костю́м **свобо́ден**   The suit is **too loose**
Рукава́ **коротки́**   The sleeves are **too short**

Adjectives that have no short forms

(a) adjectives in -ск- (e.g. **физи́ческий** 'physical')

(b) adjectives of time (e.g. **ле́тний** 'summer')and place (e.g. **за́дний** 'back')

(c) adjectives that denote materials/substances (e.g. **стально́й** 'steel')

(d) 'animal' adjectives of the type **во́лчий** 'wolf's'

! Note: **рад** 'is glad' has no *long* form.

The comparative degree

(a) Most Russian adjectives have *two* comparatives.

(b) One comparative (the 'long' form) combines **бо́лее** 'more' with the long adjective, normally precedes the noun, and defines and describes it: **бо́лее широ́кая пло́щадь** 'a broader square'. (**Ме́нее** 'less' is used in reverse comparisons: **ме́нее** серьёзный кри́зис 'a **less** serious crisis'.)

(c) The other ('short') comparative is a one-word form in **-ee** (colloquially **-ей**) or **-e** that follows the noun and is linked to it by a form of the verb 'to be': **Э́то кре́сло удо́бнее** 'This armchair is more comfortable'.

The long form of the comparative adjective

(a) Almost every Russian adjective makes its long-form comparative with **бо́лее** + positive adjective:

  счастли́вый челове́к a **happy** man
  бо́лее счастли́вый челове́к a **happier** man
  тру́дная зада́ча a **difficult** task
  бо́лее тру́дная зада́ча a **more difficult** task

(b) **Бо́лее** is invariable, but adjective and noun agree in gender (masculine, feminine, or neuter), number (singular or plural), and in case:

Masculine:	**бо́лее ва́жный** вопро́с	a **more important** question
Feminine:	**бо́лее бога́тая** же́нщина	a **richer** woman
Neuter:	**бо́лее дли́нное** письмо́	a **longer** letter
Plural:	**бо́лее чи́стые** пля́жи	**cleaner** beaches

One-word long comparatives

(a) Three pairs of opposites have one-word long comparatives (**бо́лее** plays no part in their formation):

ста́рший elder, senior   **мла́дший** younger, junior
бо́льший bigger   **ме́ньший** smaller
лу́чший better   **ху́дший** worse

(b) **Ста́рший** is used mainly of people: ста́рший брат/класс/лейтена́нт/ста́ршее поколе́ние 'elder brother/senior class/senior lieutenant/older generation', as is its opposite, **мла́дший**. Like **лу́чший** 'better, best' and **ху́дший** 'worse, worst' they can also function as superlatives. For objects, **бо́лее ста́рый** is used: Он купи́л бо́лее ста́рую маши́ну 'He bought an **older** car'.

(c) A fourth pair, **вы́сший** 'higher', **ни́зший** 'lower' have some non-comparative functions: **вы́сшая матема́тика** 'higher mathematics', **вы́сшее уче́бное заведе́ние** 'higher teaching establishment' (cf. *superlative* usage in **в вы́сшей сте́пени** 'to the highest degree', **ни́зшее зва́ние** 'lowest rank').

The short form comparative in -ее (colloquially -ей)

(a) The short (predicative) form of most comparatives is made by adding **-ee** to the stem of the adjective. The short form does not decline and is the same for all genders and the plural:

Докла́д **интере́снее**   The report **is more interesting**
Ле́кция **интере́снее**   The lecture **is more interesting**
Э́то сло́во **интере́снее**   This word **is more interesting**
Фа́кты **интере́снее**   The facts **are more interesting**

(b) Adjectives with monosyllabic stems add stressed **-ée** to the stem:

Э́тот вопро́с **важне́е**   This question **is more important**
Э́та у́лица **длинне́е**   This street **is longer**
Э́та кни́га **нужне́е**   This book **is more necessary**
Э́тот ма́льчик **умне́е**   This boy **is cleverer**
Боксёр **сильне́е**   The boxer **is stronger**

One or two adjectives with stems of more than one syllable also do this:

Э́тот чемода́н **тяжеле́е**   This suitcase **is heavier**

Short-form comparatives in –e, with consonant change

The following consonant changes occur in the formation of short-form comparatives:

в-вл, г-ж, д-ж, з-ж, к-ч, с-ш, ст-щ, т-ч

Short forms of this type end in a single unstressed **-e**. Sometimes **к** is by-passed and the preceding consonant changed (e.g. **бли́же** 'is closer', from бли́зкий 'close', with з changing to **ж** and **к** omitted):

Long form		Short form	
бли́зкий	'close'	Река́ **бли́же**	The river **is closer**
бога́тый	'rich'	Челове́к **бога́че**	The man **is richer**
высо́кий	'high'	Гора́ **вы́ше**	The mountain **is higher**
гла́дкий	'smooth'	О́зеро **гла́же**	The lake **is smoother**
гро́мкий	'loud'	Мото́р **гро́мче**	The engine **is louder**
густо́й	'thick'	Лес **гу́ще**	The forest **is thicker**
дешёвый	'cheap'	Биле́ты **дешевле**	The tickets **are cheaper**
дорого́й	'dear'	Бензи́н **доро́же**	Petrol **is dearer**
жи́дкий	'thin, weak'	Чай **жи́же**	The tea **is weaker**
коро́ткий	'short'	Рукава́ **коро́че**	The sleeves **are shorter**
кре́пкий	'strong'	Чай **кре́пче**	The tea **is stronger**
круто́й	'steep'	Холм **кру́че**	The hill **is steeper**
лёгкий	'easy, light'	Зада́ча **ле́гче**	The task **is easier**
ме́лкий	'shallow'	Река́ **ме́льче**	The river **is shallower**
молодо́й	'young'	Врач **моло́же**	The doctor **is younger**
мя́гкий	'soft'	Поду́шка **мя́гче**	The cushion **is softer**
ни́зкий	'low'	Це́ны **ни́же**	Prices **are lower**
просто́й	'simple'	Уро́к **про́ще**	The lesson **is simpler**
стро́гий	'strict'	Учи́тель **стро́же**	The teacher **is stricter**
твёрдый	'hard, firm'	Его́ шаг **тве́рже**	His step **is firmer**
ти́хий	'quiet'	Ве́чер **ти́ше**	The evening **is quieter**
то́лстый	'thick'	Том **то́лще**	The volume **is thicker**
туго́й	'tight'	Струна́ **ту́же**	The string **is tighter**
у́зкий	'narrow'	Тонне́ль **у́же**	The tunnel **is narrower**
чи́стый	'clean'	Посу́да **чи́ще**	The crockery **is cleaner**

Other short forms

There are a few other short forms that undergo consonant change (see preceding page), e.g. péзче from péзкий 'sharp'.

Some very common forms in -e do not conform to the standard consonant changes:

большо́й 'big'	Дом бо́льше	The house **is bigger**
глубо́кий 'deep'	Óзеро глу́бже	The lake **is deeper**
ма́ленький 'small'	Ко́мната ме́ньше	The room **is smaller**
плохо́й 'bad'	Рабо́та ху́же	The work **is worse**
сла́дкий 'sweet'	Пиро́г сла́ще	The pie **is sweeter**
ста́рый 'old'	Моря́к ста́рше	The sailor **is older**
то́нкий 'thin'	Та́лия то́ньше	The waist **is thinner**
хоро́ший 'good'	Го́лос лу́чше	The voice **is better**
широ́кий 'broad'	У́лица ши́ре	The street **is broader**

Note (a) ста́рше 'is older' is used of people, старе́е of objects.

(b) some adjectives have irregular one-word long-form comparatives *and* irregular short forms:

	One-word comparatives		Short forms	
большо́й 'big'	бо́льший	'bigger'	бо́льше	'is bigger'
ма́ленький 'small'	ме́ньший	'smaller'	ме́ньше	'is smaller'
плохо́й 'bad'	ху́дший	'worse'	ху́же	'is worse'
хоро́ший 'good'	лу́чший	'better'	лу́чше	'is better'
ста́рый 'old'	ста́рший	'older'	ста́рше	'is older'

(c) молодо́й 'young' has long-form comparative мла́дший 'younger', short-form comparative моло́же 'is younger'.

Adjectives in -ский

Adjectives in **-ский** (e.g. траги́ческий 'tragic') have no comparative short forms, but, in common with some other adjectives which have no short forms, they either use a synonym, or the long form, or a version that *does* have a short form (e.g. траги́чный 'tragic' with the comparative short form **траги́чнее** 'is/are more tragic').

Constructions with the comparative degree

(a) Standard comparison: nominative + **short-form** comparative + *genitive*:

Он моло́же меня́   He is **younger** than me
Пи́во деше́вле вина́   Beer **is cheaper** than wine

> **Note:** An alternative short-form construction with чем (Он моло́же, чем я) is less commonly used, though with a **long-form** comparative it is the *norm*: Он живёт в бо́льшем до́ме, чем мы 'He lives in a **bigger** house than we do', as it is when the second item for comparison is one of the possessive pronouns его́ 'his', её 'her', or их 'their': Моя́ маши́на нове́е, **чем** его́ 'My car is newer **than** his'.

(b) A difference (in measurement, age, etc.) between two items for comparison is expressed by **на** + accusative case:

Она́ **на три го́да** ста́рше меня́   She is **three years** older than me
Он **на два сантиме́тра** вы́ше отца́   He is **two centimetres** taller than father

> **Note:** The instrumental (тремя́ года́ми etc.) is a rarer alternative to на + accusative.

(c) **В** + a form of раз 'time' is used to render a difference in terms of a multiple ('twice as big' etc.):

Он **в два ра́за** (вдво́е) бога́че сы́на   He is **twice as rich** as his son

(d) 'The ... the ...' is rendered as Чем ..., тем ...:

Чем ни́же це́ны на то́пливо, **тем лу́чше**   **The lower** fuel prices are, the better

(e) 'Much' + comparative is rendered by **намно́го** (намно́го лу́чше 'much better'), **гора́здо** (гора́здо вы́ше 'much taller'), **мно́го** (мно́го деше́вле 'much cheaper'), or **куда́** (куда́ интере́снее 'much more interesting'), and 'even, still' + comparative by **ещё**: ещё лу́чше 'even better'.

The superlative degree

(a) The standard method of forming the superlative of an adjective is to precede a noun phrase (long adjective + noun) by **са́мый/ са́мая/са́мое/са́мые**:

Masculine	**са́мый** о́стрый нож	the **sharpest** knife
Feminine	**са́мая** бога́тая страна́	the **richest** country
Neuter	**са́мое** вку́сное блю́до	the **tastiest** dish
Plural	**са́мые** изве́стные писа́тели	the **most famous** writers

(b) **Са́мый** declines and agrees with nouns and adjectives in gender, number, and case:

	Masculine Singular	Feminine Singular
Nom.	са́м-**ый** о́стрый нож	са́м-**ая** бога́тая страна́
Acc.	са́м-**ый** о́стрый нож	са́м-**ую** бога́тую страну́
Gen.	са́м-**ого** о́строго ножа́	са́м-**ой** бога́той страны́
Dat.	са́м-**ому** о́строму ножу́	са́м-**ой** бога́той стране́
Instr.	са́м-**ым** о́стрым ножо́м	са́м-**ой** бога́той страно́й
Prep.	са́м-**ом** о́стром ноже́	са́м-**ой** бога́той стране́

Note: Neuter forms decline like masculine, except in the nominative/accusative (neuter са́мое вку́сное блю́до).

	Plural	
Nom.	са́м-**ые** о́стрые ножи́	са́м-**ые** бога́тые стра́ны
Acc.	са́м-**ые** о́стрые ножи́	са́м-**ые** бога́тые стра́ны
Gen.	са́м-**ых** о́стрых ножей́	са́м-**ых** бога́тых стран
Dat.	са́м-**ым** о́стрым ножа́м	са́м-**ым** бога́тым стра́нам
Instr.	са́м-**ыми** о́стрыми ножа́ми	са́м-**ыми** бога́тыми стра́нами
Prep.	са́м-**ых** о́стрых ножа́х	са́м-**ых** бога́тых стра́нах

Other forms of the superlative

Some one-word irregular comparatives can also be used as superlatives: **лу́чший** 'better, best' (**лу́чший** куро́рт 'the best spa'), **ху́дший** 'worse, worst', **ста́рший** 'older, oldest', **мла́дший** 'younger, youngest', *see page 57*. (Sometimes they combine with са́мый: **са́мая лу́чшая** бума́га 'the very best paper'.)

The predicative superlative

(a) **Са́мый** is also used in forming a predicative superlative:

Э́тот дом **са́мый ма́ленький**   This house **is the smallest**
Э́та зада́ча **са́мая лёгкая**   This task **is the easiest**

(b) Another way of expressing a predicative superlative is to combine a short-form predicative comparative (e.g. умне́е 'cleverer', серьёзнее 'more serious') with всех (genitive of все 'all, everyone') or всего́ (genitive of всё 'all, everything'):

Э́та де́вочка **умне́е всех**   This girl is **the cleverest**
Э́та пробле́ма **серьёзнее всего́**   This problem is **the most serious**

Superlatives in -ейший/-айший, наи- and наибо́лее

(a) A limited range of forms in **-ейший**, based mainly on monosyllabic roots, can either have superlative meaning (**сильне́йший** челове́к 'the strongest man') or denote an extreme manifestation (**сложне́йшая** зада́ча 'a **most complex** task', **чисте́йший** вздор 'the most **arrant** nonsense'). Forms derived from adjectives with roots in **г, к, х** undergo consonant change to **ж, ч, ш** and take **-айший** (**кратча́йший** 'shortest' from 'short', note also **з-ж** in **ближа́йший** 'nearest': **ближа́йшая** больни́ца 'the nearest hospital').

(b) Indeclinable **наибо́лее** is somewhat official and normally combines with adjectives with roots of more than one syllable: **наибо́лее логи́чное** реше́ние 'the **most logical** solution'. Declinable one-word superlatives in **наи-** are formal: **наилу́чший** сорт 'the **very best** brand', **наибо́льшая** эффекти́вность '**maximum** effectiveness'.

Note: For вы́сший 'highest', *see page 57*.

The pronoun

Pronouns are words that substitute for nouns or noun phrases. They sub-divide into:

(a) *Personal pronouns* (я 'I', ты 'you' (singular, familiar), он 'he, it', она́ 'she, it', оно́ 'it', мы 'we', вы 'you' (plural, formal), они́ 'they').

(b) *The reflexive pronoun* себя́.

(c) *Demonstrative pronouns* (э́тот 'this', тот 'that').

(d) *Possessive pronouns* (pronominal adjectives) (мой 'my, mine', твой 'your, yours' (familiar), его́ 'his, its', её 'her, hers, its', наш 'our, ours', ваш 'your, yours', их 'their, theirs').

(e) *The reflexive possessive pronoun* свой.

(f) *Interrogative and relative pronouns* (кто 'who', что 'what', како́й 'which', кото́рый 'who, which', чей 'whose').

(g) *Indefinite pronouns* (кто́-то 'someone', кто́-нибудь 'anyone', что́-то 'something', что́-нибудь 'anything', etc.).

(h) *Quantifying pronouns* (весь 'all' etc.).

(i) *Emphatic pronouns* (сам 'oneself', са́мый 'the very').

(j) *Negative pronouns* (никто́, ничто́, никако́й, ниче́й, не́кого, не́чего).

I Personal pronouns

The personal pronouns decline as follows:

Nom.	Acc.	Gen.	Dat.	Instr.	Prep.
я	мен-я́	мен-я́	мн-е	мн-ой	мн-е
ты	теб-я́	теб-я́	теб-е́	тоб-о́й	теб-е́
он	его́	его́	ем-у́	им	нём
она́	ёе	ёе	ей	ей	ней
оно́	его́	его́	ем-у́	им	нём
м-ы	н-ас	н-ас	н-ам	н-а́ми	н-ас
в-ы	в-ас	в-ас	в-ам	в-а́ми	в-ас
они́	их	их	им	и́ми	них

Functions and features of the personal pronouns я, ты, он, она́, оно́

(a) **Я** takes first-person singular forms of a verb:

Я чита́ю и пишу́   I **read** and **write**

It is of common gender, used for either male or female speakers:

Я рад   I am glad   **Я рабо́тал**   I worked (masc.)
Я ра́да   I am glad   **Я рабо́тала**   I worked (fem.)

(b) **Ты** takes second-person singular forms of a verb:

Ты зна́ешь э́того челове́ка?   Do you **know** this person?

It is used in addressing relatives, close friends and colleagues, children, subordinates, animals, etc. Like **я**, it is of common gender:

Ты согла́сен? Do you **agree**?   **Ты опозда́л** You **are late** (masc.)
Ты согла́сна? Do you **agree**?   **Ты опозда́ла** You **are late** (fem.)

The pronoun **ты** is usually omitted when the second-person singular verb is used in the impersonal meaning 'one':

Не зна́ешь, что де́лать   **One doesn't know** what to do

(c) **Он/Она́** relate, respectively, to masculine and feminine nouns (animate or inanimate):

Он игра́л в футбо́л   He **played** football
Она́ больна́   She **is ill**
Э́то наш дом. **Он но́вый**   This is our house. **It** is new
Где ло́жка? **Она́** в я́щике   Where is the spoon? **It** is in the drawer

(d) **Оно́** relates to neuter nouns:

Бе́лое мо́ре? **Оно́** на се́вере   The White Sea? **It** is in the north

! **Note:** The oblique cases of **он она́ оно́** take initial **н-** after a preposition: от **него́** 'from **him**', к **нему́** 'to **him**', с **ним** 'with **him**'; до **нёе** 'before **her**', к **ней** 'to **her**', пе́ред **ней** 'before **her**' etc. (*see also page 65*).

Functions and features of the personal pronouns мы, вы, они

(a) **Мы** combines with first-person plural forms of verbs and the plural of past-tense forms and short adjectives:

Мы аплоди́руем   We **applaud**
Мы зна́ли   We **knew**
Мы гото́вы   We **are ready**

(b) **Вы** can refer to one person (if used in polite speech) or more than one, combining with the second-person plural of verbs, the plural past tense and plural short adjectives:

Вы игра́ете в те́ннис?   **Do** you **play** tennis?
Вы пообе́дали?   **Have** you **dined**?
Вы дово́льны?   **Are** you **pleased**?

When **вы** combines with the *long* form of an adjective, **тако́й** or **оди́н**, a distinction is made between singular and plural:

Кто вы тако́й/така́я?   Who **are you?** (male/female singular)
Кто вы таки́е?   Who **are you?** (plural)
Вы оди́н/одна́?   Are you **alone?** (male/female singular)
Вы одни́?   Are you **alone?** (plural)
Вы сме́лый/сме́лая   You are **daring**   (male/female singular)
Вы сме́лые   You are **daring**   (plural)

! Note: When used as a polite form (e.g., in letters), **Вы** is capitalized for one addressee (but uncapitalized for a number of addressees).

(c) **Они́** combines with third-person plural forms of verbs and short adjectives:

Они́ помога́ют/отдыха́ли/голодны́   They **help/relaxed/are hungry**

The oblique cases of **они́** take initial **н-** when governed by a preposition: среди́ **них** 'among them', к **ним** 'towards them', ме́жду **ни́ми** 'between them'.

Они́ is omitted in general statements, when no named individuals are indicated:

Здесь стро́ят мост   **They are building** a bridge here

! Note: pronouns pair with nouns or other pronouns, using the preposition **с** + instrumental case:
они́ с отцо́м   he/she/they **and father**
мы с ва́ми   you **and I**
мы с ним   he **and I**

The reflexive pronoun себя

The reflexive pronoun declines as follows:

Nom.	non-existent
Acc.	себ-я́
Gen.	себ-я́
Dat.	себ-е́
Instr.	соб-о́й
Prep.	себ-е́

(a) **Себя** refers back to the subject of the clause (i.e. the subject and **себя** denote the same person), rendering English 'myself', 'himself', 'herself', 'ourselves', 'yourself/yourselves', 'themselves'. No distinction is made in respect of person or number:

Я зна́ю **себя́**   I know **myself**
Ты зна́ешь **себя́**   You know **yourself**
Он/Она́ зна́ет **себя́**   He/She knows **himself/herself**
Мы зна́ем **себя́**   We know **ourselves**
Вы зна́ете **себя́**   You know **yourself/yourselves**
Они́ зна́ют **себя́**   They know **themselves**

(b) The pronoun is more versatile than the reflexive verb ending **-ся/-сь** (*see page 137*), since it can express the indirect object in the dative, combine with prepositions, and render other relationships:

Она́ сши́ла **себе́** пла́тье   She made **herself** a dress
Он привлёк **к себе́** внима́ние   He drew attention to **himself**
Они́ разгова́ривали **ме́жду собо́й**   They conversed among **themselves**
Он дово́лен **собо́й**   He is pleased with **himself**

(c) Particular care must be taken not to be misled by English use of a personal pronoun when Russian requires the *reflexive* pronoun:

Он взял меня́ **с собо́й**   He took me **with him**
Я посади́л её **ря́дом с собо́й**   I sat her **next to me**
Закро́й дверь **за собо́й**   Close the door **behind you**

(d) Do not confuse **себя́** with the *emphatic* pronoun **сам** 'oneself' (*see page 77*).

The demonstrative pronoun э́тот 'this'

(a) Demonstrative pronouns indicate the person or thing referred to.

(b) Э́тот 'this' declines as follows, with soft endings in the masculine and neuter singular instrumental and the whole of the plural:

	Masculine	Feminine	Neuter	Plural
Nom.	э́тот	э́т-а	э́т-о	э́т-и
Acc.	э́тот	э́т-у	э́т-о	э́т-и
Gen.	э́т-ого	э́т-ой	э́т-ого	э́т-их
Dat.	э́т-ому	э́т-ой	э́т-ому	э́т-им
Instr.	э́т-им	э́т-ой	э́т-им	э́т-ими
Prep.	э́том	э́т-ой	э́т-ом	э́т-их

(c) The declined forms must not be confused with э́то 'this is, these are':

э́тот заво́д **this** factory	Э́то заво́д This **is** a factory
э́та ма́рка **this** stamp	Э́то ма́рка This **is** a stamp
э́то молоко́ **this** milk	Э́то молоко́ This **is** milk
э́ти ре́ки **these** rivers	Э́то ре́ки These **are** rivers

(d) **Note** the idioms:

Всё де́ло в э́том   **That is** just the point

Что вы хоти́те э́тим сказа́ть?   What do you mean **by that**?

(e) Э́тот is used to distinguish something close at hand from something further away (rendered by тот 'that', *see page 68*):

Он живёт в э́том и́ли в том до́ме?   Does he live in **this** house or **that one**?

(f) Э́тот са́мый means 'this very':

Нам нужна́ э́та са́мая ка́рта   We need **this very** map

(g) The animate-accusative rule applies:

Вы зна́ете э́того челове́ка?/э́тих люде́й?   Do you know **this person/these people**?

The demonstrative pronoun тот 'that'

(a) **Тот** declines as follows, with soft endings in the masculine and neuter singular instrumental and the whole of the plural:

	Masculine	*Feminine*	*Neuter*	*Plural*
Nom.	тот	т-а	т-о	т-е
Acc.	тот	т-у	т-о	т-е
Gen.	т-ого́	т-ой	т-ого́	т-ех
Dat.	т-ому́	т-ой	т-ому́	т-ем
Instr.	т-ем	т-ой	т-ем	т-е́ми
Prep.	т-ом	т-ой	т-ом	т-ех

(b) It denotes spatial distancing:

> Они́ жи́ли по **ту** сто́рону реки́   They lived on **that** side of the river

or temporal distancing:

> В **тот** день бы́ло хо́лодно   It was cold **that** day

(c) It can also mean 'he, she, the latter', resolving ambiguity:

> Ва́ня обрати́лся к Ко́ле, но **тот** не отреаги́ровал   Vanya addressed Kolya, but **he** (Kolya) didn't react

(d) **Кто** is used as a relative pronoun to **тот** and **те**:

> **Тот, кто** знал, отве́тил   **The one who** knew answered
> (*but* **Та, кото́рая** зна́ла, отве́тила   **She who** knew answered)
> Я поблагодари́л **тех, кто** помо́г   I thanked **those who** helped

(e) **Что** is used as a relative pronoun to **то**:

> Я был удивлён **тем, что** он сказа́л   I was surprised by what he said

! Note: тот же (са́мый) 'the same', не тот 'the wrong', ни тот ни друго́й 'neither':
> Они́ се́ли в **тот же** са́мый ваго́н   They got into **the same** carriage
> Он набра́л **не тот** но́мер   He dialled **the wrong** number
> **Ни тот ни друго́й** не знал   **Neither** of them knew

Clauses linked by то, что 'what' (= that which)

То, что он сказа́л, рассерди́ло меня́   **What** (**that which**) he said angered me.

Note:

(a) The construction with **то, что** is especially common where a verb or adjective governs an oblique case or prepositional phrase:

Зави́сеть от + *genitive*

Э́то зави́сит **от того́, что** вы име́ете в виду́   It depends **what** you have in mind

Ве́рить + *dative*

Я ве́рю **тому́, что** он сказа́л   I believe **what** he said

(b) The construction may be equivalent to English preposition + -ing:

Благода́рен за + *accusative*

Я благода́рен ей **за то, что** она́ мне помогла́   I am grateful to her **for helping** me

Горди́ться + *instrumental*

Он горди́тся **тем, что** он её оте́ц   He is proud **of being** her father

Что́бы + past tense

When intention or purpose is expressed rather than fact, **что́бы** + past tense is used instead of **что** (*see pages 135–136*):

Добива́ться + *genitive*

Он добива́лся **того́, что́бы** она́ подписа́ла контра́кт   He tried **to get her to sign** the contract

Compare **то, что**, denoting a **fact**:

Он доби́лся **того́, что** она́ подписа́ла контра́кт   He **got her to sign** the contract

The possessive pronouns мой, твой, наш, ваш

(a) The possessive pronoun **мой** 'my, mine' declines as follows:

	Masculine	Feminine	Neuter	Plural
Nom.	мой	мо-я́	мо-ё	мо-и́
Acc.	мой	мо-ю́	мо-ё	мо-и́
Gen.	мо-его́	мо-е́й	мо-его́	мо-и́х
Dat.	мо-ему́	мо-е́й	мо-ему́	мо-и́м
Instr.	мо-и́м	мо-е́й	мо-и́м	мо-и́ми
Prep.	мо-ём	мо-е́й	мо-ём	мо-и́х

Note: Твой declines like мой.

(b) The possessive pronoun **наш** 'our, ours' declines as follows:

	Masculine	Feminine	Neuter	Plural
Nom.	наш	на́ш-а	на́ш-е	на́ш-и
Acc.	наш	на́ш-у	на́ш-е	на́ш-и
Gen.	на́ш-его	на́ш-ей	на́ш-его	на́ш-их
Dat.	на́ш-ему	на́ш-ей	на́ш-ему	на́ш-им
Instr.	на́ш-им	на́ш-ей	на́ш-им	на́ш-ими
Prep.	на́ш-ем	на́ш-ей	на́ш-ем	на́ш-их

(c) The possessive pronoun **ваш** declines like **наш**. It is spelt **Ваш** in polite contexts (e.g., letters, but **ваш** if addressed to more than one person).

(d) All the possessive pronouns observe the animate accusative = genitive rule in the masculine singular and the whole of the plural:

> Он зна́ет **моего́ бра́та, твоего́ отца́, на́шего дя́дю, ва́ших племя́нников и племя́нниц**   He knows **my brother, your father, our uncle, your nephews and nieces**

(e) The pronouns are used both adjectivally (e.g. **моя́** ка́рта 'my map') and pronominally (e.g. **Э́та** ка́рта–**моя́** 'This map is **mine**').

The third-person possessive pronouns eró 'his, its', ëe 'her, its', их 'their'

(a) The third person possessive pronouns **eró**, **ëe**, and **их** are indeclinable and invariable, whatever the gender, number, or case of the noun they refer to:

eró отéц, **eró** мать, **eró** друзья́	**his** father, **his** mother, **his** friends
ëe брат, **ëe** сестра́, **ëe** письмо́	**her** brother, **her** sister, **her** letter
их дом, **их** ко́мната, **их** де́ти	**their** house, **their** room, **their** children
Я интересу́юсь **eró** карти́нами	I am interested in **his** paintings
Я ве́рю **ëe** сестре́	I believe **her** sister
Она́ вы́шла за́муж за **их** бра́та	She married **their** brother

(b) **Eró**, **ëe**, and **их** also refer to objects:

Наш дом ста́рый. **Eró** исто́рия ухо́дит в про́шлый век   Our house is old. **Its** history goes back to last century

Пра́га - столи́ца Че́хии. **Ёё** населе́ние бы́стро растёт   Prague is the capital of the Czech Republic. **Its** population is growing fast

Я смотрю́ на дере́вья. **Их** ли́стья опада́ют   I look at the trees. **Their** leaves are falling

Note: The initial **н-** that precedes **personal** pronouns eró, ëe, and их in the meaning, respectively, 'him', 'her', and 'them' when governed by prepositions (*see page 64*), **never** precedes the possessive pronouns eró 'his', ëe 'her', and их 'their', thus:

Personal pronouns	*Possessive pronouns*
от **него́** from him	*but* от **eró** дру́га from his friend
для **нёё** for her	*but* для **ëe** до́чери for her daughter
с **ни́ми** with them	*but* с **их** сестро́й with their sister

(c) The pronouns are also used pronominally (e.g. Э́тот дом – ëe 'This house is hers').

The reflexive possessive pronoun свой

(a) **Свой** declines like **мой** and **твой** and refers back to subjects (nouns or pronouns) of any gender or either number:

Он потеря́л **свою́** кни́гу	He has lost **his** book
Она́ потеря́ла **свою́** кни́гу	She has lost **her book**
Они́ потеря́ли **свои́** кни́ги	They have lost **their** books

(b) When there is a **third-person** subject, it is *essential* to differentiate between **свой** and **его́** 'his', **её** 'her', **их** 'their', otherwise the wrong meaning will be conveyed (Он забы́л **свой** но́мер телефо́на means 'He has forgotten **his** (**own**) telephone number', while 'Он забы́л **его́** но́мер телефо́на' means 'He has forgotten **his** (**someone else's**) telephone number'.

(c) The possessive pronouns **его́, её,** and **их** (*not* свой) may constitute part of a multiple **subject**:

Мой брат и **его́** друг обе́дают	My brother and **his** friend are having lunch

(d) They may also refer to the subject of a new clause:

Она́ сказа́ла, что **её** брат бо́лен	She said **her** brother was ill

(e) With **first-person** or **second-person** subjects (**я, ты, мы,** or **вы**), мой, твой, наш, and ваш *can* be used, but **свой** is *preferred*:

Я показа́л **свой** (мой) па́спорт	I showed **my** passport
Мы кра́сили **свой** (наш) дом	We were painting **our** house
Вы нашли́ **свою́** (ва́шу) су́мку?	Have you found **your** bag?

(f) In references to parts of the body, possessive pronouns are usually omitted altogether:

Он вытира́ет ру́ки	He is drying **his** hands
Я поре́зал па́лец	I cut **my** finger

! **Note:** свой, своя́, своё, свои́ are used to denote possession ('my own', 'his own', etc.):

У меня́ **свой** компью́тер	I have **my own** computer
У него́ **своя́** моби́лка	He has **his own** mobile
У вас **свои́** лы́жи	You have **your own** skis

The interrogative and relative pronouns кто and что

(a) **Кто** and **что** decline as follows:

Nom.	кт-о	чт-о
Acc.	к-ого́	чт-о
Gen.	к-ого́	ч-его́
Dat.	к-ому́	ч-ему́
Instr.	к-ем	ч-ем
Prep.	к-ом	ч-ём

(b) **Кто** 'who' combines with masculine singular predicates (Кто го́лоден? 'Who **is hungry?**). It can be extended by **тако́й**: Кто вы тако́й/така́я/таки́е? 'Who are you?' (respectively, of a male, a female, and a group). Note the logical consistency of **Кем** ты хо́чешь быть? '**What** [literally 'Who'] do you want to be?'

(c) **Кто** also functions as a **relative** pronoun to other pronouns (**тот, те, все, никто́**, etc.):

> **Тот, кто** отве́тил пра́вильно, получи́л пре́мию **The one who** answered correctly received a prize
>
> Не зна́ю **никого́, кто** бы так хорошо́ говори́л I don't **anyone who** speaks so well

(d) **Те, кто** and **все, кто** can take a singular or a plural predicate:

> те, кто **ушёл/ушли́** those who **left**
>
> все, кто **зна́ет/зна́ют** everyone who **knows**

(e) **Что?** 'what?' is used of objects and animals. It can be extended by **тако́е**: Что э́то **тако́е?** 'What is that?' As a **relative** pronoun, it relates back to other inanimate pronouns (**всё, то**, etc.):

> Я скажу́ вам **всё, что** зна́ю I'll tell you **all** (**that**) I know
>
> Я записа́л **то, что** он сказа́л I noted down **what** he said

(f) Relative **что** also relates back to whole clauses:

> Он у́мер, **что**, коне́чно, печа́льно **He died, which** of course is sad
>
> Снег раста́ял, **чего́** я не ожида́л **The snow melted, which** I had not expected

The interrogative and relative pronouns какóй, котóрый, and чей

(a) **Какóй?** 'which?, what kind of?' declines like **плохóй** (*see page 46*):

Какáя сегóдня погóда? **What's** the weather like today?
Какóе сегóдня числó? **What's** the date today?
Какóй сегóдня день? **What** day is it today?
Какáя у негó машúна? **What** kind of car has he got?
Какóй дом ваш? **Which** house is yours?

> **!** Note: the colloquial **что за**: Что за погóда сегóдня? **What's** the weather like today?' Что за шляпа! 'What a hat!'

(b) **Какóй** is also used in exclamations:

Какáя рáдость! **What** joy!

(c) **Котóрый** 'who, which' declines like **бéлый** (*see page 44*). It relates to animate and inanimate nouns, agreeing with them in gender and number:

дом, **котóрый** стоúт на углý the house **which** stands on the corner
кáрта, **котóрая** висúт на стенé the map **that** hangs on the wall
окнó, **котóрое** закрыто the window **that** is shut
дéти, **котóрые** ýчатся the children **who** are studying

However, the *case* of **котóрый** is determined by the grammar of its own clause, and **not** by its antecedent:

Он женúлся на **жéнщине, с котóрой** познакóмился на балý He married **a woman with whom** he became acquainted at a dance
Я говорúл с **ученикóм, котóрого** исключúли из шкóлы I was talking to **the pupil** (**whom**) they had expelled from school

(d) The genitive forms **котóрого, котóрой**, and **котóрых** mean 'whose' (masculine, feminine, and plural, respectively):

водúтель, машúна **котóрого** в гаражé the driver **whose** car is in the garage
дéвушка, женúх **котóрой** за гранúцей the girl **whose** fiancé is abroad
ученикú, результáты **котóрых** высóкие the pupils **whose** results are impressive

(e) **Что** is sometimes used as relative pronoun to a noun:

Компью́тер, **что** зави́с   The computer **that** crashed

but **кото́рый** is preferable, and the norm.

(f) The use of **кото́рый** as an *interrogative* is limited largely to the phrases **Кото́рый час?** (= **Ско́лько вре́мени?**) 'What is the time?' and **В кото́ром часу́?** (= **Во ско́лько?**) 'At what time?'

(g) **Чей** 'whose' declines as follows:

	Masculine	Feminine	Neuter	Plural
Nom.	чей	чь-я	чь-ё	чь-и
Acc.	чей	чь-ю	чь-ё	чь-и
Gen.	чь-его́	чь-ей	чь-его́	чь-их
Dat.	чь-ему́	чь-ей	чь-ему́	чь-им
Instr.	чь-им	чь-ей	чь-им	чь-и́ми
Prep.	чь-ём	чь-ей	чь-ём	чь-их

(h) It is used as an interrogative pronoun, appearing mainly in the nominative case:

Чей э́то дом?   **Whose** house is that?
Чья э́то ко́мната?   **Whose** room is that?
Чьё э́то кольцо́?   **Whose** ring is that?
Чьи э́то конькѝ?   **Whose** skates are those?

(i) It can also mean 'whose' in a relative meaning, as an alternative to кото́рого, кото́рой, кото́рых (*see page 74*):

же́нщина, **чей** муж заболе́л   the woman **whose** husband fell ill

The indefinite pronouns кто́-то/кто́-нибудь, что́-то/ что́-нибудь, како́й-то/како́й-нибудь, че́й-то/че́й-нибудь

(a) The pronouns in **-то** refer to definite persons or objects whose identity is unkown to or has perhaps been forgotten by the speaker. Their existence is not in question, but identification is either impossible or not desirable:

Кто́-то стучи́т в дверь **Someone** is knocking at the door (but I do not know who it is, or will not say)

Они́ **о чём-то** говори́ли, но я не знал, о чём и́менно They were talking about **something**, but I did not know about what exactly

Он принёс **каку́ю-то** кни́гу, но я забы́л, как она́ называ́лась He brought **some** book **or other**, but I forget what it was called

Учи́тельница проверя́ла **чью́-то** тетра́дь The teacher was marking **someone's** exercise book

(b) The pronouns in **-нибудь** are used:

(i) of persons or things not yet defined or selected, and thus not yet in place:

Я до́лжен обрати́ться к **кому́-нибудь** за по́мощью I must turn to **someone** (not yet designated) for help

Я куплю́ ей **что́-нибудь**, но ещё не реши́л, что и́менно I will buy her **something**, but haven't yet decided what exactly

Она́ хо́чет, что́бы я спел **каку́ю-нибудь** наро́дную пе́сню She wants me to sing **some** folk song **or other** (still to be selected)

(ii) when a repeated action involves different persons or objects on different occasions:

Ка́ждый день он приноси́л **ка́кую-нибудь** газе́ту Every day he brought **some** newspaper **or other** (a different one on each occasion)

The pronouns весь, це́лый, сам, са́мый

(a) **Весь** 'all, all the' declines as follows:

	Masculine	Feminine	Neuter	Plural
Nom.	весь	вс-я	вс-ё	вс-е
Acc.	весь	вс-ю	вс-ё	вс-е
Gen.	вс-его́	вс-ей	вс-его́	вс-ех
Dat.	вс-ему́	вс-ей	вс-ему́	вс-ем
Instr.	вс-ем	вс-ей	вс-ем	вс-е́ми
Prep.	вс-ём	вс-ей	вс-ём	вс-ех

Це́лый 'a whole' and **са́мый** 'the very' decline like **бе́лый** (*see page 44*).

(b) **Весь** means 'the whole', **це́лый** 'a whole' (Он съел **всю** ды́ню 'He ate **the whole** melon', Он съел це́лую ды́ню 'He ate **a whole** melon'). Plural **все** means 'all the' (**все** города́ '**all the** towns'), plural **це́лые** means 'whole' (**це́лые** города́ '**whole** towns').

(c) **Все** also means 'everyone'. It takes a plural predicate (Все зна́ют 'Everyone **knows**') and the relative pronoun кто (все, кто 'everyone who' – *see page 73*). **Всё** means 'everything' and takes the relative pronoun что (всё, что 'everything that').

(d) The emphatic pronoun **сам** 'oneself' declines as follows:

	Masculine	Feminine	Neuter	Plural
Nom.	сам	сам-а́	сам-о́	са́м-и
Acc.	сам	сам-у́	сам-о́	сам-и́х
Gen	сам-ого́	сам-о́й	сам-ого́	сам-и́х
Dat.	сам-ому́	сам-о́й	сам-ому́	сам-и́м
Instr.	сам-и́м	сам-о́й	сам-и́м	сам-и́ми
Prep.	сам-о́м	сам-о́й	сам-о́м	сам-и́х

It is used to personalize: Я **сам** реши́л э́ту зада́чу 'I solved this problem **myself**', or to emphasize: Мы говори́ли с **сами́м** мини́стром 'We spoke to the minister **himself**', and must not be confused with **са́мый**, which denotes spatial or temporal limit: Мы живём у **са́мой** реки́ 'We live **right by** the river'. Он рабо́тает до **са́мой** но́чи 'He works **right through to** nightfall'.

The negative pronouns никто́, ничто́, никако́й, ниче́й

(a) **Никто́** 'no one, nobody' declines like **кто** (*see page 73*) and takes a masculine singular predicate (Никто́ не **гото́в** 'No one's **ready**'). It combines with the negative particle **не**, except in one-word answers (**Кто** пришёл? 'Who came?' **Никто́** 'No one'):

Никто́ **не** зна́ет   Nobody knows
Я никого́ **не** зна́ю   I don't know anyone
Он никому́ **не** помога́ет   He doesn't help anyone

Prepositions appear between **ни** and the oblique case form:

Она́ **ни на кого́** не смо́трит   She's not looking **at anyone**

(b) Russian can accumulate negatives (unlike English, which reverts to *positive* pronouns [and *adverbs, see page 180*] after the first negative):

Никто́ никогда́ ничего́ не зна́ет   **No one ever** knows **anything**

(c) **Ничто́** 'nothing' declines like **что** (*see page 73*). It also combines with the negative particle **не**:

Ничто́ его́ **не** волну́ет   Nothing worries him
Ничего́ **не** произошло́   Nothing happened
Он ничего́ **не** зна́ет   He **doesn't** know anything
Он ничему́ **не** ве́рит   He **doesn't** believe anything

! **Note:** As indicated under **никто́**, above, negatives can accumulate:
Никто́ никогда́ ничего́ не говори́т   No one ever says anything

(d) Prepositions come between **ни** and oblique cases of **что**:

Он **ни за что** не заплати́л   He **didn't** pay for **anything**

(e) **Никако́й** 'no, none at all' declines like **плохо́й** (*see page 46*). It combines with **не** or **нет** and is used mainly for emphasis (prepositions come between **ни** and oblique cases of **какой**):

Нет **никако́го** сомне́ния   There is **no** doubt **at all**

(f) **Ниче́й** 'no one's' declines like **чей** (*see page 75*) and combines with **не** (unless used as a predicate: Этот щено́к **ниче́й** 'This puppy isn't anybody's'). Prepositions appear between **ни** and the relevant form of **чей**.

The pronouns не́кого and не́чего

(a) The declension endings of **не́кого** and **не́чего** are identical with those of **кто** and **что** (*see page 73*), but neither pronoun has a nominative case and the stress always falls on **не́-**. The pronouns indicate lack of potential for carrying out an action or process and comprise:

не́- + **case form** (**determined by following infinitive**) + **infinitive**:

Не́кого спроси́ть   There is no one to ask
Не́кем любова́ться   There is no one to admire
Не́чего де́лать   There is nothing to do
Не́чем горди́ться   There is nothing to be proud of

(b) Prepositions appear between **не́** and the case form of the pronoun:

Не́ **с** кем дружи́ть   There is no one to be friends with
Не́ **к** кому обраща́ться   There is no one to turn to
Не́ **о** чем ду́мать   There is nothing to think about

(c) There is a past-tense equivalent with **бы́ло**, and a future-tense equivalent with **бу́дет**:

Не́чего **бы́ло** де́лать   There **was** nothing to do
Не́ с кем **бу́дет** дружи́ть   There **will be** no one to be friends with

and an opposite, affirmative construction in **есть/бы́ло/бу́дет**:

Есть с кем игра́ть   There **is** someone to play with
Бы́ло/бу́дет кого́ спроси́ть   There **was/will be** someone to ask

(d) The logical **subject** of a verb (that is to say, the person who performs the action referred to) appears in the *dative*:

Ему́ не́чего де́лать   He has nothing to do
Нам не́ с кем бы́ло посове́товаться   We had no one to consult

(e) If the **negative pronoun** is the logical subject of the verb, then it appears in the dative:

Не́кому мыть маши́ну   There is **no one** to wash the car

The numeral

I Cardinal numerals (one, two, three, etc.)

0	ноль/нуль	18	восемна́дцать
1	оди́н, одна́,	19	девятна́дцать
	одно́, одни́	20	два́дцать
2	два, две	30	три́дцать
3	три	40	со́рок
4	четы́ре	50	пятьдеся́т
5	пять	60	шестьдеся́т
6	шесть	70	се́мьдесят
7	семь	80	во́семьдесят
8	во́семь	90	девяно́сто
9	де́вять	100	сто
10	де́сять	200	две́сти
11	оди́ннадцать	300	три́ста
12	двена́дцать	400	четы́реста
13	трина́дцать	500	пятьсо́т
14	четы́рнадцать	600	шестьсо́т
15	пятна́дцать	700	семьсо́т
16	шестна́дцать	800	восемьсо́т
17	семна́дцать	900	девятьсо́т

1,000	ты́сяча
2,000	две ты́сячи
5,000	пять ты́сяч
1,000,000	миллио́н
2,000,000	два миллио́на
5,000,000	пять миллио́нов
1,000,000,000	миллиа́рд/биллио́н
1,000,000,000,000	триллио́н

Notes on the form and formation of cardinal numerals

(a) Of numerals 11-19, only 11 (одиннадцать) and 14 (четырнадцать) are *not* stressed on the first -**a**-.

(b) The numerals 50–80 have a central, but not a final soft sign. 50 and 60 have final stress, 70 and 80 initial stress.

(c) Тысяча 'thousand' can be written 1000, 1.000, or 1 000 (but *never* with a comma).

(d) Compound cardinal numerals are formed by placing simple numerals in sequence: двадцать один '21', три тысячи триста сорок пять 'three thousand three hundred and forty-five'.

Cardinals as serial numbers

(a) Apart from indicating quantity, cardinals can also denote numbers in a series or sequence: комната (номер) девять 'room (number) nine', Казанская, 6 '6 Kazan Street', дом двенадцать, квартира сто сорок 'house number twelve, apartment one hundred and forty', рейс двадцать четыре 'flight number twenty-four'.

(b) Telephone and fax numbers are read as follows: два ноля семь – ноль девяносто пять – четыреста девяносто семь – двадцать один шестьдесят пять: 007 (Russian Federation) – 095 (Moscow) – 497 2165 (seven-digit local number), i.e. they are read as words, *not* (as in English) as individual digits.

Биллион

Both миллиард and биллион mean 'one thousand million' (English 'billion' can mean 'one thousand million' or 'a million million').

Approximation

Approximation is rendered by inverting numeral and noun: дня три 'about three days' (prepositions are placed centrally: дня через три 'in about three days' time').

Ноль/нуль 'nought, zero'

(a) **Ноль** and **нуль** decline like soft-sign masculine nouns:

вы́ше/ни́же нуля́   above/below **zero**
начина́ть с нуля́   to start **from scratch**

(b) They govern the genitive (singular or plural):

ноль **внима́ния**   zero **attention**
ноль **гра́дусов**   zero **degrees**

Оди́н, одна́, одно́, одни́ 'one'

(a) Оди́н declines with hard endings except for masculine and neuter instrumental and the whole of the plural, which have soft endings:

	Masculine	Feminine	Neuter	Plural
Nom.	оди́н	одн-а́	одн-о́	одн-и́
Acc.	оди́н	одн-у́	одн-о́	одн-и́
Gen.	одн-ого́	одн-ой	одн-ого́	одн-и́х
Dat.	одн-ому́	одн-ой	одн-ому́	одн-и́м
Instr.	одн-и́м	одн-ой	одн-и́м	одн-и́ми
Prep.	одн-о́м	одн-ой	одн-о́м	одн-и́х

(b) Numeral and noun agree in gender, number, and case:

оди́н костю́м   **one** suit
одна́ ла́мпа   **one** lamp
одно́ по́ле   **one** field
одни́ са́нки   **one** sledge
цена́ **одного́ биле́та**   the price **of one ticket**
Он купи́л **одну́ ды́ню**   He bought **one melon**
Она́ дви́нула **одно́й руко́й**   She moved **one arm**

(c) Оди́н can also mean 'the same' and 'alone, by oneself':

Они́ служи́ли в **одно́м полку́**   They served in **the same regiment**
Он живёт **оди́н**   He lives **alone**

(d) 'One of' is rendered as **оди́н из** + genitive:

Он был **одни́м из** мои́х учителе́й   He was **one of** my teachers

(e) Compound numerals ending with **один** also take a singular noun and predicate:

Два́дцать одна́ де́вушка записа́лась на ку́рсы   Twenty-one **girls enrolled** for the course

(f) All numerals in a compound decline:

Съе́хались делега́ты из **тридцати́ одно́й** страны́   Delegates from **thirty-one** countries convened

(g) The masculine animate-accusative = genitive rule applies to **один** individually or as final element in a compound:

Она́ встре́тила **одного́ ученика́**   She met **one pupil**
Уго́нщики уби́ли **пятьдеся́т одного́** пассажи́ра   The hijackers killed **fifty-one passengers**

(h) **Одни́ ... други́е** means 'Some ... others':

Одни́ за, **други́е** про́тив   **Some** are for, **others** against

Полтора́/полторы́ 'one and a half'

(a) Полтора́ is used with *masculine* and *neuter* nouns, полторы́ with *feminine* nouns. Both take the genitive singular:

полтора́ **дня**   a **day** and a half
полтора́ **очка́**   a **point** and a half
полторы́ **неде́ли**   a **week** and a half

(b) Полтора́/полторы́ share the oblique case полу́тора, which agrees with **plural** forms of the noun:

ме́ньше полу́тора **киломе́тров**   less than **a kilometre** and a half

в полу́тора **часа́х** лёта от Брюссе́ля   **an hour and a half's** flight from Brussels

> **!** Note: два с полови́ной часа́ 'two and a half hours', пять с полови́ной часо́в 'five and a half hours', etc.

Два/две 'two', три 'three', четы́ре 'four'

(a) The numerals два/две, три, and четы́ре take the genitive singular of nouns when the numerals themselves are in the nominative/accusative case.

(b) Два is used with *masculine* and *neuter* nouns, две with *feminine* nouns. Both take the genitive singular:

два шага́   two **paces**
два ме́ста   two **places**
две де́вушки   two **girls**

(c) Три and четы́ре are used with masculine, feminine, or neuter nouns and also take the genitive singular:

три/четы́ре словаря́   three/four **dictionaries**
три/четы́ре зда́ния   three/four **buildings**
три/четы́ре ко́шки   three/four **cats**

(d) Adjectives qualifying masculine and neuter nouns appear in the genitive *plural* after два, три, четы́ре, those qualifying feminine nouns in the *nominative* plural after две, три, четы́ре:

два ме́стных по́езда   two **local** trains
три больши́х облака   three **large** clouds
четы́ре чи́стые руба́шки   four **clean** shirts

(e) The same rule applies to *compound* numerals ending with два/две, три, ог четы́ре:

со́рок два дождли́вых дня   forty-two **rainy days**
три́дцать три откры́тых окна́   thirty-three **open windows**
два́дцать четы́ре но́вые ма́рки   twenty-four **new stamps**

Declension of два/две, три, and четы́ре

(a) 2–4 decline as follows:

Nom.	дв-а/дв-е	тр-и	четы́р-е
Acc.	дв-а/дв-е	тр-и	четы́р-е
Gen.	дв-ух	тр-ёх	четыр-ёх
Dat.	дв-ум	тр-ём	четыр-ём
Instr	дв-умя́	тр-емя́	четырь-мя́
Prep.	дв-ух	тр-ёх	четыр-ёх

(b) The declined forms agree with nouns and adjectives in the same case of the **plural** (e.g. двух, трёх, четырёх agree with the genitive plural of the noun, двум, трём, четырём with the dative plural):

Они шли около **двух дней**   They walked for about **two days**
Он кончил к **трём часам**   He had finished by **three o'clock**
между **двумя большими домами**   between **two large houses**
в **четырёх картонных коробках**   in **four cardboard boxes**

(c) All components of compound numerals decline:

один из **тридцати трёх** залов   one of the **thirty-three** halls
в **двадцати двух** странах   in **twenty-two** countries

(d) The animate accusative = genitive rule affects 2, 3, and 4:

Он встретил **двух друзей**   He met **two friends**
Она наказала **трёх девочек**   She punished **three girls**
Она кормит **четырёх коров**   She feeds **the four cows**

(e) The rule does *not* apply, however, when they form part of compound numerals:

Я видел пятьдесят **два солдата**   I saw fifty-**two soldiers**

Оба/обе 'both'

Оба takes the genitive singular of masculine and neuter nouns and the genitive *plural* of adjectives, обе the genitive singular of feminine nouns and the *nominative* plural of adjectives:

оба **взрослых сына**   both **grown-up sons**
обе **северные столицы**   both **northern capitals**

The numerals пять 'five' and above

(a) The numerals пять 'five' and above take the genitive plural of nouns, when the numerals themselves are in the nominative/accusative case:

пять книг   five **books**
сто звёзд   a hundred **stars**
тридцать заводов   thirty **factories**
тысяча дней   a thousand **days**

(b) However, compound numerals ending in **один, одна, одно** take the nominative singular of a noun and those in **два/две, три, четыре** take the genitive singular of a noun (*see pages 82–84*):

сорок **один** кандидат   forty-**one** candidates
сорок **два** кандидата   forty-**two** candidates
сорок **три** кандидата   forty-**three** candidates
сорок **четыре** кандидата   forty-**four** candidates
сорок **пять** кандидатов   forty-**five** candidates

The numerals пять 'five' and above decline, and agree in their oblique cases with nouns **in the same case of the plural** (e.g. instrumental пятью agrees with the instrumental plural of a noun). All parts of a compound numeral decline:

в трёхстах двадцати двух реках   in **322 rivers**

Declension type I: пять 'five'

Пять declines like a feminine singular soft-ending noun (*see page 25*), with end stress in declension:

Nom./Acc.	пять
Gen./Dat./Prep.	пят-и́
Instr.	пять-ю́

Likewise шесть 'six', семь 'seven', восемь 'eight' (genitive/dative/prepositional восьми, instrumental восьмью or восемью), девять 'nine', десять 'ten', двадцать 'twenty', тридцать 'thirty':

рабочие **пяти** заводов   the workers **of five factories**
к **шести** часам   by **six** o'clock
город с **восьмью** парками   a town with **eight parks**
в **двадцати** магазинах   in **twenty** shops

Declension type II: 11-19 (as пять (*see page 86*), but with stem stress)

This applies to the numerals **одиннадцать** 'eleven' through to **девятнадцать** 'nineteen':

команды **двенадцати кораблей**   the crews **of twelve ships**
Он помог **четырнадцати детям**   He helped 14 **children**
дом с **шестнадцатью квартирами**   a house with **sixteen flats**

Declension type III: 50–80

These numerals decline as follows, with *medial* stress in oblique cases:

Nom./Acc.	пятьдеся́т
Gen./Dat./Prep.	пяти́дссят-и
Instr.	пятью́десять-ю

Likewise **шестьдеся́т** '60', **се́мьдесят** '70', **во́семьдесят** '80':

бо́льше **шести́десяти рубле́й**   more than **sixty roubles**
го́род с **семью́десятью теа́трами**   a city with **70 theatres**

Declension type IV: со́рок 'forty', девяно́сто 'ninety', сто 'hundred'

Each of these numerals has a single oblique case in -**a**. Their genitive/dative/instrumental/prepositional cases are **сорок-а́**, **девяно́ст-а**, and **ст-а**:

оди́н из **сорока́ госте́й**   one of **the forty guests**
Он заплати́л **ста рабо́чим**   He paid a **hundred workers**
в **девяно́ста лагеря́х**   in **ninety camps**

The animate accusative rule

Only the numerals **оди́н** 'one', **два/две** 'two', **о́ба/о́бе** 'both' (genitive-animate accusative **обо́их/обе́их**), **три** 'three', and **четы́ре** 'four' and numerals ending in **оди́н** are affected by the animate accusative = genitive rule (also the collective numerals *see page 89*). The numerals 5–100 are *not* affected, thus:

Я ви́жу **одного́ ма́льчика**   I see **one boy**
Я ви́жу **двух де́вочек**   I see **two girls**
Я ви́жу **пять/со́рок солда́т**   I see **five/forty soldiers**

Declension type V: 200–900

(a) Both parts of the numerals двести, триста, четыреста decline, the first part like два/две, три, четыре, the second part with plural noun endings:

Nom./Acc.	двест-и	трист-а	четырест-а
Gen.	двухсот	трёхсот	четырёхсот
Dat.	двумст-ам	трёмст-ам	четырёмст-ам
Instr.	двумяст-ами	тремяст-ами	четырьмяст-ами
Prep.	двухст-ах	трёхст-ах	четырёхст-ах

(b) Likewise, both parts of пятьсот, шестьсот, семьсот, восемьсот, девятьсот decline, the first part like пять, шесть, семь, восемь, девять, the second part with plural noun endings:

Nom./Acc.	пятьсот
Gen.	пятисот
Dat.	пятист-ам
Instr.	пятьюст-ами
Prep.	пятист-ах

цена двухсот сигар   the price **of two hundred cigars**
с тремястами танками   with **300 tanks**
в пятистах деревнях   in **500 villages**

Declension type VI: тысяча '1,000', миллион 'million', миллиард/ биллион 'thousand million', триллион 'trillion'

These numerals decline like nouns (тысяча like a feminine noun, the rest like masculine nouns) and can appear in multiples (две тысячи 'two thousand', десять миллионов 'ten million', etc.). They are followed by the **genitive plural**, *whatever their own case*:

с двумя тысячами **солдат**   with two thousand **soldiers**
в миллионе **семей**   in a million **families**

I The collective numerals

(a) The collective numerals comprise **дво́е** 'two', **тро́е** 'three', **че́тверо** 'four', **пя́теро** 'five', **ше́стеро** 'six', **се́меро** 'seven', **во́сьмеро** 'eight', **де́вятеро** 'nine', **де́сятеро** 'ten'. They take the genitive plural, when the numerals themselves are in the nominative/accusative case, and are widely used with plural-only nouns:

дво́е **су́ток**   two **days and nights**
тро́е **са́нок**   three **sledges**
че́тверо **носи́лок**   four **stretchers**
пя́теро **часо́в**   five **clocks**

(b) Collective numerals cannot appear in compounds. Instead, synonyms are used (e.g. день 'day' for су́тки 'day, twenty-four-hour period': со́рок два **дня** 'forty-two **days**'), or circumlocutions such as **в коли́честве** 'numbering' (в коли́честве сорока́ двух 'numbering forty-two').

(c) Although the collective numerals decline (дво́е, двои́х, двои́м, двои́ми, двои́х, likewise тро́е; че́тверо, четверы́х, четверы́м, четверы́ми, четверы́х, likewise пя́теро, ше́стеро, се́меро, во́сьмеро, де́вятеро, де́сятеро), their oblique cases are not used with the oblique cases of plural-only nouns; the oblique cases of cardinal numerals are used instead, thus:

дво́е воро́т   **two** gates

but:

У **двух** воро́т стоя́ли солда́ты   Soldiers stood at the **two** gates

(d) The collective numerals are also used with **де́ти** 'children' (**дво́е дете́й** 'two children', **тро́е дете́й** 'three children'), with **ребя́та** 'children', **вну́ки** 'grandchildren', and with **близнецы́** (**че́тверо близнецо́в** 'quadruplets'). They are also used with masculine animate nouns, as an alternative to cardinal numerals (**два** студе́нта/**дво́е** студе́нтов 'two students'), and when an animate noun is omitted from a numeral phrase: Нас **пя́теро** 'There are **five** of us', ко́мната на **двои́х** 'a room for two'.

Singular or plural predicate

The use of singular or plural predicate with numerals and numeral phrases depends on various factors:

The **plural** is preferred:

(a) when a deliberate action is performed:

Тро́е моряко́в **спасли́** ребёнка   The three sailors **saved** the child.

Не́сколько челове́к **трениру́ются**   A few people **are training**

(b) with short adjectives:

Два из костю́мов ему́ **велики́**   Two of the suits **are too big** for him

(c) with о́ба/о́бе 'both':

О́ба дру́га **жени́лись**   Both friends **got married**

A **singular** predicate is usual:

(a) when the verb denotes existence or state:

В ко́мнате **бы́ло** пять челове́к   There **were** five people in the room

На столе́ **лежи́т** три кни́ги   Three books **are lying** on the table

(b) with a passive construction or concept:

Уби́то семь пассажи́ров   Seven passengers **have been killed**

Поги́бло три же́нщины   Three women **have perished**

(c) in expressions denoting the passing of time:

Пройдёт не́сколько неде́ль   A few weeks **will pass**

Мне **испо́лнилось** со́рок лет   I have **turned** forty

Мно́го 'many/much', **ма́ло/немно́го** 'not much, few', **ско́лько?** 'how many, how much?', **сто́лько** 'so many, so much' and **нема́ло** 'not a little, not a few' almost always take a singular predicate: У неё **бы́ло** мно́го/ма́ло де́нег 'She **had** a lot of/not much money'. **Большинство́** 'majority' takes a singular predicate unless followed by an animate noun in the genitive plural, when it takes a *plural* predicate: Большинство́ рабо́чих **бастова́ли** 'Most workers **were on strike**'.

I Ordinal numerals (numerals that indicate order, position, or sequence)

1st	пе́рвый -ая -ое -ые	15th	пятна́дцатый -ая -ое -ые
2nd	второ́й -а́я -о́е -ы́е	16th	шестна́дцатый -ая -ое -ые
3rd	тре́тий -ья -ье -ьи	17th	семна́дцатый -ая -ое -ые
4th	четвёртый -ая -ое -ые	18th	восемна́дцатый -ая -ое -ые
5th	пя́тый -ая -ое -ые	19th	девятна́дцатый -ая -ое -ые
6th	шесто́й -а́я -о́е -ы́е	20th	двадца́тый -ая -ое -ые
7th	седьмо́й -а́я -о́е -ы́е	30th	тридца́тый -ая -ое -ые
8th	восьмо́й -а́я -о́е -ы́е	40th	сороково́й -а́я -о́е -ы́е
9th	девя́тый -ая -ое -ые	50th	пятидеся́тый -ая -ое -ые
10th	деся́тый -ая -ое -ые	60th	шестидеся́тый -ая -ое -ые
11th	оди́ннадцатый -ая -ое -ые	70th	семидеся́тый -ая -ое -ые
12th	двена́дцатый -ая -ое -ые	80th	восьмидеся́тый -ая -ое -ые
13th	трина́дцатый -ая -ое -ые	90th	девяно́стый -ая -ое -ые
14th	четы́рнадцатый -ая -ое -ые	100th	со́тый -ая -ое -ые

200th	двухсо́тый -ая -ое -ые
300th	трёхсо́тый -ая -ое -ые
400th	четырёхсо́тый -ая -ое -ые
500th	пятисо́тый -ая -ое -ые
600th	шестисо́тый -ая -ое -ые
700th	семисо́тый -ая -ое -ые
800th	восьмисо́тый -ая -ое -ые
900th	девятисо́тый -ая -ое -ые
1,000th	ты́сячный
2,000th	двухты́сячный -ая -ое -ые
3,000th	трёхты́сячный -ая -ое -ые
4,000th	четырёхты́сячный -ая -ое -ые
5,000th	пятиты́сячный -ая -ое -ые
1,000,000th	миллио́нный -ая -ое -ые
2,000,000th	двухмиллио́нный -ая -ое -ые
1,000,000,000th	триллио́нный -ая -ое -ые

Ordinal numerals: some notes on formation

(a) Only the *final* component of a compound ordinal numeral is an ordinal. The rest are cardinals: сто **пятидеся́тый** посети́тель 'the hundred and **fiftieth** visitor'.

(b) The initial components of **пятидеся́тый** 'fiftieth' to **восьмидеся́тый** 'eightieth', and **двухсо́тый** 'two-hundredth' to **девятисо́тый** 'nine-hundredth' are in the *genitive* case. This also occurs in multiples of **ты́сячный** 'thousand' (e.g. **сорокаты́сячный** 'forty thousandth').

(c) Exceptions include девяно́сто 'ninety' and сто 'hundred', which do *not* appear in the genitive case when functioning as initial components of a compound ordinal numeral: **девяностоты́сячный** 'ninety thousandth', **стоты́сячный** 'hundred thousandth'. This principle (that the first numeral component in a compound appears in the genitive case except for девяно́сто 'ninety' and сто 'hundred' [note also **одно-**, as in **одноле́тний** 'one-year']) applies more generally: **пятиле́тие** 'fifth anniversary', **сорокачеты́рёхле́тний** мужчи́на 'a forty-four-year-old man', **столе́тие** 'century, centenary'.

Abbreviated ordinal numerals

Abbreviations end in the final letter of the ordinal, thus: **1-й** for пе́рвый 'first', unless the last letter but one is a consonant, when the last two letters of the ordinal appear in the abbreviation: собы́тия **2-го** (for второ́го) дня 'events of the second day'.

Declension of ordinal numerals

Ordinal numerals decline like adjectives (*see page 44*). **Тре́тий** 'third' declines as follows:

	Masculine	*Feminine*	*Neuter*	*Plural*
Nom.	тре́тий	тре́ть-я	тре́ть-е	тре́ть-и
Acc.	тре́тий	тре́ть-ю	тре́ть-е	тре́ть-и
Gen.	тре́ть-его	тре́ть-ей	тре́ть-его	тре́ть-их
Dat.	тре́ть-ему	тре́ть-ей	тре́ть-ему	тре́ть-им
Instr.	тре́ть-им	тре́ть-ей	тре́ть-им	тре́ть-ими
Prep.	тре́ть-ем	тре́ть-ей	тре́ть-ем	тре́ть-их

Using ordinal numerals

(a) Like adjectives, ordinal numerals agree with nouns in gender, case, and number:

во время **Второй мировой войны** during the **Second World War**

один из **моих первых друзей** one of **my first friends**

(b) An ordinal numeral is sometimes used where English would have a cardinal:

урок **первый** lesson **one**

страница сто **седьмая** page **one hundred and seven**

глава **третья** chapter **three**

четвёртая программа channel **four**

сорок первый размер size **forty-one**

шестнадцатый ряд row **sixteen**

пятый автобус the number **five** bus

(c) In numbering *rooms*, either cardinals *or* ordinals may be used:

комната тридцать **три**/тридцать **третья** room thirty-three

(d) Ordinals combine with **по** + dative (compare use of a superlative in English) in indicating *relative dimension*:

третья **по высоте** гора the third **highest** mountain

Fractions and decimals

Cardinals and ordinals are used in the formation of fractions: **одна пятая** 'one fifth', семь и **четыре седьмых** 'seven and four sevenths'. The dependent noun appears in the genitive *singular*: пять и две пятых **километра** 'five and two fifths **of a kilometre**'. Decimals are based on tenths (0,1 or одна десятая = 0.1 or 'one tenth'), etc. (Russian uses **commas** in forming decimals.)

Roman numerals

Roman numerals are used of centuries (**XXI** век 'the **21st** century'), and of important events: **X** Конгресс 'The **10th** Congress'.

Telling the time

Кото́рый час? Ско́лько вре́мени? 'What's the time?'

(a) These questions can be answered using cardinal numerals only:

три пятна́дцать   *three fifteen*

(b) The twenty-four-hour clock is commonly used:

шестна́дцать два́дцать   *twenty past four p.m., 16.20*
два́дцать два ноль пять   *five past ten p.m., 22.05*

(c) **Час** is used for 'one o'clock' and cardinal numerals + часа́/часо́в for subsequent hours:

час   *one o'clock*
два часа́/три часа́/четы́ре часа́   *two/three/four o'clock*
пять часо́в to **двена́дцать часо́в**   *five o'clock to 12 o'clock*

(d) Before or after the hour, either the 24-hour system is used or:

(i) up to the half hour the construction 'so many minutes of the next hour' (represented by the genitive of an ordinal numeral):

пять (мину́т) тре́тьего   *five past two*
де́сять (мину́т) тре́тьего   *ten past two*
че́тверть тре́тьего   *quarter past two*
два́дцать (мину́т) тре́тьего   *twenty past two*
два́дцать пять (мину́т) тре́тьего   *twenty-five past two*
полови́на тре́тьего (полтре́тьего)   *half past two*

(ii) after the half hour, **без** + genitive:

без двадцати́ пяти́ (мину́т) три   *twenty-five to three*
без двадцати́ (мину́т) три   *twenty to three*
без че́тверти три   *a quarter to three*
без десяти́ (мину́т) три   *ten to three*
без пяти́ (мину́т) три   *five to three*

! **Note:** мину́т is mandatory only with numerals that are *not* multiples of пять, thus: без семи́ **мину́т** четы́ре 'seven **minutes** to four', but без десяти́ (мину́т) четы́ре 'ten minutes to four'.

В кото́ром часу́? Во ско́лько? 'At what time?'

(a) These questions are answered by prefacing times up to and including the half hour by **в**: **в семь часо́в** 'at seven o'clock', **в**

чётверть пе́рвого 'at quarter past twelve', **в полвосьмо́го** (or **в половине восьмо́го** 'at half-past seven'), etc.

(b) If there is another preposition present, the **в** is omitted, e.g., **о́коло пяти́ часо́в** 'at about five o'clock'. Times after the half-hour are left unchanged: **без двадцати́ пяти́ мину́т де́сять** 'twenty-five to ten' and '*at* twenty-five to ten'.

(c) The day (twenty-four hours) is divided up as follows:

час/два часа́/три часа́ **но́чи**   *one/two/three o'clock* **in the morning/a.m.**

четы́ре часа́   *through to*   оди́ннадцать часо́в **утра́**   *four o'clock to eleven o'clock* **in the morning/a.m.**

час/два часа́/три часа́/четы́ре часа́/пять часо́в **дня**   *one/two/ three/four/five o'clock* **in the afternoon/p.m.**

шесть часо́в   *through to*   оди́ннадцать часо́в **ве́чера**   *six o'clock to eleven o'clock* **in the evening/p.m.**

Како́е число́? 'What is the date?'

The question is answered using a neuter ordinal in the nominative case (the name of the *month* is in the genitive: **Сего́дня девя́тое ма́я** 'It's the ninth of May').

Како́го числа́? 'On what date?'

The question is answered using the **genitive** of a neuter ordinal (the *month* and the *year* also appear in the genitive case): **два́дцать четвёртого декабря́ ты́сяча девятьсо́т девяно́сто девя́того го́да** 'on the twenty-fourth of December 1999'.

В како́м году́? 'In which year?'

(a) The question is answered by using **в** + an ordinal numeral in the **prepositional case** (only the *final* component is an ordinal: the rest are cardinal numerals in the nominative case):

в две ты́сячи двадца́том году́   *in 2020*

(b) If any detail is added, ordinal and year appear in the **genitive case**:

в ма́рте две ты́сячи пя́того го́да   *in March 2005*

в пя́тницу тре́тьего ма́я две ты́сячи второ́го го́да   *on Friday 3 May 2002*

The verb

A verb is a part of speech that expresses an action (**он пи́шет** 'he is writing') or state (**она́ стои́т** 'she is standing'). A Russian verb can be transitive, requiring an object in the accusative case to complete it (Она́ включи́ла ла́мпу 'She **switched on** the lamp'), or intransitive, not requiring an object to complete it (Он **спал** 'He was asleep').

I The conjugations

There are two patterns of conjugation: the **first** conjugation and the **second** conjugation.

I The first conjugation

First-conjugation verbs subdivide into those with present-future stems ending in a vowel and those with present-future stems ending in a consonant. The present-future stem of a verb is revealed by removing the last two letters of the third-person plural. Thus, the stem of **чита́ть** 'to read', third-person plural **чита́-ют**, ends in the vowel **а**, and the stem of **писа́ть** 'to write', third-person plural **пи́ш-ут**, ends in the consonant **ш**.

Vowel stems

First-conjugation verbs with vowel stems include:
(a) very many verbs in **-ать** and **-ять** (e.g. чита́ть 'to read', теря́ть 'to lose')
(b) all verbs in **-авать** (e.g. дава́ть 'to give')
(c) all verbs in -**овать** and **-евать** (e.g. голосова́ть 'to vote', плева́ть 'to spit')
(d) very many verbs in **-еть** (e.g. име́ть 'to have')
(e) a few verbs in **-ить** (e.g. пить 'to drink')
(f) some verbs in **-ыть** (e.g. мыть 'to wash')
(g) a few verbs in **-уть** (e.g. дуть 'to blow')

First-conjugation endings

Verbs of the first conjugation add the following endings to the stem: **-ю, -ешь, -ет, -ем, -ете, -ют**

> **Note:** (a) -ю and -ют are usually replaced by -у and -ут after a consonant.
> (b) ю and я are replaced, respectively, by у and а after ж, ч, ш, or щ.
> (c) in the conjugation of some verbs, -е is replaced by -ё under stress.

First-conjugation verbs with vowel stems

(a) Verbs in -ать/-ять

Verbs in **-ать**	Verbs in **-ять** (end-stressed)	Verbs in **-ять** (stem-stressed)
игра́ть 'to play'	**стреля́ть** 'to shoot'	**се́ять** 'to sow'
я игра́-ю	стреля́-ю	се́-ю
ты игра́-ешь	стреля́-ешь	се́-ешь
он игра́-ет	стреля́-ет	се́-ет
мы игра́-ем	стреля́-ем	се́-ем
вы игра́-ете	стреля́-ете	се́-ете
они́ игра́-ют	стреля́-ют	се́-ют

> **Note:** (i) Stem-stressed verbs in **-ять** include **ла́ять** 'to bark' and **та́ять** 'to melt' (intransitive). They conjugate like **се́ять** 'to sow' (however, stem-stressed **ка́шлять** 'to cough' conjugates like **стреля́ть** 'to shoot').
> (ii) **смея́ться** 'to laugh' conjugates смею́сь, смеёшься, смеётся, смеёмся, смеётесь, смею́тся (*see pages 137, 138*).

(b) Verbs in -авать

These include **дава́ть** 'to give' and its compounds, as well as compounds of **-знава́ть** and **-става́ть**:

дава́ть 'to give'	**признава́ть** 'to acknowledge'	**встава́ть** 'to get up'
я да-ю́	призна-ю́	вста-ю́
ты да-ёшь	призна-ёшь	вста-ёшь
он да-ёт	призна-ёт	вста-ёт
мы да-ём	призна-ём	вста-ём
вы да-ёте	призна-ёте	вста-ёте
они́ да-ю́т	призна-ю́т	вста-ю́т

(c) Verbs in -овать/-евать

Conjugation of **испо́льзовать** 'to use' and **воева́ть** 'to wage war':

я испо́льзу-ю	я вою́-ю
ты испо́льзу-ешь	ты вою́-ешь
он испо́льзу-ет	он вою́-ет
мы испо́льзу-ем	мы вою́-ем
вы испо́льзу-ете	вы вою́-ете
они́ испо́льзу-ют	они́ вою́-ют

! **Note:** (i) Some verbs take -ё- under stress: **жева́ть** 'to chew' (жую́, жуёшь), **плева́ть** 'to spit' (плюю́, плюёшь).
(ii) Secondary imperfective verbs in -евать (verbs that derive from a perfective verb by the insertion of a suffix, e.g. **надева́ть** 'to put on' and **успева́ть** 'to have time to, manage') conjugate like **игра́ть** 'to play'.

(d) Verbs in -еть

The verb **уме́ть** 'to know how to' conjugates as follows:

я уме́-ю	мы уме́-ем
ты уме́-ешь	вы уме́-ете
он уме́-ет	они́ уме́-ют

Likewise **владе́ть** 'to own', **греть** 'to heat', **жале́ть** 'to pity', **име́ть** 'to have', **сметь** 'to dare', and many verbs derived from adjectives: **богате́ть** 'to get rich' (from бога́тый 'rich'), **красне́ть** 'to blush' (from кра́сный 'red'), **полне́ть** 'to put on weight' (from по́лный 'stout'), **старе́ть** 'to age' (from ста́рый 'old'), as well as a few verbs derived from nouns: **сироте́ть** 'to be orphaned' (from сирота́ 'orphan').

The verb **петь** 'to sing' conjugates as follows:

я по-ю́	мы по-ём
ты по-ёшь	вы по-ёте
он по-ёт	они́ по-ю́т

(e) Verbs in -ить

The verb **пить** 'to drink' conjugates as follows:

я пь-ю	мы пь-ём
ты пь-ёшь	вы пь-ёте
он пь-ёт	они пь-ют

Likewise **бить** 'to hit', **лить** 'to pour', **шить** 'to sew'.

The verb **брить** 'to shave' (transitive) conjugates as follows:

я бре́-ю	мы бре́-ем
ты бре́-ешь	вы бре́-ете
он бре́-ет	они бре́-ют

(f) Verbs in -ыть

The verb **мыть** 'to wash' conjugates as follows:

я мо́-ю	мы мо́-ем
ты мо́-ешь	вы мо́-ете
он мо́-ет	они мо́-ют

Likewise **рыть** 'to dig', and compounds of **-крыть**.

(g) Verbs in -уть

The only common verb in this category is **дуть** 'to blow':

я ду́-ю	мы ду́-ем
ты ду́-ешь	вы ду́-ете
он ду́-ет	они ду́-ют

First-conjugation verbs with consonant stems

(a) Verbs with consonant change throughout conjugation

The following consonant changes occur throughout the conjugation of a number of first-conjugation verbs with stems ending in consonants:

з–ж	к–ч	м–мл	п–пл
ре́зать	**пла́кать**	**дрема́ть**	**щипа́ть**
'to cut'	'to weep'	'to doze'	'to pinch'
я ре́ж-у	пла́ч-у	дремл-ю́	щипл-ю́
ты ре́ж-ешь	пла́ч-ешь	дре́мл-ешь	щи́пл-ешь
он ре́ж-ет	пла́ч-ет	дре́мл-ет	щи́пл-ет
мы ре́ж-ем	пла́ч-ем	дре́мл-ем	щи́пл-ем
вы ре́ж-ете	пла́ч-ете	дре́мл-ете	щи́пл-ете
они́ ре́ж-ут	пла́ч-ут	дре́мл-ют	щи́пл-ют

с–ш	ск–щ	т–ч	х–ш
писа́ть	**иска́ть**	**пря́тать**	**маха́ть**
'to write'	'to look for'	'to hide'	'to wave'
я пиш-у́	ищ-у́	пря́ч-у	маш-у́
ты пи́ш-ешь	и́щ-ешь	пря́ч-ешь	ма́ш-ешь
он пи́ш-ет	и́щ-ет	пря́ч-ет	ма́ш-ет
мы пи́ш-ем	и́щ-ем	пря́ч-ем	ма́ш-ем
вы пи́ш-ете	и́щ-ете	пря́ч-ете	ма́ш-ете
они́ пи́ш-ут	и́щ-ут	пря́ч-ут	ма́ш-ут

! **Note:** (i) others in the series include **каза́ться** (кажу́сь, ка́жешься) 'to seem', **скака́ть** (скачу́, ска́чешь) 'to gallop', **сы́пать** (сы́плю, сы́плешь) 'to pour', **чеса́ть** (чешу́, че́шешь) 'to scratch', **плеска́ть** (плещу́, пле́щешь) 'to splash', **шепта́ть** (шепчу́, ше́пчешь) 'to whisper'.
(ii) **колеба́ться** 'to hesitate' conjugates with stress on the stem throughout (коле́блюсь, коле́блешься).

(b) Other first-conjugation verbs in -ать with stems ending in consonants

брать	éхать	ждать	жать	звать
'to take'	'to travel'	'to wait'	'to press'	'to call'
бер-у́	éд-у	жд-у	жм-у	зов-у́
бер-ёшь	éд-ешь	жд-ёшь	жм-ёшь	зов-ёшь
бер-ёт	éд-ет	жд-ёт	жм-ёт	зов-ёт
бер-ём	éд-ем	жд-ём	жм-ём	зов-ём
бер-ёте	éд-ете	жд-ёте	жм-ёте	зов-ёте
бер-у́т	éд-ут	жд-ут	жм-ут	зов-у́т

лгать	нача́ть	рвать	слать	стать
'to tell lies'	'to begin'	'to tear'	'to send'	'to become'
лг-у	начн-у́	рв-у	шл-ю	ста́н-у
лж-ёшь	начн-ёшь	рв-ёшь	шл-ёшь	ста́н-ешь
лж-ёт	начн-ёт	рв-ёт	шл-ёт	ста́н-ет
лж-ём	начн-ём	рв-ём	шл-ём	ста́н-ем
лж-ёте	начн-ёте	рв-ёте	шл-ёте	ста́н-етс
лг-ут	начн-у́т	рв-ут	шл-ют	ста́н-ут

(c) Verbs in -оть, -нуть, -ереть, -нять

боро́ться	ги́бнуть	тере́ть	заня́ть	снять
'to struggle'	'to perish'	'to rub'	'to occupy'	'to take off'
бор-ю́сь	ги́бн-у	тр-у	займ-у́	сним-у́
бо́р-ешься	ги́бн-ешь	тр-ёшь	займ-ёшь	сни́м-ешь
бо́р-ется	ги́бн-ет	тр-ёт	займ-ёт	сни́м-ет
бо́р-емся	ги́бн-ем	тр-ём	займ-ём	сни́м-ем
бо́р-етесь	ги́бн-ете	тр-ёте	займ-ёте	сни́м-ете
бо́р-ются	ги́бн-ут	тр-ут	займ-у́т	сни́м-ут

! **Note:** коло́ть 'to chop' conjugates like боро́ться, запере́ть 'to lock' and умере́ть 'to die' like тере́ть, поня́ть 'to understand' like заня́ть, подня́ть to pick up' like снять. Приня́ть 'to accept' conjugates приму́, при́мешь, при́мет, при́мем, при́мете, при́мут. Most end-stressed verbs in -нуть take -ё- in conjugation (e.g. верну́, вернёшь from верну́ть 'to return' (transitive).

(d) Additional first-conjugation verbs with consonant stems

быть 'to be'	взять 'to take'	деть 'to put'	жить 'to live'	плыть 'to swim'
бу́д-у	возьм-у́	де́н-у	жив-у́	плыв-у́
бу́д-ешь	возьм-ёшь	де́н-ешь	жив-ёшь	плыв-ёшь
бу́д-ет	возьм-ёт	де́н-ет	жив-ёт	плыв-ёт
бу́д-ем	возьм-ём	де́н-ем	жив-ём	плыв-ём
бу́д-ете	возьм-ёте	де́н-ете	жив-ёте	плыв-ёте
бу́д-ут	возьм-у́т	де́н-ут	жив-у́т	плыв-у́т

! **Note:** **деть** appears mostly in compounds, e.g. **наде́ть** 'to put on', **оде́ться** 'to dress (oneself)'.

(e) First-conjugation verbs in –ти

These verbs can be subdivided in accordance with the stem consonants that appear in conjugation:

-д- stems вести́ 'to lead'	-з- stems везти́ 'to convey'	-с- stems нести́ 'to carry'	-т- stems мести́ 'to sweep'	-ст- stems расти́ 'to grow'
вед-у́	вез-у́	нес-у́	мет-у́	раст-у́
вед-ёшь	вез-ёшь	нес-ёшь	мет-ёшь	раст-ёшь
вед-ёт	вез-ёт	нес-ёт	мет-ёт	раст-ёт
вед-ём	вез-ём	нес-ём	мет-ём	раст-ём
вед-ёте	вез-ёте	нес-ёте	мет-ёте	раст-ёте
вед-у́т	вез-у́т	нес-у́т	мет-у́т	раст-у́т

! **Note:** **идти́** 'to go' (иду́, идёшь), **ползти́** 'to crawl' (ползу́, ползёшь), **цвести́** 'to bloom' (цвету́, цветёшь).

(f) Verbs in -сть/-зть

These can also be subdivided in accordance with their stem consonants:

-д- stems		-з- stems	
класть		**лезть**	
'to put, place'		'to climb'	
клад-у́	клад-ём	лез-у	ле́з-ем
клад-ёшь	клад-ёте	ле́з-ешь	ле́з-ете
клад-ёт	клад-у́т	ле́з-ет	ле́з-ут

> **!** Note: **красть** 'to steal' and **упа́сть** 'to fall' conjugate like **класть**, while **сесть** 'to sit down' conjugates ся́ду, ся́дешь, ся́дет, ся́дем, ся́дете, ся́дут.

(g) Verbs in -чь

Some verbs in **-чь** conjugate with **-г-** in the first person singular and third person plural, and **-ж-** before **-е-/-ё-**, others alternate **-к-** and **-ч-** in analogous positions:

г–ж	г–ж	г–ж	к–ч
стричь	**лечь**	**мочь**	**печь**
'to cut (hair)'	'to lie down'	'to be able'	'to bake'
стриг-у́	ля́г-у	мог-у́	пек-у́
стриж-ёшь	ля́ж-ешь	мо́ж-ешь	печ-ёшь
стриж-ёт	ля́ж-ет	мо́ж-ет	печ-ёт
стриж-ём	ля́ж-ем	мо́ж-ем	печ-ём
стриж-ёте	ля́ж-ете	мо́ж-ете	печ-ёте
стриг-у́т	ля́г-ут	мо́г-ут	пек-у́т

> **!** Note: **жечь** 'to burn' (transitive) conjugates: жгу, жжёшь, жжёт, жжём, жжёте, жгут, **течь** 'to flow' has third-person forms only: течёт, теку́т.

I The second conjugation

Verbs of the second conjugation add the following endings to the present-future stem:

> **-ю, -ишь, -ит, -им, -ите, -ят**

!
Note: ю is replaced by у and я by а after ж, ч, ш, or щ.

Second-conjugation verbs comprise:

(a) all verbs in **-ить**, except for those with monosyllabic infinitives and one or two others

(b) many verbs in **-еть** (some of which describe sounds)

(c) some verbs in **-ать** (some of which describe sounds)

(d) **боя́ться** 'to fear' and **стоя́ть** 'to stand':

Verbs in -ить	Verbs in -еть	Verbs in -ать	Verbs in -ять
звони́ть	**смотре́ть**	**слы́шать**	**боя́ться**
'to ring'	'to look'	'to hear'	'to fear'
звон-ю́	смотр-ю́	слы́ш-у	бо-ю́сь
звон-и́шь	смо́тр-ишь	слы́ш-ишь	бо-и́шься
звон-и́т	смо́тр-ит	слы́ш-ит	бо-и́тся
звон-и́м	смо́тр-им	слы́ш-им	бо-и́мся
звон-и́те	смо́тр-ите	слы́ш-ите	бо-и́тесь
звон-я́т	смо́тр-ят	слы́ш-ат	бо-я́тся

Second-conjugation verbs in **-еть** include: **блесте́ть** (блести́т, блестя́т) 'to shine', **боле́ть** (боли́т, боля́т) 'to hurt', **ви́деть** (ви́жу, ви́дишь) 'to see', **висе́ть** (виси́т, вися́т) 'to hang' (intransitive), **горе́ть** (гори́т, горя́т) 'to burn' (intransitive), **греме́ть** (греми́т, гремя́т) 'to thunder', **зави́сеть** (зави́сит, зави́сят) 'to depend', **кипе́ть** (кипи́т, кипя́т) 'to boil' (intransitive), **сиде́ть** (сижу́, сиди́шь) 'to sit'.

Those in **-ать** include: **держа́ть** (держу́, де́ржишь) 'to hold', **дрожа́ть** (дрожу́, дрожи́шь) 'to tremble', **дыша́ть** (дышу́, ды́шишь) 'to breathe', **крича́ть** (кричу́, кричи́шь) 'to shout', **лежа́ть** (лежу́, лежи́шь) 'to lie', **молча́ть** (молчу́, молчи́шь), 'to be silent', **спать** (сплю, спишь) 'to sleep', **стуча́ть** (стучу́, стучи́шь 'to knock').

!
Note: Some of the verbs are used in the third person only.

Consonant change

A regular feature of second-conjugation verbs is consonant change in the first-person singular. The following changes take place:

д-ж	з-ж	с-ш
буди́ть	вози́ть	гаси́ть
'to awaken'	'to convey'	'to extinguish'
буж-у́	вож-у́	гаш-у́
бу́д-ишь	во́з-ишь	га́с-ишь
бу́д-ит	во́з-ит	га́с-ит
бу́д-им	во́з-им	га́с-им
бу́д-ите	во́з-ите	га́с-ите
бу́д-ят	во́з-ят	га́с-ят

т-ч	т-щ	ст-щ
тра́тить	посети́ть	чи́стить
'to spend'	'to visit'	'to clean'
тра́ч-у	посещ-у́	чи́щ-у
тра́т-ишь	посет-и́шь	чи́ст-ишь
тра́т-ит	посет-и́т	чи́ст-ит
тра́т-им	посет-и́м	чи́ст-им
тра́т-ите	посет-и́те	чи́ст-ите
тра́т-ят	посет-я́т	чи́ст-ят

! **Note:** also б-бл (e.g. люблю́, лю́бишь, from люби́ть 'to love'), в-вл (e.g. ловлю́, ло́вишь, from лови́ть 'to catch'), м-мл (e.g. кормлю́, ко́рмишь, from корми́ть 'to feed'), п-пл (e.g. ступлю́, сту́пишь, from ступи́ть 'to step').

Consonant change (continued)

Some of the commonest verbs that undergo a consonant change
in the first-person singular of second-conjugation verbs include:

б-бл: **люби́ть** 'to love', **употреби́ть** 'to use'

в-вл: **лови́ть** 'to catch', **ста́вить** 'to stand' (transitive)

д-ж: **ви́деть** 'to see', **води́ть** 'to lead', **е́здить** 'to travel', **сади́ться**
'to sit down', **сиде́ть** 'to sit', **ходи́ть** 'to go'

з-ж: **изобрази́ть** 'to depict'

м-мл: **корми́ть** 'to feed'

п-пл: **купи́ть** 'to buy', **спать** 'to sleep'

с-ш: **кра́сить** 'to paint', **носи́ть** 'to carry', **проси́ть** 'to request'

ст-щ: **прости́ть** 'to forgive', **пусти́ть** 'to let go'

т-ч **встре́тить** 'to meet', **заме́тить** 'to notice', **лете́ть** 'to fly',
отве́тить 'to answer', **плати́ть** 'to pay'

т-щ **запрети́ть** 'to forbid'

Stress change in verbs of the second conjugation

Stress changes from the ending on to the stem in the conjugation
of many second-conjugation verbs (beginning with the second
person singular).

The following are some of the commonest verbs affected:
буди́ть (бужу́, бу́дишь) 'to awaken', **держа́ть** (держу́, де́ржишь)
'to hold', **дыша́ть** (дышу́, ды́шишь) 'to breathe', **жени́ться**
(женю́сь, же́нишься) 'to marry' (of a man), **кури́ть** (курю́,
ку́ришь) 'to smoke', **лови́ть** (ловлю́, ло́вишь) 'to catch', **люби́ть**
(люблю́, лю́бишь) 'to love', **носи́ть** (ношу́, но́сишь) 'to carry',
плати́ть (плачу́, пла́тишь) 'to pay', **получи́ть** (получу́,
полу́чишь) 'to receive', **проси́ть** (прошу́, про́сишь) 'to request',
пусти́ть (пущу́, пу́стишь) 'to let go', **служи́ть** (служу́, слу́жишь)
'to serve', **смотре́ть** (смотрю́, смо́тришь) 'to look', **суди́ть** (сужу́,
су́дишь) 'to judge', **учи́ть** (учу́, у́чишь) 'to teach', **учи́ться** (учу́сь,
у́чишься) 'to learn', **ходи́ть** (хожу́, хо́дишь) 'to go', **шути́ть**
(шучу́, шу́тишь) 'to joke'.

Irregular verbs

Four verbs do not conform to the pattern of either conjugation:

бежа́ть 'to run'	есть 'to eat'	хоте́ть 'to want'	дать 'to give'
бег-у́	ем	хоч-у́	дам
беж-и́шь	ешь	хо́ч-ешь	дашь
беж-и́т	ест	хо́ч-ет	даст
беж-и́м	ед-и́м	хот-и́м	дад-и́м
беж-и́те	ед-и́те	хот-и́те	дад-и́те
бег-у́т	ед-я́т	хот-я́т	дад-у́т

The past tense

(a) The masculine past tense is formed by replacing the infinitive ending **-ть** or **-сть** by **-л** (for exceptions, *see page 108*):

игра́-ть	спеши́-ть	пе-ть	е-сть
'to play'	'to hurry'	'to sing'	'to eat'
он игра́-л	он спеши́-л	он пе-л	он е-л
'he played'	'he hurried'	'he sang'	'he ate'

(b) The feminine, neuter, and plural are formed by adding **-а, -о,** and **-и** to the masculine form:

он игра́-л	она́ игра́-ла	оно́ игра́-ло	они́ игра́-ли
'he played'	'she played'	'it played'	'they played'

(c) The past tense agrees with the subject in gender and number (i.e. singular or plural), thus, of a male subject, masculine forms are used:

я, ты, он   рабо́та-л   'I, you, he worked'

and of a female subject, feminine forms:

я, ты, она́   рабо́та-ла   'I, you, she worked'

while plural forms are used for **мы** 'we', **вы** 'you', and **они́** 'they'

мы, вы, они́   рабо́та-ли   'we, you, they worked'

Verbs that have no л in the masculine past tense

These include (note that л reappears in the feminine, neuter, and plural forms):

(a) verbs in **-чь**, e.g. **мочь** 'to be able', **течь** 'to flow':

мог могла́ могло́ могли́

Likewise **бере́чь** 'to take care of' (берёг берегла́ берегло́ берегли́), etc.

тёк текла́ текло́ текли́

Likewise **печь** 'to bake', etc.

(b) verbs in **-ти**: **везти́** 'to convey', **нести́** 'to carry', **расти́** 'to grow' (intransitive):

вёз везла́ везло́ везли́
нёс несла́ несло́ несли́
рос росла́ росло́ росли́

Likewise **спасти́** 'to save' (спас, спасла́, спасло́, спасли́).

> ❗ **Note:** verbs in -ти with -д- or -т- stems *do* have л in the masculine past: **идти́** 'to go', past шёл, шла, шло, шли; **вести́** 'to lead', past вёл, вела́, вело́, вели́.

(c) Verbs in **-нуть** that denote change in state, location, e.g. **замёрзнуть** 'to freeze' (intransitive):

замёрз замёрзла замёрзло замёрзли

Likewise **исче́знуть** 'to disappear', **поги́бнуть** 'to perish', **привы́кнуть** 'to get used to'.

(d) verbs in **-ере́ть**, e.g. **запере́ть** 'to lock', **тере́ть** 'to rub', **умере́ть** 'to die':

за́пер заперла́ за́перло за́перли
тёр тёрла тёрло тёрли
у́мер умерла́ у́мерло у́мерли

(e) verbs in **-зть** (e.g. **лезть** 'to climb', past лез, ле́зла, ле́зло, ле́зли) and compounds of **-шиби́ть** (e.g. **ошиби́ться** 'to make a mistake', past оши́бся, оши́блась, оши́блось, оши́блись).

I The future tense

The imperfective (*see page 111*) future of the verb consists of the relevant forms of the future tense of the auxiliary verb **быть** 'to be' and the *imperfective* infinitive of the verb (**never** the perfective infinitive). Thus, the imperfective future of **рабо́тать** 'to work' is:

я бу́ду	рабо́тать	I will	work
ты бу́дешь	рабо́тать	you will	work
он/она́ бу́дет	рабо́тать	he/she will	work
мы бу́дем	рабо́тать	we will	work
вы бу́дете	рабо́тать	you will	work
они́ бу́дут	рабо́тать	they will	work

As well as acting as an auxiliary verb in forming the future of other verbs, the future of **быть** 'to be' is a future in its own right:

я бу́ду	в Москве́	I will be	in Moscow
ты бу́дешь	рад/ра́да	you will be	glad
он/она́ бу́дет	хи́миком	he/she will be	a chemist
мы бу́дем	за́няты	we will be	busy
вы бу́дете	за грани́цей	you will be	abroad
они́ бу́дут	приглашены́	they will be	invited

! **Note:** The *perfective* future is formed simply by conjugating a perfective verb.

As in English, the *present* tense is often used in Russian with future meaning, especially with verbs of beginning or finishing, and with verbs of motion:

Уро́к **начина́ется** в шесть часо́в   The lesson **begins** at six o'clock

Конгре́сс **зака́нчивается** за́втра   The congress **ends** tomorrow

Сего́дня ве́чером мы **идём** в кино́   This evening **we are going** to the cinema

Мы **прилета́ем** в Хитро́у в час но́чи   We **fly** into Heathrow at 1 a.m.

The imperative

The singular **familiar** form of the imperative is formed by adding:

(a) **-й** to a vowel stem (the third-person plural minus the last two letters), e.g. **играть** 'to play':

Infinitive	3rd person plural	Stem	Imperative
играть	игра-ют	игра-	игра-й! 'play!'

(b) **-и** to the consonant stem of a verb with *fixed end stress* in conjugation (e.g. **брать** 'to take', беру́, берёшь, **говори́ть** 'to speak', говорю́, говори́шь), or *mobile* stress in conjugation (e.g. **суди́ть** 'to judge', сужу́, су́дишь)

брать	бер-у́т	бер-	**бери́!** 'take!'
говори́ть	говор-я́т	говор-	**говори́!** 'speak!'
суди́ть	су́д-ят	суд-	**суд-и́!** 'judge!'

(c) **-ь** to a stem with *fixed* stem stress in conjugation and ending in a single consonant, e.g. **дви́нуть** 'to move':

дви́нуть	дви́н-ут	двин-	**двин-ь!** 'move!'

Stress in imperatives of more than one syllable is on the same syllable as the first-person singular, e.g. **писа́ть** 'to write':

писа́ть 'to write'   пишу́ 'I write'   пиши́! (imperative) 'write!'

> **!** **Note:** (a) The verb **дава́ть** and its compounds, and compounds of -**става́ть** and -**знава́ть** form their imperatives from the infinitive: дава́й! 'give!', встава́й! 'get up!'
>
> (b) The imperative of **пить** 'to drink' is пей! (likewise бей! from **бить** 'to strike', лей! from **лить** 'to pour', шей! from **шить** 'to sew').
>
> (c) Compounds of -**езжа́ть** and -**éхать** share an imperative in -**езжа́й**.

The **plural** and **formal** form of the imperative is made by adding -**те** to the singular form: игра́йте! 'play!' (to a number of people or someone one addresses as вы). Useful imperatives include:

иди́(те)!	go, come!	смотри́(те)!	look!
слу́шай(те)!	listen!	не забу́дь(те)!	don't forget!
жди́(те)!	wait!		

The **third-person** imperative comprises the particle **пусть** + third-person singular or plural of a verb: **Пусть** он идёт 'let him go', **Пусть** они́ попро́буют 'let them try'.

I The aspect: preliminary remarks

Almost all Russian verbs have two aspects, an **imperfective** and a **perfective**.

The aspects are formed either:

(a) by prefixation:

Imperfective	Perfective	Meaning
петь	с-петь	'to sing'

(b) by pairing a first conjugation verb (imperfective) with a second conjugation verb (perfective) :

включ-**а́ть** включ-**и́ть** 'to switch on'

(c) by inserting a syllable, e.g. -**ва**-, into the perfective:

наде-**ва́**-ть наде́ть 'to put on'

In a few cases, imperfective and perfective are from different roots, e.g. imperfective **лови́ть**, perfective **пойма́ть** 'to catch'.

Imperfective verbs have a past, present, and future, e.g. **звони́ть** 'to ring':

Past	Present	Future
он звони́л	он звони́т	он бу́дет звони́ть

while perfectives have past and future only, e.g. **позвони́ть** 'to ring' :

он позвони́л ——— он позвони́т

The **imperfective** aspect denotes:

(a) an action that was, is, or will be in progress ('he was, is, will be ringing'), or

(b) a **repeated** or **habitual** action ('he used to ring, rings, will ring').

The **perfective** aspect indicates **completion** of an action in the past ('he made, has made, had made a call') or **intention to complete** an action in the future ('he will make a call, will have made a call'). A **result** is often implied (e.g. a message has been passed on, information is now available, etc.). (For other functions of the perfective, *see also page 119*.)

> **!** **Note:** (a) A number of verbs have an **imperfective aspect only** (e.g. наблюда́ть 'to observe', состоя́ть 'to consist of'). Some have a **perfective** only (e.g. хлы́нуть 'to gush'). A small number have the same form for imperfective and perfective, e.g. испо́льзовать 'to use'.
> (b) Imperfective and perfective differ only in aspect, **not** in meaning.

Prefixation in the formation of the perfective

(a) Prefixation is one of the principal methods of deriving a perfective from an imperfective. The addition of a perfective prefix results, not in a change of *meaning*, but only in a change of *aspect*. Thus, both imperfective **писа́ть** (письмо́) and perfective **написа́ть** (письмо́) mean 'to write (a letter)', but the past, present, and future of **писа́ть** (**я писа́л, пишу́, бу́ду писа́ть** письмо́) imply writing in progress ('I was writing, am writing, will be writing a letter') or repetition ('I used to write, write, will [often] write a letter'), while the past and future of perfective **написа́ть** (**я написа́л, напишу́** письмо́) denote the completion of an act of writing in the past ('I wrote, have written, had written a letter) or intention to complete an act of writing in the future ('I will write, will have written a letter, will get a letter written').

(b) The commonest of the perfective prefixes is **по-**, which can express:

(i) a *completed* action or process:

Она́ **покра́сила** сте́ны   She **painted** the walls
Мы **помы́ли** маши́ну   We **washed** the car

(ii) an *instantaneous* action:

Он **поре́зал** па́лец   He **cut** his finger
Я **поблагодари́л** его́   I **thanked** him

> **!** **Note:** (i) In different contexts, the prefix по- (like some others) may imply different types of action. Thus, Она́ посмотре́ла на меня́ 'She looked at me' may be described as instantaneous, while Она́ посмотре́ла фильм 'She watched a film' denotes a completed action.
> (ii) For 'submeanings' of perfectives in по-, *see page 115*.

Other perfective prefixes

Other perfective prefixes include the following:

- **вз-/вс-**

  Вода́ **вскипе́ла**   The water **has boiled**

  Он **вспаха́л** по́ле   He **ploughed up** the field

- **вы-** (always *stressed* as a perfective prefix, but always *unstressed* as an imperfective prefix except for imperfective вы́глядеть 'to look, appear'):

  Он **вы́гладил** руба́шку   He **ironed** the shirt

  Она́ **вы́купала** дете́й   She **bathed** the children

Also вы́пить 'to drink', вы́расти 'to grow', вы́стрелить 'to shoot', вы́учить 'to learn'.

- **за-**

  Он **заплати́л** за биле́ты   He **paid** for the tickets

Also зажа́рить 'to fry'.

- **из-/ис-**

  Я **истра́тил** свои́ де́ньги   I **have spent** (all) my money

- **на-** (with verbs that denote writing, drawing, and some others):

  Она́ **напи́шет** письмо́   She **will write** a letter

  Ребёнок **нарисова́л** дом   The child **drew** a house

  Она́ **научи́ла** меня́ петь   She **taught** me to sing

Also накорми́ть 'to feed', напеча́тать 'to print, type'.

- **под(о)-** is confined mainly to the verb ждать 'to wait':

  Я подожду́, пока́ он не придёт   I **will wait** until he arrives

Perfective prefixes (continued)

● **при-** (with **гото́вить** 'to prepare', and some others):

Я **пригото́влю** у́жин   I **will prepare** dinner

Also **пригрози́ть** 'to threaten'.

● **про-**

Она́ **прочита́ла** всю кни́гу   She **read** the whole book

Also проголосова́ть 'to vote'.

● **раз-/рас-** express division, or the reversal of a process:

Они́ **раздели́ли** иму́щество   They **divided up** the property
Снег **раста́ял**   The snow **melted**

Others include разбуди́ть 'to awaken'.

● **с-**

Она́ **споёт** а́рию   She **will sing** an aria
Я **спря́тал** ключ   I **hid** the key

Others include свари́ть 'to boil' (transitive), совра́ть 'to tell a lie',
сде́лать 'to do, make', съесть 'to eat', сыгра́ть 'to play', слома́ть
'to break', сшить 'to sew, make'.

● **у-** is used with verbs of perception, and some others:

Я **услы́шал** её го́лос   I **heard** her voice
Он **укра́л** часы́   He **stole** a watch

Also уви́деть 'to catch sight of', утону́ть 'to drown' (intransitive).

A number of different prefixes (**вз-/вс-, из-/ис-, об-, раз-/рас-**) are
used to denote the onset of an *emotion*:

Он **взволнова́лся**   He **got worried, excited**
Она́ **испуга́лась**   She **took fright**
Она́ **обра́довалась**   She **rejoiced**
Он **рассерди́лся** на меня́   He **got angry** with me

> **!** **Note:** Other perfective prefixes are used with isolated verbs: **о-** in **овдове́ть** 'to
> be widowed', **от-** in **отреаги́ровать** 'to react', **пере-** in **переночева́ть** 'to spend
> the night', etc.

Submeanings of the perfective prefixes за- and по-

Some prefixed perfectives in **за-** have a submeaning of **inception**: Он замолчáл 'He fell silent', Онá заболéла 'She fell ill', Ребёнок заплáкал 'The child burst into tears'. This also applies to a number of perfectives in **по-**: Он побежáл 'He broke into a run'. In addition, many prefixed perfectives in по- have the submeaning of **short duration**: Он поспáл 'He had a nap', Онá посидéла 'She sat for a while', etc. (*see also page 126*).

Imperfective and perfective aspects differentiated by conjugation

(a) A number of aspectual pairs comprise a *first-conjugation* imperfective in -**ать** or -**ять** and a *second-conjugation* perfective in -**ить** or -**еть**. Most of the verbs are prefixed:

Imperfective	Perfective	Meaning
включ-áть	включ-и́ть	'to switch on'
вступ-áть	вступ-и́ть	'to enter, join'
загор-áться	загор-éться	'to catch fire'
измен-я́ть	измен-и́ть	'to alter'
объясн-я́ть	объясн-и́ть	'to explain'
повтор-я́ть	повтор-и́ть	'to repeat'
сообщ-áть	сообщ-и́ть	'to report'

(b) In some cases, the perfective is stressed on the stem:

довер-я́ть	довéр-ить	'to entrust'
назнач-áть	назнáч-ить	'to appoint'
наруш-áть	нарýш-ить	'to infringe'
улучш-áть	улýчш-ить	'to improve'

(c) A few unprefixed verbs also belong in the series:

брос-áть	брóс-ить	'to throw'
конч-áть	кóнч-ить	'to finish'
реш-áть	реш-и́ть	'to decide'

Consonant mutation in the imperfective aspect

The following consonant mutations occur *regularly* in the imperfective aspect of aspectual pairs comprising *first*-conjugation imperfective and *second*-conjugation perfective:

Mutation	Perfective	Imperfective	Meaning
б: бл	осла́б-ить	ослабл-я́ть	'to weaken'
в: вл	удиви́ть	удивля́ть	'to surprise'
д: ж	оби́деть	обижа́ть	'to offend'
д: жд	обсуди́ть	обсужда́ть	'to discuss'
з: ж	возрази́ть	возража́ть	'to object'
п: пл	скрепи́ть	скрепля́ть	'to staple'
с: ш	согласи́ться	соглаша́ться	'to agree'
ст: ск	пропусти́ть	пропуска́ть	'to miss'
ст: щ	прости́ть	проща́ть	'to forgive'
т: ч	встре́тить	встреча́ть	'to meet'
т: щ	защити́ть	защища́ть	'to protect'

Note: (a) the **ст: ск** alternation is confined to perfective пусти́ть/imperfective пуска́ть 'to let go' and its compounds.

(b) The **п: пл** mutation does not affect perfective ступи́ть/ imperfective ступа́ть 'to step' and compounds.

(c) The mutations also affect the *first-person singular* of the **perfective** verbs: Я осла́блю дисципли́ну 'I will slacken discipline', Я удивлю́ его́ 'I will surprise him', Я оби́жу их 'I will offend them', Я возражу́ про́тив э́того 'I will object to this', Я скреплю́ бума́ги 'I will staple the papers together', Я встре́чу госте́й 'I will meet the guests', Я соглашу́сь на э́то 'I will agree to this', Я пропущу́ по́езд 'I will miss the train', Я прощу́ оши́бку 'I will forgive the mistake', Я защищу́ диссерта́цию 'I will defend my dissertation'.

(d) the first-person singular of обсуди́ть 'to discuss' is обсужу́ 'I will discuss' (despite imperfective обсужда́ть), and this also applies to a number of other verbs with **д** in the perfective infinitive and **жд** in the imperfective infinitive.

Secondary imperfectives based on first-conjugation verbs

Most verbs have a 'neutral' perfective, that is to say, imperfective and perfective have the same *meaning*, e.g. игра́ть/сыгра́ть 'to play', but a different aspect. However, many verbs also take prefixes that change both their aspect (which changes to perfective) **and** their meaning. The new perfectives then acquire imperfectives through the insertion of a syllable. Thus, проигра́ть (a derivative of игра́ть 'to play') means 'to lose', and its imperfective is formed by inserting the syllable **-ыв-** and shifting the stress back onto the stem, thus:

Root verb 'to play'	Perfective compound	Secondary imperfective	Meaning
игра́ть	проигра́ть	прои́грывать	'to lose'

Likewise подписа́ть 'to sign' (a derivative of писа́ть 'to write'), imperfective подпи́сывать, etc.

> **Note:** (a) the stem vowel -o- is usually replaced by -a- in the secondary imperfective: зарабо́тать 'to earn', imperfective зараба́тывать, and -e- by -ё-: причеса́ть 'to comb', imperfective причёсывать.
> (b) many perfective compounds based on monosyllabic verbs form imperfectives with -ва-: уби́ть 'to kill', imperfective убива́ть. Others insert -и- or -ы-: убра́ть 'to clear away', imperfective убира́ть, назва́ть 'to name', imperfective называ́ть.

Secondary imperfectives based on second-conjugation verbs

These are formed in the same way as those derived from first-conjugation verbs (including stress shift and stem-vowel change -o- to -a-). The suffix **-ив-** is inserted into the perfective infinitive:

Root verb 'to look'	Perfective compound	Secondary imperfective	Meaning
смотре́ть	осмотре́ть	осма́тривать	'to examine'

> **Note:** (a) secondary imperfectives based on second-conjugation verbs are affected by consonant mutation, for example: расплати́ться 'to settle up', imperfective распла́чиваться (for other consonant changes, *see page 116*).
> (b) when two vowels appear in sequence in the perfective, e.g. накле́ить 'to affix', the secondary imperfective is formed with the suffix -ва-. Thus, the imperfective of накле́ить is накле́ивать.

Perfectives in -нуть

(a) A number of imperfective verbs with the ending **-ать**
(sometimes **-ять** or **-еть**) form their perfectives using the suffix
-ну-. Many of the perfectives denote a single instantaneous
action:

Imperfective	Perfective	Meaning
гляде́ть	гля́нуть	to glance
дви́гать	дви́нуть	to move
засыпа́ть	засну́ть	to fall asleep
исчеза́ть	исче́знуть	to disappear
каса́ться	косну́ться	to touch
крича́ть	кри́кнуть	to shout
просыпа́ться	просну́ться	to wake up
пры́гать	пры́гнуть	to jump
стуча́ть	сту́кнуть	to bang
улыба́ться	улыбну́ться	to smile
хло́пать	хло́пнуть	to slam

(b) Others include достига́ть/**дости́гнуть** 'to achieve', замерза́ть/
замёрзнуть 'to freeze' (intransitive), ка́шлять/**ка́шлянуть** 'to
cough', отдыха́ть/**отдохну́ть** 'to relax', подчёркивать/
подчеркну́ть 'to underline', привыка́ть/**привы́кнуть** 'to get used
to'.

Irregular aspectual pairs

Imperfective	Perfective	Meaning
брать	взять	to take
говори́ть	сказа́ть	to say
класть	положи́ть	to place, put
ложи́ться	лечь	to lie down
переса́живаться	пересе́сть	to change vehicles
сади́ться	сесть	to sit down
станови́ться	стать	to become

I Functions of the verbal aspects

(a) The fundamental difference between the aspects (*see also page 111*) is that the imperfective is used to denote actions that are either:

● in progress: Он **плати́л** за биле́ты 'He **was paying** for the tickets'

● or repeated: Он **всегда́** плати́л за биле́ты 'He **always** paid for the tickets',

while the perfective denotes:

● a single completed action: Он **заплати́л** за биле́ты 'He **paid/has paid/had paid** for the tickets'.

(b) As we have seen, the imperfective has a past, present, and future (e.g. **он плати́л/пла́тит/бу́дет плати́ть** 'he was paying/pays/will be paying'), while the perfective has a past and future (e.g. **он заплати́л/ запла́тит** 'he paid/will pay'), but *no* present.

(c) The perfective aspect is often *resultative*; compare the non-resultative *imperfective*:

Он **подмета́л** пол   He **was sweeping** the floor (an action incomplete and *in progress*), and the resultative *perfective*:

Он **подмёл** пол   He **has swept** the floor (*result* – the floor is clean)

(d) The perfective is thus said to move the action forward (e.g. Ему́ **вы́дали** ви́зу 'They issued him with a visa' – so now he can buy a ticket, go to Russia, etc.), while the imperfective describes action in progress (e.g. Ему́ **выдава́ли** ви́зу 'They were issuing him with a visa': the formalities were in process).

(e) Perfectives also have other functions

(i) Some denote the **beginning** of an action (*see also page 115*):

Она́ **запоёт**   She **will start singing**

(ii) Others denote an **instantaneous** action:

Он **чихну́л**   He **sneezed**

(iii) Some (mainly prefixed **по-**, with no imperfective counterparts, *see also page 115*) denote an action **of short duration**:

Я **постою́** здесь немно́го   I **will stand** here for a while

The present tense

(a) Only the *imperfective* aspect can be used in the present tense (a conjugated perfective verb has *future* meaning). Unlike English, which distinguishes actions in progress ('He **is putting on** his coat') from habitual actions ('He **puts on** his coat'), the *Russian* present tense can express either meaning. The difference between durative action and habitual action may be conveyed by context:

Сейча́с он надева́ет пальто́   He is putting on his coat **now**

Он **всегда́** надева́ет пальто́   He **always** puts on his coat

> **Note:** *See pages 150–154 for the verbs of motion, which* do *distinguish between action in progress (*Я иду́ в шко́лу *'I* **am on my way** *to school'), and habitual and other types of action (*Он хо́дит в шко́лу *'He* **goes** *to school').*

(b) The present tense also:

(i) conveys facts:

Дон **впада́ет** в Азо́вское мо́ре   The Don **empties** into the Sea of Azov

(ii) is used to denote an action that began in the past and continues in the present (English uses the past continuous: 'have/has been -ing'):

Я **рабо́таю** здесь уже́ два го́да   I **have been working** here for two years

Она́ уже́ давно́ **живёт** в Ки́еве   She **has been living** in Kiev for a long time

> **Note:** Use of the past tense here would correspond to the English *pluperfect* with 'had': Она́ уже́ давно́ **жила́** в Ки́еве   She **had been living** in Kiev for a long time

In a *negative* version of the construction with давно́ не, the present tense may imply permanency and the past tense a temporary state:

Я давно́ **не ем** мя́са   I **have not eaten** meat for a long time (have given it up entirely)

Я давно́ **не ел** мя́са   I **have not eaten** meat for a long time (but may do so again)

The present tense (continued)

The present tense of the verb **быть** 'to be' is either:
(a) 'understood':

Я гото́в/Она́ дово́льна   I **am** ready/She **is** pleased

or (b) replaced by a verb specific to a particular context:

Он **слу́жит** в а́рмии   He **is** ('serves') *in the army*

Они́ **у́чатся** в университе́те   They **are** ('are studying') *at university*

> **!** **Note:** In definitions and more official contexts, the verb **явля́ться** 'to be' is sometimes used (*see also page 42*): Он **явля́ется** чле́ном профсою́за   He **is** a *member of the TU*

Есть 'is/are, there is/are' is very commonly used to emphasize existence or availability: **Есть** биле́ты   **There are** tickets

Indirect or reported speech

In Russian, if the speaker's words were in the present tense, the present tense is used to report them. Thus, Я **не зна́ю** 'I **don't know**' is reported in Russian using the *present* tense (and in English using the *past*):

Он сказа́л, что **не зна́ет**   He said he **didn't know**

Similarly:

Я ду́мал, что он **понима́ет** её   I thought he **understood** her

Он наде́ялся, что я **забо́чусь** о ней   He hoped I **was looking after** her

Я узна́л, что она́ **и́щет** сы́на   I learnt she was **looking for** her son

The historic present

Like English, Russian has a *historic present*, which is used to make past occurrences more vivid:

В 1835 году́ Го́голь **пи́шет** <<*Нос*>>   In 1835 Gogol **writes** *The Nose*

Future meaning

In some instances (*see page 109*), the present can be used with future meaning:

За́втра мы **идём** в го́сти   Tomorrow we **are going** visiting

Aspect in the past tense: the imperfective

(a) A function of the imperfective past is to denote that an action was in progress at a particular time:

Учи́тель **проверя́л** тетра́ди   The teacher **was marking** the exercise books

(b) The durative element of the action may be reinforced by an adverb of time such as **до́лго** 'for a long time':

Он до́лго бри́лся   He **took a long time** to shave

(c) A whole series of imperfectives can be used to describe a scene, with actions appearing in indeterminate order:

Вчера́ мы **отдыха́ли** в па́рке: **игра́ли** в футбо́л, **слу́шали** ра́дио   Yesterday we **relaxed** in the park: **played** football, **listened** to the radio

(d) Imperfectives can also denote *concurrent* actions:

Она́ **расска́зывала**, а я **слу́шал**   She **narrated**, and I **listened**

(e) Imperfective and perfective can coexist in the same sentence, the imperfective denoting an action in progress, the perfective the completion of a process:

Мы **гуля́ли**, пока́ не **стемне́ло**   We **walked** until it **grew dark**

(f) Conversely, a completed action (perfective) can be set against the background of an action in progress (imperfective):

Пока́ она́ **гото́вила** у́жин, я **накры́л** на стол   While she **was cooking** dinner, I **laid** the table

(g) Care must be taken in selecting the correct aspect in sentences with **когда́** 'when', **в то вре́мя как** 'while', **по́сле того́ (,) как** 'after', etc. Compare use of the imperfective for simultaneous actions in:

Когда́ он **проща́лся** с ней, он поцелова́л её в лоб
When he **said goodbye** to her (i.e. *was saying* goodbye to her) he kissed her on the forehead

and of the perfective for consecutive actions in:

Когда́ он **попроща́лся** с ней, он сел в маши́ну и уе́хал
When he **had said goodbye** to her he got into his car and drove off

Aspect in the past tense: imperfective (continued)

Frequency

(a) The imperfective past also indicates frequency:

> Он обы́чно **задава́л** мно́го вопро́сов   He **used to ask** many questions
> Ка́ждый раз, когда́ он **входи́л**, все **встава́ли**   Every time he **came in** everyone **got up**

(b) The idea of habitual action may be reinforced by an adverb or adverbial phrase (**ча́сто** 'often', **ча́ще всего́** 'more often than not', **иногда́** 'sometimes', **всегда́** 'always', **обы́чно** 'usually', **раз в год** 'once a year', etc.):

> Он **всегда́** запира́л дверь   He **always** locked the door
> **Иногда́** она́ купа́лась в о́зере   **Sometimes** she swam in the lake
> **Обы́чно** он опа́здывал   **Usually** he was late
> Они́ отмеча́ли пра́здник **раз в год**   They marked the festival **once a year**

(c) The *perfective* is used if an action is repeated a number of times in close succession:

> Шофёр **просигна́лил** два́жды   The driver **hooted** twice

(d) When, however, the repeated actions are spaced out, with substantial intervals between the repeats, the imperfective must be used:

> Я не́сколько раз **перечи́тывал** *Анну Каре́нину*   I **have re-read** *Anna Karenina* several times

An action and its reverse

The imperfective past is also used to indicate that an action occurred and was then reversed or cancelled:

> Кто́-то **включа́л** свет   Someone **has had the light on** (but now it is off again)
> Он **надева́л** костю́м   He **put on** the suit (and has now taken it off again)

Она́ уезжа́ла на про́шлой неде́ле *She* **went away** *last week*
(and has now returned)

Я **брал** кни́гу в библиоте́ке I **took** *a book out of the library* (and
have now returned it)

> **Note:** Use of *perfectives* here would mean, respectively, that the light has been
> switched on and is *still* on (Кто́-то **включи́л** свет), that he has put on and *is*
> *still* wearing the suit (Он **наде́л** костю́м), that she went away last week and is
> *still* away (Она́ **уе́хала** на про́шлой неде́ле), and that I have not yet returned
> the library book (Я **взял** кни́гу в библиоте́ке).

Imminent events

The imperfective past is used to record an event that was about
to take place:

Парохо́д **отплыва́л** в два часа́ *The steamer* **was due to sail** *at*
two o'clock

Мы **отправля́лись** в похо́д *We* **were about to set out** *on a hike*

'Statement of fact'

The imperfective past is used to express a 'statement of fact'. In
this type of construction, a question or statement appears in the
vaguest of contexts, with no emphasis on completion or
non-completion:

Вы **чита́ли** *Де́тство*? Да, **чита́ла** **Have** *you (ever)* **read**
Childhood? *Yes,* **I have**

Вы **встреча́ли** Ма́шу? Да, ка́жется, **встреча́л** **Have** *you (ever)*
met *Masha? Yes, I believe* **I have**

> **Note:** The use of the *perfective* in such contexts would imply that, for example,
> you were *told* to read *Childhood* and ought to have read it, alternatively the
> speaker would like to have it if you have finished with it (Вы **прочита́ли**
> *Де́тство*? **Did** you **read/have you finished** *Childhood?*); or that you were
> *expected to* or *had agreed to* meet Masha and *should have* met her (Вы
> **встре́тили** Ма́шу? '**Did** you **meet** Masha?).

The perfective past

Completed actions or processes

(a) The perfective past is used to denote the completion of an action or process. A *result* is often implied (*see also page 111*):

Они **обменялись** адресами   They **exchanged** addresses (as a *result,* they have each other's address, can keep in touch, etc.)

Он **вымыл** посуду   He **washed** the dishes (as a *result,* they are clean)

Он **поужинал**   He **dined** (as a *result,* he is no longer hungry)

(b) Perfectives may appear as a succession of completed actions or processes:

Когда дождь **кончился**, мы **пошли** гулять   When the rain **stopped** we **went** for a walk

Как только он **поднялся** на трибуну, **раздались** аплодисменты   As soon as he **mounted** the rostrum, applause **rang out**

Note: A perfective indicating successful completion may be preceded by imperfectives that denote *attempts* to complete:

Он **поступал** в университет и, кажется, **поступил**   He applied for university and apparently got in

Она **сдавала** и **сдала** зачёт   She **took** and **passed** the test

Он **решал** и наконец **решил** кроссворд   He **tackled** and finally **solved** the crossword

Instantaneous actions

Some perfectives, mainly with the prefixes **вз-/вс-**, **раз-/рас-**, or **у-**, or the suffix **-ну-** (*see page 118*), denote instantaneous actions, often introduced by adverbs such as **вдруг** 'suddenly', **сразу** 'all at once', **мгновенно** 'instantly':

Сразу **вспыхнула** забастовка   A strike **flared up** all at once

Вдруг я **увидел** сигнал   Suddenly I **caught sight of** the signal

Мгновенно **раздался** выстрел   Instantly a shot **rang out**

Он **кашлянул**   He **gave a cough**

Actions of short duration

A number of verbs, mainly prefixed **по-** and with no
imperfectives, denote actions of short duration, sometimes
reinforced by the adverb **немно́го** 'a little' (*see also page 119*):

Она́ **поговори́ла** со мной   She **had a chat** with me
Мы **поигра́ли** немно́го в   We **played** chess **for a while**
ша́хматы
Она́ **почита́ла**   She **read for a while**

> **!** Note: Compare the neutral perfective **прочита́ть**, which denotes completion of
> an action: Она́ **прочита́ла** расска́з   She read the story

Inceptive verbs

A number of perfective verbs prefixed **за-**, and a few in **по-**,
denote the *beginning* of an action or process (*see also page 119*):

заболе́ть   to fall ill
запе́ть   to start singing
зазвони́ть   to start ringing
почу́вствовать (боль)   to start feeling (pain)
полюби́ть   to take a liking to

Many inceptive perfectives have no imperfective. However,
заболе́ть 'to fall ill' has the secondary imperfective заболева́ть
and запе́ть 'to start singing' the secondary imperfective запева́ть.

Aspect in the negative past: imperfective and perfective

The negated *imperfective* past can describe:

(a) a continuous negative state, sometimes reinforced by durative adverbs that automatically produce imperfectives, such as **всё** 'still' or **до́лго** 'for a long time':

> Он всё не **звони́л**   He still **didn't phone**
>
> Она́ до́лго **не реаги́ровала**   She **took** a long time **to react**

(b) repeated occurrences or non-occurrences, sometimes reinforced by frequentative adverbs:

> Он ча́сто **не отвеча́л**   He often **didn't answer**
>
> Она́ обы́чно **не жа́ловалась**   She **didn't** usually **complain**

Use of aspect in denoting a single negated occurrence

(a) In describing a single occurrence, a negated *imperfective* expresses a categorical denial that the action took place at all:

> Я никако́го письма́ **не получа́л**   I **didn't receive** any letter at all

(b) The negated *perfective* indicates:

(i) that the action *did* take place but **was not completed**:

> Дом ещё **не постро́или**   They **haven't finished building** the house

(ii) that the action was *expected* or *might* have been expected to take place, but did not:

> Я **не взял** фотоаппара́т в доро́гу   I **didn't take** my camera on the trip (even though I usually do)

> **!** Note: that *imperfective* usage: Я не брал фотоаппара́т 'I **didn't take** the camera' simply negates the action.

(iii) that the action has not taken place but, again, *is expected to*:

> Она́ ещё **не верну́лась**   She **hasn't** yet **returned**

> **!** Note: that imperfective usage: Она́ совсе́м не возвраща́лась 'She **did not return at all**' expresses a categorial denial that the action took place.

Aspect in the future

A future action in progress

The imperfective is used to denote a future action in progress:

Что вы **бу́дете де́лать** за́втра ве́чером? What **will you be doing** tomorrow evening?

Я **бу́ду смотре́ть** телеви́зор I **will be watching** television

> **Note:** A *perfective* answer would also be possible (implying a completed action): **Мы пое́дем** за́ город 'We **are going to drive** into the country'.

Repeated actions

The imperfective is used to denote future repeated actions:

Я всегда́ **бу́ду отдыха́ть** в Со́чи I **will** always **holiday** in Sochi

Intention to complete an action

(a) The perfective is used to denote intention to complete an action:

Я **напишу́** сочине́ние I **will write** the essay

(b) Perfectives may appear in sequence, each action following completion of the previous action:

Поза́втракаю и **пойду́** на рабо́ту I **will have breakfast** and **go** to work

Use of either aspect in a future context

(a) Sometimes either aspect is possible in a future context, the imperfective emphasizing *the progress of the action*:

Ле́том мы **бу́дем де́лать** ремо́нт в до́ме In the summer **we will be carrying out** repairs in the house

while the perfective anticipates *successful completion*:

Ле́том мы **сде́лаем** ремо́нт в до́ме In the summer we **will carry out** repairs in the house

(b) Different aspects can co-exist in the same sentence, the perfective expressing completion, the imperfective the durative nature of an action:

Поу́жинаю, пото́м **бу́ду смотре́ть** телеви́зор I **will have supper** and then **watch** television

Other future usage: the 'logical' future

Russian uses the future tense after **когда** 'when', **как то́лько** 'as soon as', **пре́жде(,) чем** 'before', **е́сли** 'if', **пока́ не** 'until', when future action is indicated (unlike English, which uses the *present* tense):

Когда́ он **ко́нчит**, поблагодари́ его́   When he **finishes**, thank him

Как то́лько **узна́ю**, скажу́ вам   As soon as I **hear** I'll tell you

Пре́жде чем он **подпи́шется**, он просмо́трит контра́кт   Before he **signs** he will look through the contract

Е́сли **бу́дешь покупа́ть** цветы́, купи́ и мне   If you **are buying** flowers, buy some for me too

Я подожду́, пока́ она́ не **придёт**   I'll wait until she **arrives**

The future in indirect or reported speech

The future tense is used to report a statement that was itself expressed in future terms. Thus, the statements Я **закро́ю** дверь 'I **will close** the door' and Я **бу́ду перепи́сываться** с ним 'I **will correspond** with him' are reported using the *future*:

Он сказа́л, что **закро́ет** дверь   He said he **would close** the door

Она́ сказа́ла, что **бу́дет перепи́сываться** с ним   She said she **would correspond** with him

Note: If two or more future clauses are to be reported, English uses 'would' in reporting the first, and subsequently switches to the past tense. Russian, however, used the future in both cases. Thus, the statement Я **переведу́** статью́, е́сли вы **пришлёте** её 'I **will translate** the article if you **send** it' is reported using the future of *both* verbs:

Он сказа́л, что **переведёт** статью́, е́сли я **пришлю́** её
He said he **would translate** the article, if I **sent** it (literally 'He said he **will translate** the article if I **will send** it')

Polite requests

The *negative* perfective future is sometimes used in polite requests:

Прости́те, вы **не подви́нетесь** немно́го?   Excuse me, **could** you **move over** a bit?

Aspect in the imperative

The imperfective imperative is used to issue:

(a) a general injunction:

Соблюдáй прáвила!　**Observe** the rules!

(b) a frequentative instruction:

Пéйте молокó кáждый день!　**Drink** milk every day!

Note: The *perfective* may be used where an action is to be repeated a number of times in swift succession:

Повторú этот звук нéсколько раз!　**Repeat** this sound several times!

(c) a request to continue an action:

Продолжáйте, я вас слýшаю!　**Go on**, I'm listening!

The imperative in the context of a single action

(a) In the context of a single action, the *perfective* is used to order implementation:

Переведúте эту фрáзу!　**Translate** this phrase!

and the *imperfective* to order non-implementation:

Не переводúте эту фрáзу!　**Don't translate** this phrase!

(b) The imperfective is also used:

(i) to express an *invitation* to guests on social occasions:
Заходúте! '*Come in!*', **Садúтесь!** '*Sit down!*', **Раздевáйтесь!**
'*Take off your hat and coat!*'

(ii) in concurring with a request, e.g.: **Мóжно повéсить пальтó!**
'May I hang up my coat?' **Вéшайте, вéшайте!** 'Hang it up by all means!' or issuing a reminder: Тебé нýжно позвонúть отцý.
Звонú скорéй! 'You've got to ring Dad. Hurry up and **ring**!'

> **Note:** The negative *perfective* is used to issue warnings against potentially harmful behaviour, combined with a concern that the action might occur by mistake: **Не упадúте!** 'Mind you don't fall', **Не споткнúтесь!** 'Mind you don't trip!', **Не забýдьте** 'Mind you don't forget!'. The imperative may be preceded by **смотрú!**: **Смотрú, не пролéй** вóду! 'Mind you don't spill the water!'

Aspect in the infinitive

The *imperfective* infinitive is used to denote

(a) continuous actions:

Ей ну́жно бу́дет **отдыха́ть** ме́сяц   She will need **to rest** for a month

(b) repeated actions:

Сто́ит **проверя́ть** зре́ние раз в год   It is worth **having** your eyes **checked** annually

Note: When **всегда́** 'always' or another frequentative adverb qualifies a verb or short adjective, however, the frequentative element is absorbed by the verb or adjective and the following infinitive may be in the *perfective* aspect:

Она́ всегда́ гото́ва **помо́чь**   She is always ready **to help**
Я всё забыва́ю **принести́** фотогра́фии   I keep on forgetting **to bring** the photographs

Completed actions

(a) The perfective infinitive is used to denote a single completed action:

Он реши́л **вы́звать** врача́   He decided **to call out** the doctor

(b) The imperfective infinitive is used, however, if **не** appears between the auxiliary verb and the infinitive:

Он реши́л **не вызыва́ть** врача́   He decided **not to call out** the doctor

(c) Since the underlying meaning of **разду́мывать/разду́мать** is 'to decide *not* to' it takes an *imperfective* infinitive:

Она́ разду́мала **танцева́ть**   She changed her mind about **dancing** (decided not to dance)

(d) The imperfective infinitive is also used

(i) after **не ну́жно** 'there is no need to' and **не на́до** 'you mustn't, you shouldn't', and other words that imply *inadvisability*:

Не ну́жно **спра́шивать**   There is no need **to ask**
Не на́до **налива́ть** ему́ во́дку   You shouldn't **pour** him vodka
Нет смы́сла **остана́вливаться**   There's no point in **stopping**

(ii) to denote habitual actions, learned skills, (dis)inclinations, etc.:

Он научи́лся **стреля́ть** He learnt **to shoot**
Она́ привы́кла **ждать** She has got used to **waiting**
Он уме́ет **води́ть** маши́ну He knows how **to drive** a car

(iii) after verbs that denote beginning, continuing, or finishing:

Она́ начала́ **гла́дить** бельё She began **to iron** the linen
Я продолжа́л **переводи́ть** текст I continued **to translate** the text
Он переста́л **жа́ловаться** He has stopped **complaining**

Aspect of the infinitive with words of necessity, obligation

(a) **Мочь** 'to be able' combines with the *perfective* aspect to denote completion of a single action:

Ты мо́жешь **взять** фотоаппара́т You can **take** the camera

while **мочь не** takes the *perfective* in the meaning 'may/might not' and the *imperfective* in the meaning 'need/needs not':

Он мо́жет **не прие́хать** He may/might **not come**
Он мо́жет **не встава́ть** He need **not get up**

(b) **До́лжен/должна́/должно́/должны́** 'must, should, ought to, is/are supposed to' also take the perfective in denoting anticipation of the completion of a single action:

Он до́лжен **встре́тить** её He is supposed **to meet** her

while **не до́лжен** takes the *perfective* in the meaning 'is unlikely to' and the *imperfective* in the meaning 'not obliged to':

Она́ не должна́ **простуди́ться** She shouldn't **catch cold** (she only got her feet wet)
Она́ не должна́ **встреча́ть** его́ She doesn't have **to meet** him (if she doesn't want to)

(c) **Нельзя́** takes the *perfective* in the meaning 'it is impossible' and the *imperfective* in the meaning 'you're not allowed to':

Отсю́да нельзя́ **позвони́ть** You can't **ring** from here (it is impossible, there is no phone)
Отсю́да нельзя́ **звони́ть** You're not allowed **to ring** from here (it is forbidden)

Aspect in the infinitive (conclusion)

(a) With **пора́** 'it is time to':

Пора́ 'it is time to' combines with the *imperfective* infinitive:

Пора́ **зака́нчивать** рабо́ту   It is time **to finish** work

In the meaning 'it is desirable to' it takes the *perfective* infinitive:

Пора́ **поко́нчить** с э́тим злом   It is time **to have done** with this evil

(b) With verbs of motion:

(i) The imperfective infinitive is the norm:

Он пошёл **собира́ться**   He went off **to pack his things**
Пойдём **накрыва́ть** на стол   Let's go and **lay** the table

(ii) The *perfective* is possible, however, if there is special emphasis on completion of an action: Он пошёл в магази́н **купи́ть** кни́гу 'He went to the shop **to buy** a book' (compare use of the *imperfective* infinitive in Он пошёл **покупа́ть** пода́рки 'He went to buy some presents', with emphasis on a *series of activities*).

(iii) The perfective infinitive after verbs of motion is also common with actions of short duration in **по-**:

Она́ вы́шла **посиде́ть** на во́здухе   She went out to **sit** in the open air **for a while**

(c) With **не хоте́ть** 'not to want to':

(i) The imperfective infinitive is widely used after **не хоте́ть**:

Я не хоте́л **переодева́ться**   I didn't want **to change my clothes**

especially with emphatic adverbs:

Я совсе́м не хочу́ **ложи́ться**   I have no wish whatsoever **to go to bed**

(ii) However, the perfective is usual when an undesirable action has taken place *unintentionally*:

Я не хоте́л вас **оскорби́ть**   I didn't mean **to insult** you

and when **не** is not *strictly* negative:

Ты не хо́чешь **приня́ть уча́стие?**   Wouldn't you [= would you] like **to take part?**

The conditional mood

(a) An English conditional consists of a main, **'would'** clause and an **'if'** clause ('if' + the past tense):

I **would** go **if** I had time

(b) The conditional describes a situation that does not exist ('I would go' implies that I **cannot** go', 'if I had time' implies that I **do not** have time), but that *could* exist given the right conditions.

(c) Use of the past tense in the English conditional is purely conventional: reference is not really to the past. Special forms are used by some speakers, e.g. 'if I were you'. The conditional can also be used with pluperfect meaning:

I **would** have gone **if** I had had time

(d) The Russian conditional construction is similar to the English. It comprises a main clause (past tense + **бы**):

Я поéхал бы   I would go

and an 'if' clause (**éсли бы** + past tense):

éсли бы у меня́ бы́ло вре́мя   if I had time

> **Note:** (a) The main clause may precede the éсли clause, or vice versa.
> (b) A comma appears between the two clauses: Я поéхал бы, éсли бы у меня́ бы́ло вре́мя 'I would go if I had time'.
> (c) The same construction is used in the pluperfect, e.g. Éсли бы у меня́ была́ маши́на, я отвёз бы вас на вокза́л 'If I **had** a car I **would** take you to the station' *or* 'If I **had had** a car I **would have** taken you to the station'.

(e) The conditional is thus used in an *unreal* situation that might, however, be reversed by a change in circumstances:

Éсли бы я был нача́льником, я дал бы вам приба́вку к зарпла́те   If I **were** the boss I **would give** you a rise

> **Note:** (i) The conjunction éсли 'if' can appear in other, non-conditional, types of construction, e.g. with a finite future tense: Éсли ты егó уви́дишь, скажи́ ему́, что я звони́л 'If you see him, tell him I rang'.
> (ii) 'Would' is not always the marker of a conditional construction: it also appears in reported speech: 'He promised he **would** help' Он обеща́л, что помо́жет (*see page 129*) and in past habitual (imperfective) contexts: 'He would always be late' Он всегда́ опа́здывал (*see also page 123*).

The subjunctive mood

(a) The verb **хоте́ть** 'to want' is followed by an infinitive when the subject does not change:

Я хочу́ **получи́ть** ви́зу   I want **to get** a visa.

(b) When the subject does change, however, the *subjunctive* is used. This involves replacement of the infinitive by **что́бы** + the past tense (a comma appears between **хоте́ть** and **что́бы**):

Я хочу́, **что́бы он получи́л** ви́зу   I want **him to get** a visa

(c) As in the conditional (*see page 134*), use of the past tense is purely conventional: the construction bears no relation to the past.

(d) Other tenses of хоте́ть can be used:

Я **хоте́л/захочу́**, что́бы он получи́л ви́зу   I **wanted/will want** him to get a visa

(e) Хоте́ть can be replaced by verbs and other words that denote wish or desire: **тре́бовать/по-** 'to demand', **за то/про́тив того́** 'in favour of/against', **наста́ивать/настоя́ть** 'to insist', **ва́жно** 'it is important', etc. *English* equivalents use constructions other than the 'accusative and infinitive' construction used with 'to want' (I want **him to vote**):

Я **тре́бую, что́бы** он согласи́лся   I **demand** he should consent
Она́ **за то, что́бы** все уча́ствовали   She is **in favour of** everyone participating
Он **настоя́л (на том)**, что́бы мы говори́ли по-ру́сски   He **insisted** we (should) speak Russian
Ва́жно, что́бы лю́ди не забы́ли о войне́   **It is important** that people should not forget about the war

> **!** Note: The **что́бы** construction is also used with **говори́ть/сказа́ть** 'to say, tell':
> Она́ сказа́ла, что́бы я не беспоко́ился 'She **said I shouldn't** worry'.

The subjunctive of purpose

(a) In a variant of the subjunctive construction, action is taken to achieve a desired result. Resolve is expressed in a number of set phrases: **де́лать всё, что́бы** 'to do everything to ensure that', **следи́ть за тем, что́бы** 'to see to it that', **добива́ться того́, что́бы** 'to try to get (someone to do something)':

Врач де́лает всё, что́бы больно́й попра́вился   The doctor **is doing all she can** to ensure that the patient **recovers**

Она́ следи́т за тем, что́бы де́ти не голода́ли   She **sees to it that** the children **do not go hungry**

Мы добива́емся того́, что́бы все стра́ны подписа́ли догово́р   We **are trying to get** all countries **to sign** the treaty

(b) The set phrases (де́лать всё, что́бы, etc.) may be replaced by virtually any action, the purpose of which is expressed by the second clause:

Он купи́л компью́тер, **что́бы** его́ сын **мог** по́льзоваться Интерне́том   He bought a computer **so that** his son **can** use the Internet

Закро́й дверь, **что́бы** шум **не меша́л** отцу́ рабо́тать   Close the door, **so that** the noise **does not stop** father working

Она́ наде́ла сви́тер на ребёнка, **что́бы** он **не простуди́лся**   She put a sweater on the child, **so that** he **should not catch a cold**

> **Note:** If the subject does not change, что́бы + *infinitive* is used: Она́ наде́ла сви́тер, что́бы не простуди́ться 'She put on a sweater **so as not to catch cold**'.

The subjunctive of hypothesis

The particle **бы** + past tense is used in hypothetical, unreal situations:

Нет ни одно́й страны́, где бы он не побыва́л   There is not a single country **where** he **has not spent some time**

Concessive constructions

Interrogative pronouns and adverbs (кто, что, где, куда́, etc.) + **бы ни** + past tense render English 'whoever', 'whenever', 'however', etc.

Что бы он ни де́лал, он никогда́ не забыва́л свои́х роди́телей   **Whatever** he **did**, he never forgot his parents

Reflexive verbs

Reflexive verbs conjugate like non-reflexive verbs, but with the ending **-ся** added to forms ending in a consonant or **-й**, and **-сь** to forms ending a vowel, e.g. **купа́ться** 'to bathe (oneself)':

Present tense	я купа́юсь	ты купа́ешься	он купа́ется
	мы купа́емся	вы купа́етесь	они́ купа́ются
Imperative	купа́йся!	купа́йтесь!	
Past tense	он купа́лся	она́ купа́лась	оно́ купа́лось
			они́ купа́лись

! Note: **-сь** is added to the imperative ending **-и: Верни́сь!** 'Return!'

'True' reflexives

'True' reflexives (e.g. **мы́ться** 'to wash [oneself]') are verbs in which the subject of the verb and the reflexive ending (-ся/-сь) refer to the same person, that is to say, the subject of the verb performs the action on himself/herself. Most of these verbs refer to preparation, dressing, washing, etc.:

бри́ться/по-   to shave (oneself)
гото́виться/при-   to prepare (oneself)
купа́ться/вы́-, ис-   to bathe (oneself)
мы́ться/вы́-, по-   to wash (oneself)
одева́ться/оде́ться   to get dressed
переодева́ться/переоде́ться   to get changed
причёсываться/причеса́ться   to do one's hair (or have it done)
раздева́ться/разде́ться   to get undressed

! Note: (a) English is usually a poor guide to Russian usage, since it hardly ever uses the reflexive particle 'self' with such verbs except for emphasis, e.g, 'She dresses **herself**' (of a small child).
(b) All the above verbs can be used transitively, *without* a reflexive ending, compare Она́ купа́ет **ребёнка** 'She is bathing the child' and Она́ купа́ется 'She is bathing (herself)'.
(c) Other true reflexives include **ложи́ться** 'to lie down' and **сади́ться** 'to sit down'.

Reciprocal meanings of reflexive verbs

Some reflexive verbs denote that two or more people are participating in a reciprocal action, thus:

Мы ча́сто **встреча́емся**   We often **meet** (each member of the group meets the rest)

Other reciprocals include:

ви́деться/у-   to see each other
мири́ться/по-   to make it up
обнима́ться/обня́ться   to embrace (each other)
объединя́ться/объедии́ться   to unite (together)
руга́ться/по-   to quarrel
собира́ться/собра́ться   to gather (together)
целова́ться/по-   to kiss (each other)

Note: (a) English is, again, not a reliable guide to Russian usage, since English reciprocal verbs normally omit 'each other' or 'one another': Они́ поцелова́лись 'They kissed' ('each other' understood).

(b) all the verbs in the group can be used transitively, without the reflexive ending:

Он **поцелова́л** де́вушку   He **kissed** the girl (compare reciprocal Они́ поцелова́лись They kissed (each other))

(c) Some verbs express reciprocal meanings through the pronoun друг дру́га 'each other': Они́ лю́бят друг дру́га 'They love each other', Мы ве́рим друг дру́гу 'We believe each other'.

Verbs which are only formally reflexive

A number of verbs have reflexive endings but no discernible reflexive meaning: беспоко́иться/по- 'to be worried', боя́ться 'to fear', волнова́ться/вз- 'to get excited', горди́ться 'to be proud', любова́ться/ по- 'to admire', наде́яться/по- 'to hope', нра́виться/ по- 'to please', признава́ться/призна́ться 'to confess', пыта́ться/ по- 'to try', ра́доваться/об- 'to rejoice', смея́ться 'to laugh', сомнева́ться 'to doubt', удивля́ться/удиви́ться 'to be surprised', улыба́ться, улыбну́ться, to 'smile'.

Intransitive reflexive verbs

(a) Many transitive verbs can be made *in*transitive by the addition of a reflexive ending. Compare transitive **конча́ть/ко́нчить** 'to end':

Он **конча́ет** рабо́ту   He **finishes** work

(where accusative **рабо́ту** is the object of **конча́ет**), and:

Рабо́та **конча́ется**   Work **ends**

(where nominative **рабо́та** 'work' has become the grammatical *subject* of **конча́ется** 'ends').

(b) Other reflexive intransitives include: начина́ться/нача́ться 'to begin' (Уро́к **начина́ется** 'The lesson begins'), продолжа́ться 'to continue' (Дождь **продолжа́ется** 'The rain continues'), увели́чиваться/ увели́читься 'to increase' (Дохо́д **увели́чивается** 'Revenue increases'), ухудша́ться/ху́дшиться 'to deteriorate' (Ситуа́ция **ху́дшилась** 'The situation has deteriorated'), открыва́ться/откры́ться 'to open' (Магази́н **открыва́ется** 'The shop opens').

Passive reflexive verbs

Passive verbs can also be created by adding reflexive endings to transitive verbs. However, unlike reflexive intransitive verbs:

(a) Generally speaking, only *imperfective* verbs can function as passives, e.g. from запреща́ть 'to ban':

Кури́ть **запреща́ется**   Smoking is **forbidden**

(b) Agent words appear in the *instrumental* case (this does not occur with reflexive intransitives):

Дом **стро́ится** рабо́чими   The house **is being built** by workers

(c) the subject of a reflexive passive can be *animate*:

Дире́ктор **назнача́ется** коми́ссией   The director **is appointed** by a commission

> **!** **Note:** Verbs that do not take the *accusative case* cannot function as either reflexive transitives or reflexive passives. Thus, 'We are helped' is rendered as **Нам помога́ют** ('They help us').

Impersonal constructions

Impersonal constructions occur in the following contexts:

(a) references to the weather or the environment:

Стемне́ло   It grew dark
О́сенью **света́ет** по́здно   **Dawn comes** late in autumn

(b) references to personal well-being, indispositon, inclination.
The person appears in the accusative case in some phrases, in the
dative in others:

Его́ тошни́т   **He** feels sick
Ей хо́чется спать   **She** feels sleepy
Мне повезло́   **I** am in luck
Нам удало́сь победи́ть   **We** succeeded in winning
Вам придётся подожда́ть   **You** will have to wait

(c) references to an external, natural force:

Дом **уда́рило мо́лнией**   The house **was struck by lightning**

(d) with the second-person singular of a verb (English 'one',
colloquially 'you'), usually without the pronoun ты:

Никогда́ не **зна́ешь**, к чему́ он кло́нит   **You** never **know** (one
never knows) what he is getting at

(e) with the third-person plural of a verb (without the pronoun
они́), sometimes identifying with authority or officialdom:

Про́сят не кури́ть   No smoking

otherwise appearing in set formulas:

Как вас **зову́т?**   What's your name?
Говоря́т, что он поги́б   **They say** he has perished

(f) Sometimes, where the subject is clearly singular, use of the
third-person plural is purely conventional:

Меня́ **разбуди́ли** на рассве́те   **I was awakened** at dawn
Тебя́ **про́сят** к телефо́ну   **You are wanted** on the phone

Participles

The present active participle

Formation

The present active participle is formed from the third-person plural of *imperfective* verbs. Final **-т** is replaced by masculine **-щий**, feminine **-щая**, neuter **-щее**, and plural **-щие**:

Infinitive	3rd-person plural	Participle (masculine)
знать 'to know'	зна́ю-т	зна́ю-щий
сиде́ть 'to sit'	сидя́-т	сидя́-щий
вести́ 'to lead'	веду́-т	веду́-щий

Participles from reflexive verbs take the ending **-ся**:

бри́ться 'to shave' бре́ю-тся бре́ющ-ийся

Stress in participles from first-conjugation verbs is as in the third-person plural:

писа́ть 'to write' пи́шу-т пи́шущий

and from second-conjugation verbs, as in the infinitive:

смотре́ть 'to look' смо́тря-т смотря́щий

> **!** **Note:** Exceptions include лю́бящий from люби́ть 'to love'.

Usage

The present participle declines like **о́бщий** 'common' (*see page 47*).
(a) As a single participle it precedes the noun it refers to, agreeing with it in gender, number, and case:

Зал по́лон **чита́ющих студе́нтов**   The hall is full **of reading students**

(b) In a participial construction it replaces **кото́рый** + present tense and can either (i) follow or (ii) precede the noun:

(i) Он подхо́дит к **же́нщине, стоя́щей** (=, **кото́рая стои́т**) в углу́

(ii) Он подхо́дит к **стоя́щей в углу́ же́нщине**

He goes up to **the woman (who is) standing** in the corner

> **!** **Note:** Some participles also function as adjectives: теку́щие собы́тия 'current events', others as nouns: начина́ющий 'beginner'.

The past active participle

(a) The past active participle is formed by replacing the masculine past tense -л of imperfective and perfective verbs by -вший, -вшая, -вшее, and -вшие. Thus, the participle (masculine) from читáть/прочитáть 'to read' is formed:

Infinitive	Past tense	Participle
(про)читáть	(про)читá-л	(про)читá-вший

Participles from reflexive verbs take the ending -ся: боя́вшийся from боя́ться 'to fear'.

(b) If there is no -л in the masculine past tense of a verb, -ший, -шая, -шая, -шие are added to the masculine past (with some exceptions, such as исчéзнувший from исчéзнуть 'to disappear'). Thus, the participle from зажéчь 'to ignite' is formed:

зажéчь   зажёг   зажёг-ший

(c) The past active participle declines like хорóший 'good' (see page 47). It replaces котóрый + the past tense, is preceded by a comma:

дом, находи́вшийся (= , котóрый находи́лся) в цéнтре гóрода
the house **(which was) situated** in the town centre

and agrees with the noun it refers to in gender, number, and case:

Я читáю **кни́гу, получи́вшую** (= , котóрая получи́ла) приз
I am reading **the book that won** a prize

The imperfective passive participle

(a) The imperfective passive participle is formed by adding adjectival endings to the *first-person plural* of an **imperfective transitive** verb. Thus, the participle (masculine) from исполня́ть 'to perform' is formed:

Infinitive	First-person plural	Participle
исполня́ть	исполня́-ем	исполня́ем-ый

(b) The participle declines like бéлый 'white' (see page 44) and replaces an *accusative* relative pronoun and an imperfective transitive verb, agreeing with the noun it refers to in gender, case, and number:

Я интересу́юсь **тéмой, обсуждáемой** (=, котóрую обсуждáют *or* , котóрая обсуждáется) в Дýме   I am interested **in the subject which they are discussing** or **which is being discussed** in the Duma

The perfective passive participle (short form)

(a) The perfective passive participle is formed from perfective *transitive* verbs. The masculine *short-form* participle from most infinitives in **-ать/-ять** is made by replacing **-ать/-ять** by **-ан, -ана, -ано, -аны/-ян, -яна, -яно, -яны**, thus, from **прочита́ть** 'to read' and **потеря́ть** 'to lose':

Infinitive	Participle	Infinitive	Participle
прочит-а́ть	прочи́т-ан	потер-я́ть	поте́р-ян

(b) The stress falls on the syllable preceding **-ан/-ян** (except for monosyllabic дан from дать 'to give' (feminine дана́, neuter дано́, plural даны́).

(c) The participle derives from *second*-conjugation infinitives in **-ить/-еть** by replacing **-ить/-еть** by **-ён, -ена́, -ено́, -ены́** if the conjugation has *end stress* throughout, and by **-ен, -ена, -ено, -ены** if it has *fixed stem stress* or *mobile stress*):

Infinitive	Conjugation	Participle
окружи́ть 'to surround'	окружу́, -ужи́шь	окружён, -а́, ó, -ы́
нару́шить 'to disrupt'	нару́шу, -у́шишь	нару́шен, -а, -о, -ы
отложи́ть 'to postpone'	отложу́, -о́жишь	отло́жен, -а, -о, -ы

(d) Verbs in **-ить/-еть** undergo consonant change:

Infinitive	Meaning	Participle
употреби́ть	to use	употреблён
оста́вить	to leave	оста́влен
посади́ть	to plant	поса́жен
победи́ть	to win	побеждён
вы́разить	to express	вы́ражен
офо́рмить	to design the layout of	офо́рмлен
скрепи́ть	to staple	скреплён
бро́сить	to throw	бро́шен
очи́стить	to clean	очи́щен
отме́тить	to mark	отме́чен
запрети́ть	to forbid	запрещён

The perfective passive participle (short form) (continued)

Participles from verbs in -ти and -чь

These verbs form the participle by replacing third-person singular -т by -н, thus, the participles from **спасти** 'to save' and **зажечь** 'to ignite' are as follows:

Infinitive	Third-person singular	Participle
спасти	спас-ёт	спас-ён, -а́, -о́, -ы́
зажечь	зажж-ёт	зажжён -а́, -о́, -ы́

> ! **Note:** the participles укра́ден from укра́сть 'to steal', съе́ден from съесть 'to eat', and на́йден from найти́ 'to find'.

Participles in -т

Perfective transitive verbs in **-оть**, **-ыть**, **-уть**, **-ереть**, compounds of **бить** 'to strike', **вить** 'to twine', **лить** 'to pour', **пить** 'to drink', and **шить** 'to sew', compounds of **-нять** and **деть** 'to put', and other verbs that take **-м-** or **-н-** in conjugation, also **вы́брить** 'to shave' have participles in **-т**. The masculine participle is formed by removing **-ь** from the infinitive, while **-а**, **-о**, and **-ы** are added to form the feminine, neuter, and plural:

Infinitive	Meaning	Participle
проколо́ть	to puncture	проко́лот, -а, -о, -ы
закры́ть	to close	закры́т, -а, -о, -ы
тро́нуть	to touch	тро́нут, -а, -о, -ы
отпере́ть	to unlock	о́тперт, -а́, -о, -ы
уби́ть	to kill	уби́т, -а, -о, -ы
приня́ть	to accept	при́нят, -а́, -о, -ы
оде́ть	to dress	оде́т, -а, -о, -ы

> ! **Note:** (i) stress shift in some participles.
> (ii) loss of the second **-e-** of the infinitive in о́тперт, отперта́, о́тперто, о́тперты from отпере́ть 'to unlock'.

Functions of the short form perfective passive participle

The short-form perfective passive participle is a predicative form and denotes:

(a) a recently-completed action:

> Урожа́й у́бран   The harvest **has been gathered in**
>
> Его́ сын **аресто́ван**   His son **has been arrested**
>
> Пробле́ма **решена́**   The problem **has been solved**
>
> **Объя́влена** забасто́вка   A strike **has been called**
>
> **При́няты** ну́жные ме́ры   The necessary measures **have been taken**

> **!** **Note:** (i) The participle may follow or precede the noun.
>
> (ii) The agent of the action appears in the instrumental case: Го́род захва́чен **на́шими войска́ми** The city has been seized **by our troops**.

(b) a state or condition:

> Дверь **закры́та**   The door **is closed**
>
> Мы **за́няты**   We **are busy**
>
> Города́ **свя́заны** доро́гой   The towns **are linked** by a road
>
> Письмо́ подпи́сано **отцо́м**   The letter is signed **by father**

Note: Forms of the verb **быть** 'to be' also combine with the participle:

> Оши́бка **была́ заме́чена**   The mistake **was noticed** (or **had been noticed**)
>
> Кни́га **бу́дет и́здана**   The book **will be published** (or **will have been published**)
>
> Торт **был бы испечён**   The cake **would be baked** (or **would have been baked**)

The long form of the perfective passive participle

Formation

The long form of the perfective passive participle derives from the short form *masculine* in -н by the addition of **-ный, -ная, -ное, -ные**:

Infinitive	Short form (masc.)	Long form (masc.)
сде́лать 'to do'	сде́лан	сде́лан-**ный**

and from the short-form masculine in -т by adding the adjectival endings **-ый, -ая, -ое, -ые**:

поднять 'to raise' по́днят по́днят-**ый**

The long-form perfective passive participle declines like бе́лый 'white', *see page 44*).

Functions of the long form

(a) The participle can function as an attributive adjective, agreeing with the noun in gender, case, and number and preceding the noun it qualifies:

Вот оди́н из **поте́рянных** ключе́й   Here is one of the **lost** keys
Он наде́л **вы́шитую** руба́шку   He put on an **embroidered** shirt

(b) As part of a participial construction, it may

(i) follow the noun, separated from it by a comma:

Мы говори́м о письме́, **полу́ченном** сего́дня у́тром   We are talking about the letter (**which was) received** this morning
Она́ чита́ла статью́, **переведённую** с англи́йского   She was reading the article (**which had been) translated** from English

(ii) *precede* the noun, together with circumstantial detail dependent on the participle:

Все говори́ли о **запу́щенном** на околозе́мную орби́ту **спу́тнике**   Everyone was talking about the **satellite launched** into the Earth's orbit
Мы дово́льны **при́нятыми** прави́тельством **ме́рами**   We are pleased with the **measures taken** by the government

The gerund (verbal adverb)

The imperfective gerund: formation

The imperfective gerund is formed by replacing the final two letters of the *third-person plural* of a verb by -я (-а after ж, ч, ш, or щ):

Infinitive	Third-person plural	Gerund
игра́ть 'to play'	игра́-ют	игра́-я
жева́ть 'to chew'	жу-ю́т	жу-я́
вести́ 'to lead'	вед-у́т	вед-я́
иска́ть 'to seek'	и́щ-ут	ищ-а́
кури́ть 'to smoke'	ку́р-ят	кур-я́
крича́ть 'to shout'	крич-а́т	крич-а́

Note: Stress is as in the first-person singular:

Infinitive	First-person singular	Gerund
держа́ть 'to hold'	держ-у́	держ-а́

Exceptions include (a) **гля́дя** from гляде́ть 'to look', **лёжа** from лежа́ть 'to lie', **си́дя** from сиде́ть 'to sit', and **сто́я** from стоя́ть 'to stand' (b) **дава́ть** 'to give' and compounds of -**дава́ть**, -**става́ть**, and -**знава́ть** derive their gerunds from the *infinitive*:

Infinitive	Gerund	Infinitive	Gerund
дава́ть 'to give'	дава́я	встава́ть 'to get up'	встава́я

Быть 'to be', has the gerund бу́дучи.

Note: (a) Gerunds are invariable.
(b) Many common verbs have no gerunds: all verbs in -**чь**, also бежа́ть 'to run', бить 'to strike', есть 'to eat', е́хать 'to travel', ждать 'to wait for', петь 'to sing', писа́ть 'to write', хоте́ть 'to want', etc. Instead, an alternative construction must be used or a synonym found (e.g. ожида́ть 'to wait for, expect', gerund ожида́я, жела́ть 'to want, wish', gerund жела́я).

Functions of the imperfective gerund

The imperfective gerund describes an action that runs parallel to the action of the main verb (Он сиди́т, ду́мая 'He sits **thinking**') or is interrupted by it (Чита́я, я усну́л '**While reading**, I fell asleep').

The imperfective gerund may:

(a) replace a clause with **и** 'and':

Они́ сидя́т, **игра́я** (= и игра́ют) в ка́рты   They sit **playing** cards

(b) replace a clause with **когда́** 'when' or 'as':

Уходя́ (= когда́ я ухожу́), я всегда́ выключа́ю свет   **When I leave** I always turn off the light

(c) replace a clause with так как 'since':

Бу́дучи моряко́м (= так как он моря́к), он лю́бит мо́ре   **Being** a sailor, he loves the sea

(d) replace a clause with **éсли** 'if':

Критику́я (= éсли критику́ешь) па́ртию, ты критику́ешь всех нас   **By criticizing** the party you criticize all of us

(e) render English 'without' + -ing (negative gerund):

Я сосчита́л де́ньги, **не вынима́я ру́ку** из карма́на   I counted the money **without taking** my hand out of my pocket

Special features of constructions with gerunds

(a) The subject of both clauses must be the same:

Он продолжа́л писа́ть, не обраща́я внима́ния на меня́   He continued writing, without paying any attention to me

(b) A comma separates the two clauses:

Спуска́ясь под гору, я уви́дел не́сколько домо́в   Coming down the hill I caught sight of several houses

(c) The verb in the main clause may be in any tense and either aspect (e.g. perfective past):

Я **кивну́л**, дава́я поня́ть, что дово́лен   I **nodded**, indicating that I was satisfied

> **!** **Note:** Some gerunds also function as adverbs (**мо́лча** 'silently'), others as prepositions (**благодаря́** 'thanks to').

The perfective gerund

Formation

The perfective gerund is formed by replacing the ending of the perfective infinitive by **-в**:

Infinitive	Meaning	Gerund
прочита́-ть	'to read'	прочита́-в
получи́-ть	'to receive'	получи́-в

The perfective gerund is invariable. Reflexive gerunds take the ending **-вшись**:

уму́-ться 'to wash' умы́-**вшись**

Compounds of **-йти́** 'to go', **-вести́** 'to lead', and **-нести́** 'to carry' form the gerund by replacing the final two letters of the third-person plural by **-я**:

Infinitive	Meaning	Third-person plural	Gerund
найти́	'to find'	найд-у́т	найд-**я́**
унести́	'to take away'	унес-у́т	унес-**я́**

Verbs in **-чь** form the perfective gerund by adding **-ши** to the masculine past tense:

Infinitive	Meaning	Masculine past tense	Gerund
зажечь	'to ignite'	зажёг	зажёг-**ши**

Functions of the perfective gerund

The perfective gerund describes an action completed before the action of the main verb (which may be in any tense and either aspect):

Получи́в каки́е-то бума́ги, экскурсово́ды разошли́сь   **Having obtained** certain documents, the tour guides dispersed

Переведя́ э́тот текст, вы ока́жете нам услу́гу   **By translating** this text, you will be doing us a good turn

У́тром, **умы́вшись** и **побри́вшись**, он за́втракает   In the morning, **having washed and shaved**, he has breakfast

! Note: The same rules apply as to the imperfective gerund: (a) the subject of the two clauses must be the same, (b) a comma appears between the two clauses (*see page 148*).

Verbs of motion

The 12 commonest pairs of **imperfective** verbs of motion are given here in alphabetical order, with the infinitive, present, and (where appropriate) past tense of each verb. The *multidirectional* verb is first in each pair, the *unidirectional* the second:

бе́гать бе́гаю бе́гаешь бе́гает бе́гаем бе́гаете бе́гают
бежа́ть бегу́ бежи́шь бежи́т бежи́м бежи́те бегу́т 'to run'

води́ть вожу́ во́дишь во́дит во́дим во́дите во́дят
вести́ веду́ ведёшь ведёт ведём ведёте веду́т; вёл вела́ 'to take, lead, drive (a car)'

вози́ть вожу́ во́зишь во́зит во́зим во́зите во́зят
везти́ везу́ везёшь везёт везём везёте везу́т; вёз везла́ 'to take, convey'

гоня́ть гоня́ю гоня́ешь гоня́ет гоня́ем гоня́ете гоня́ют
гнать гоню́ го́нишь го́нит го́ним го́ните го́нят; гнал гнала́ гна́ло 'to drive, chase'

е́здить е́зжу е́здишь е́здит е́здим е́здите е́здят
е́хать е́ду е́дешь е́дет е́дем е́дете е́дут 'to travel'

ката́ть ката́ю ката́ешь ката́ет ката́ем ката́ете ката́ют
кати́ть качу́ ка́тишь ка́тит ка́тим ка́тите ка́тят 'to roll' (trans.)

ла́зить ла́жу ла́зишь ла́зит ла́зим ла́зите ла́зят
лезть ле́зу ле́зешь ле́зет ле́зем ле́зете ле́зут; лез ле́зла 'to climb'

лета́ть лета́ю лета́ешь лета́ет лета́ем лета́ете лета́ют
лете́ть лечу́ лети́шь лети́т лети́м лети́те летя́т 'to fly'

носи́ть ношу́ но́сишь но́сит но́сим но́сите но́сят
нести́ несу́ несёшь несёт несём несёте несу́т; нёс несла́ 'to take, carry'

пла́вать пла́ваю пла́ваешь пла́вает пла́ваем пла́ваете пла́вают
плыть плыву́ плывёшь плывёт плывём плывёте плыву́т; плыл плыла́ плы́ло 'to swim, float, sail'

по́лзать по́лзаю по́лзаешь по́лзает по́лзаем по́лзаете по́лзают
ползти́ ползу́ ползёшь ползёт ползём ползёте ползу́т; полз ползла́ 'to crawl'

ходи́ть хожу́ хо́дишь хо́дит хо́дим хо́дите хо́дят
идти́ иду́ идёшь идёт идём идёте иду́т; шёл шла 'to go' (on foot)

Multidirectional verbs of motion (ходи́ть, е́здить, etc.): habitual and repeated actions

A main function of multidirectional verbs of motion is to describe habitual action or movement, and repeated return journeys. The meaning of repetition is sometimes reinforced by a frequentative adverb (всегда́ 'always', etc.):

> Мы е́здим за грани́цу ка́ждый год   We **go** abroad every year
>
> Я ча́сто бу́ду ходи́ть на като́к   I will often **go** to the rink
>
> Ча́ще всего́ он лета́ет на самолётах Аэрофло́та   More often than not he **flies** with Aeroflot.

Note: If movement in one direction is emphasized, however (as opposed to return trips), a *unidirectional* verb is used. This often occurs (a) with когда́ 'when' (b) in a sequence of actions or when the time is given:

(a) Когда́ я иду́ на рабо́ту, я покупа́ю газе́ту   When I **am on my way to** work I buy a newspaper

(h) Ка́ждое у́тро [в 8 часо́в] я выхожу́ из до́ма и е́ду на рабо́ту   Every morning [at 8 o'clock] I leave the house and **drive** to work

(but not back again); compare Ка́ждый день я е́зжу на рабо́ту Every day I drive to work (and back).

Other functions of multidirectional verbs

(a) Multidirectional verbs also denote an action in general, an ability to perform it, a habit of performing it in a particular way, an inclination or disinclination to perform it, etc.

> Ребёнок ещё не **хо́дит**   The child cannot **walk** yet
>
> Обезья́на хорошо́ **ла́зит**   A monkey is good at **climbing**
>
> Она́ научи́лась **води́ть** маши́ну   She has learnt **to drive** a car
>
> Я люблю́ **пла́вать**   I like **swimming**
>
> Пингви́ны не уме́ют **лета́ть**   Penguins cannot **fly**
>
> Ребёнок ещё **по́лзает**   The child **is** still **crawling**
>
> Ло́шади о́чень бы́стро **бе́гают**   Horses **run** very fast
>
> Она́ хорошо́ **хо́дит** на лы́жах   She **skis** well

(b) They also describe movement in various directions: backwards and forwards, round and round, etc., on one or more occasions:

Она **ходи́ла** по магази́нам   She **went** shopping

Я **е́здил** по всей Евро́пе   I **travelled all over** Europe

В па́рке **лета́ют** комары́   Midges **are flying around** in the park

Ребёнок **по́лзает** пó полу   The child **is crawling around** on the floor

Де́ти **бе́гали** в саду́   Children **were running around** in the garden

Нас **вози́ли** по всей Гре́ции   They **took** us **all over** Greece

Гид **води́л** тури́стов по Кремлю́   The guide **took** the tourists **round** the Kremlin

Мать **носи́ла** ребёнка по спа́льне   The mother **carried** the child **up and down** the bedroom

Ма́льчики **ла́зят** по дере́вьям   The boys **are climbing around** in the trees

Use of the past tense of a multidirectional verb to denote a single return trip

The **past** tense of a multidirectional verb can be used to denote a single return journey (as well as a number of return journeys):

Я **е́здил** в о́тпуск в США   I **went** on holiday to the USA

Он неда́вно **лета́л** в Ло́ндон   Recently he **flew** to London (and back)

Вчера́ ве́чером она́ **ходи́ла** в кино́   Yesterday evening she **went** to the cinema

The imperative of multidrectional verbs of motion

The imperative of multidirectionals is normally used for negative commands:

Не **ходи́** туда́!   Don't **go** there!

Не **лета́й** вертолётом!   Don't **go** by helicopter!

Functions of unidirectional verbs of motion

Unidirectional verbs of motion (идти́, е́хать, бежа́ть, лете́ть, etc.) denote movement *in one direction*, sometimes to a named destination:

(a) in the present:

Он **идёт** по у́лице   He **is walking** down the street
Она́ **е́дет** за грани́цу   She **is going** abroad
Де́ти **бегу́т** домо́й   The children **are running** home
Обезья́на **ле́зет** на де́рево   The monkey **is climbing** a tree
Самолёт **лети́т** на се́вер   The aircraft **is flying** north
Мяч **ка́тится** по тротуа́ру   The ball **is rolling** along the pavement

> **Note:** кати́ться 'to roll' (intransitive).

(b) in the past:

По́езд **шёл** в Ки́ев   The train **was on its way** to Kiev
Мы **е́хали** за го́род   We **were driving** into the country
Парохо́д **плыл** в Я́лту   The steamer **was sailing** to Yalta
Оте́ц **лез** на кры́шу   Father **was climbing** onto the roof
Он **гна́лся** за мячо́м   He **was chasing** the ball

> **Note:** гна́ться за + instr. 'to chase after'.

(c) in the future:

Я **бу́ду е́хать** впереди́   I **will drive** in front
Когда́ мы **бу́дем идти́** ми́мо теа́тра, ку́пим биле́ты   When we **are passing** the theatre we will buy some tickets

> **Note:** (a) Маши́на **идёт** or **е́дет** 'The car is travelling along', but По́езд **идёт** 'The train is on its way', Самолёт **лети́т** 'The aircraft is flying', Парохо́д **плывёт** 'The steamer is sailing' (е́хать is not used of rail, air, or water transport). With persons, **идти́** 'to go, walk' is distinguished from **е́хать** 'to go by transport, travel'.
> (b) In denoting the immediate future, **идти́**, **е́хать**, and **лете́ть** are close in meaning to **отправля́ться** 'to set out': За́втра я **е́ду** в Москву́ 'Tomorrow I am going to Moscow/am setting out for Moscow'.
> (c) **идти́** is frequently used in the meaning 'to be in progress': **Идёт** уро́к 'A lesson is in progress', **Идёт** фильм 'A film is on', etc.

Нести́, вести́, везти́

(a) **нести́** means 'to be carrying' or 'to be taking':

Она́ **несёт** портфе́ль   She **is carrying** a briefcase
Они́ **несли́** раке́тки на корт   They **were taking** the rackets on court

(b) **вести́** means 'to be leading' or 'to be taking (on foot)'

Гид **ведёт** тури́стов по пло́щади   The guide **is leading** the tourists across the square
Он **вёл** дете́й домо́й   He **was taking** the children home

(c) **везти́** means 'to be taking, conveying (in a vehicle)':

Он **вёз** ме́бель в но́вый дом   He **was taking** furniture to the new house
Он **везёт** ребёнка в коля́ске   He **is pushing** the child in a pram

The imperative of unidirectional verbs of motion

The imperative of unidirectionals is normally used for positive commands:

Иди́ сюда́!   **Come** here!
Лети́ самолётом!   **Go** by plane!

Perfectives in по-

Perfective verbs in **по-** derive from multidirectional and unidirectional verbs of motion.
(a) Perfectives in **по-** derived from multidirectional verbs denote actions of short duration (*see also page 115*):

Я **похожу́** по вы́ставке   I will **walk round** the exhibition **for a while**
Дава́й **пое́здим** по го́роду   Let's **drive** round town for a while

(b) Those derived from unidirectionals have inceptive meaning (*see also page 115*)

Он **пошёл** в банк   He **has gone/he went** to the bank (and is not back yet. Compare Он **ходи́л** в банк   He **has been** to the bank, **he went** to the bank [and has returned])
Мы **пое́дем** за грани́цу   We **will go** abroad
Де́ти **побежа́ли** на пляж   The children **ran off** to the beach

Prefixed verbs of motion

(a) Simple verbs of motion (e.g., multidirectional **летáть**/
unidirectional **летéть** 'to fly') can combine with up to sixteen
prefixes to form compounds (e.g. **влетáть/влетéть** 'to fly into',
вылетáть/вы́лететь 'to fly out of').

(b) While simple verbs of motion are all *imperfective*, prefixed
compounds form aspectual pairs, with imperfectives based on
multidirectional verbs and perfectives based on *unidirectional*
verbs.

(c) Some simple verbs of motion form compounds without
modification of the root verb (e.g. compounds [in при-] of летáть/
летéть, носи́ть/нести́, води́ть/вести́, and вози́ть/везти́):

Imperfective	Perfective	Meaning
прилетáть	прилетéть	to arrive by air
приноси́ть	принести́	to bring (carrying)
приводи́ть	привести́	to bring (leading)
привози́ть	привезти́	to bring (by transport)

For example:

Самолёт **прилетéл**   The aircraft **arrived**
Онá **принесёт** кни́гу   She **will bring** the book
Он **приво́дит** детéй домо́й   He **brings** the children home
Привези́те мéбель!   **Bring** the furniture!

(d) Other verbs of motion modify *either* the multidirectional (MD)
or the unidirectional (UD) verb in forming compounds (in the
following, > denotes change to a modified form in the compound
stem, = denotes an absence of change):

Simple MD verb	Impf. compound stem	Simple UD verb	Pf. compound stem	Meaning
ходи́ть =	-ходи́ть	идти́ >	**-йти́**	to go, walk
éздить >	**-езжáть**	éхать =	-éхать	to travel
бéгать >	**-бегáть**	бежáть =	-бежáть	to run
плáвать >	**-плывáть**	плыть =	-плыть	to swim

The function of prefixes in forming compound verbs of motion

Prefixes commonly used in forming compounds number sixteen. They are listed here with the prepositions with which they most frequently combine (not all prefixes combine with all simple verbs of motion).

Prefix	Preposition	Meaning	Prefix	Preposition	Meaning
в-	в + acc.	into	пере-	че́рез + acc.	across
вз-/вс-	на + acc.	up onto	под-	к + dat.	up to
вы-	из + gen.	out of	при-	в/на + acc., к + dat.	arrival
до-	до + gen.	as far as	про-	ми́мо + gen.	past
за-	в/на- + acc., к + dat.	dropping in	раз-/рас- -ся/-сь	по + dat.	dispersal
на-	на + acc.	onto	с-	с + gen.	down from
об-	вокру́г	around	с- -ся/-сь		together
от-	от + gen.	away from	у-	из/с/от + gen.	away from

Note: (a) вс- and рас- are used before verbs beginning with voiceless consonants (here -ходи́ть, -плыва́ть/-плыть), otherwise вз- and раз- are used.

(b) -о- appears between в-, вз-, об-, под-, раз-, с- and -йти (войти́ 'to go in', взойти́ 'to go up', обойти́ 'to go round', etc.).

(c) a hard sign (ъ) appears between the prefixes listed in (b) and -езжа́ть/-е́хать (въезжа́ть/въе́хать 'to drive in', etc.).

(d) choice of preposition with при-, за-, and у- is determined by the dependent noun: thus при- 'arrival' and за- 'dropping by' take в or на + accusative of a *place*, к + dative of a *person*, while у- 'away from' takes из or с + genitive of a *place*, от + genitive of a *person*. For из/с, *see also pages 207, 210.*

(e) in some contexts, verbs prefixed об-, пере-, or про- take an object accusative: Он обошёл ла́герь 'He walked round the camp', Она́ переплыла́ ре́ку 'She swam across the river', Я прое́хал два киломе́тра 'I drove two kilometres'.

Prefixed verbs of motion: usage

Examples of prefixed verbs based on:

(a) -ходи́ть/-йти́ 'to go':

Она́ **вошла́** в ко́мнату   She **entered** the room
Он **дохо́дит** до угла́   He **walks as far as** the corner
Я **зайду́** к Са́ше/за Са́шей   I **will call on** Sasha/for Sasha
Она́ **отошла́** от две́ри   She **moved away from** the door
Я **перейду́ че́рез** у́лицу   I **will cross** the street
Она́ **пришла́** в шко́лу/**на** заво́д/к подру́ге   She **came to** the
  school/a factory/to see a friend

(b) -езжа́ть/-éхать 'to travel':

Он **выезжа́ет из** гаража́   He **drives out of** the garage
Он **подъéхал к** тротуа́ру   He **pulled in to** the kerb
Я **проезжа́ю ми́мо** музе́я   I **drive past** the museum
Мотоцикли́сты **разъезжа́ются**   The motorcyclists **disperse**
Велосипеди́сты **съезжа́ются**   The cyclists **meet up**
Она́ **уéхала** из Росси́и/с Ура́ла/от роди́телей   She **left**
  Russia/the Urals/her parents

Note: (i) compounds of -езжа́ть/-éхать share an imperative in
-езжа́й: въезжа́й! 'drive in!', не въезжа́й! 'don't drive in!' (*see
page 110*)

(ii) The imperfective *past* of compound verbs of motion can
denote a *single round trip*: К нам приезжа́ла тётя 'Auntie came/
has been to see us' (and has gone away again').

(iii) Examples of usage with other verbs:

Он **подбежа́л к** кио́ску   He **ran up to** the kiosk
Самолёт **взлетéл**   The plane **took off**
Она́ **доплыла́** до мо́ла   She **swam as far as** the pier
Ку́ба **выво́зит** са́хар   Cuba **exports** sugar

(iv) Some of the verbs have figurative meanings: сходи́ть/сойти́
с ума́ 'to go mad', заводи́ть/завести́ часы́ 'to wind up a clock',
приноси́ть/ принести́ по́льзу 'to bring benefit', приходи́ть/
прийти́ к вы́воду 'to come to a conclusion', etc.

I Verb list

(a) The verb list contains examples of:

(i) verbs in **-чь** (e.g. бере́чь)
(ii) verbs in **-ти** (e.g. вести́)
(iii) verbs in **-сть** (e.g. сесть)
(iv) verbs in **-оть** (e.g. боро́ться)
(v) verbs in **-ереть** (e.g. запере́ть)
(vi) verbs in **-овать** and **-евать** (e.g. бесе́довать, воева́ть)
(vii) verbs (first conjugation) with consonant change (e.g. писа́ть)
(viii) verbs (second conjugation) with consonant change (e.g. бро́сить)
(ix) second-conjugation verbs in **-ать/-ять** (e.g. стуча́ть, стоя́ть)
(x) first- and second-conjugation verbs in **-еть** (e.g. име́ть, горе́ть)
(xi) monosyllabic verbs (e.g. брать)
(xii) irregular verbs (e.g. хоте́ть)

(b) Most verbs listed are non-derivative (e.g. дать). Compound verbs are not normally given when a root verb is available (дать 'to give' appears, but not прода́ть 'to sell' or зада́ть 'to ask [a question]'). Some compounds have no commonly-used root verb, in which case a hyphenated root is given (e.g. -каза́ть).

(c) Also listed are verbs that have no **-л** in the masculine past (e.g. везти́ 'to convey', masculine past вёз).

(d) The pattern of presentation is:

(i) for all verbs – present or future conjugation, and meaning; the verb's other aspect (if available)
(ii) for selected verbs – the past tense; the government of the verb; the imperative; short forms of the perfective passive participle

! **Note:** (a) In the case of some verbs (e.g. висе́ть 'to hang'), more details of conjugation are given in the verb list, e.g., the first-person singular, than in the relevant grammatical section, *see page 104*.
(b) Absence of a first-person singular form indicates that none exists, or that none exists in the meaning given (see, for example, греме́ть 'to thunder').

бежа́ть/по- 'to run': бегу́ бежи́шь бежи́т бежи́м бежи́те бегу́т; беги́!

бере́чь/по- 'to take care of': берегу́ бережёт берегу́т; берёг берегла́; береги́!

бесе́довать 'to converse': бесе́дую бесе́дует бесе́дуют

бить/по- 'to strike': бью бьёт бьют; бей!

бледне́ть/по- 'to grow pale': бледне́ю бледне́ет бледне́ют

блесте́ть 'to shine': блещу́ блести́т блестя́т; pf. **блесну́ть**

боле́ть (+ instr.) 'to be ill (with)': боле́ю боле́ет боле́ют

боле́ть 'to hurt' (intrans.): боли́т боля́т

боро́ться (за + acc.) 'to struggle (for)': борю́сь бо́рется бо́рются; бори́сь!

боя́ться (+ gen./acc.) 'to fear': бою́сь бои́тся боя́тся; (не) бо́йся!

брать 'to take': беру́ берёт беру́т; брал брала́ бра́ло; бери́!; pf. **взять**

бри́ться/по- 'to shave' (intrans.): бре́юсь бре́ется бре́ются

бро́сить 'to throw': бро́шу бро́сит бро́сят; брось!; бро́шен; impf. **броса́ть**

буди́ть/раз- 'to awaken' (trans.): бужу́ бу́дит бу́дят; буди́!; разбу́жен

быть 'to be': бу́ду бу́дет бу́дут; был была́ бы́ло; будь!

везти́ 'to convey': везу́ везёт везу́т; вёз везла́

ве́сить 'to weigh' : ве́шу ве́сит ве́сят

вести́ 'to lead': веду́ ведёт веду́т; вёл вела́

взять 'to take': возьму́ возьмёт возьму́т; взял, взяла́ взя́ло; возьми́!; взят взята́ взя́то; impf. **брать**

ви́деть/у- 'to see': ви́жу ви́дит ви́дят

висе́ть 'to hang' (intrans.): вишу́ виси́т вися́т

владе́ть (+ instr.) 'to own': владе́ю владе́ет владе́ют

влечь 'to attract': влеку́ влечёт влеку́т; влёк влекла́; -влечён -влечена́ (in compounds)

води́ть 'to lead': вожу́ во́дит во́дят

воева́ть 'to wage war': вою́ю вою́ет вою́ют

возврати́ться 'to return' (intrans.): возвращу́сь возврати́тся возвратя́тся; impf. **возвраща́ться**

вози́ть 'to convey': вожу́ во́зит во́зят

возни́кнуть 'to arise': возни́кну возни́кнет возни́кнут; возни́к возни́кла; impf. **возника́ть**

волнова́ться/вз- 'to be excited': волну́юсь волну́ется волну́ются; (не) волну́йся!

врать/на- and **со-** 'to tell lies': вру врёт врут; врал врала́ вра́ло; (не) ври!

встава́ть 'to get up, stand up': встаю́ встаёт встаю́т; встава́й!; pf. **встать**

встать 'to get up, stand up': вста́ну вста́нет вста́нут; встань!; impf. **встава́ть**

встре́тить 'to meet': встре́чу встре́тит встре́тят; impf. **встреча́ть**

вы́глядеть (+ instr.) 'to look, appear': вы́гляжу вы́глядит вы́глядят

вы́разить 'to express': вы́ражу вы́разит вы́разят; вы́ражен; impf. **выража́ть**

вяза́ть/с- 'to tie': вяжу́ вя́жет вя́жут; -вя́зан (in compounds)

гаси́ть/за- or **по-** 'to extinguish': гашу́ га́сит га́сят; зага́шен/пога́шен

ги́бнуть/по- 'to perish': ги́бну ги́бнет ги́бнут; гиб/ги́бнул ги́бла

гла́дить/вы́- 'to iron': гла́жу гла́дит гла́дят; вы́глажен

гляде́ть (на + acc.) 'to look (at)': гляжу́ гляди́т глядя́т; pf. **гля́нуть**

гна́ться (за + instr.) 'to chase (after)': гоню́сь го́нится го́нятся; гна́лся гнала́сь

годи́ться (в + acc.) 'to be fit (for)': гожу́сь годи́тся годя́тся

голосова́ть/про- (за + acc.) 'to vote (for)': голосу́ю голосу́ет голосу́ют

горди́ться (+ instr.) 'to be proud of': горжу́сь горди́тся гордя́тся; горди́сь!

горе́ть/с- 'to burn' (intrans.): гори́т горя́т

гото́вить/при- 'to prepare': гото́влю гото́вит гото́вят; гото́вь!; пригото́влен

греме́ть/про- 'to thunder': греми́т гремя́т

греть 'to heat': гре́ю гре́ет гре́ют; -грет (in compounds)

грози́ть/при- (+ dat.) 'to threaten': грожу́ грози́т грозя́т

грузи́ть/по- 'to load': гружу́ гру́зит гру́зят; погру́жен

дава́ть 'to give': даю́ даёт даю́т; дава́й!; pf. **дать**

дави́ть (на + acc.) 'to press (upon)': давлю́ да́вит да́вят; -давлен (in compounds)

дать 'to give': дам дашь даст дади́м дади́те даду́т; дал дала́ да́ло; дай!; дан дана́; impf. **дава́ть**

де́йствовать 'to act': де́йствую де́йствует де́йствуют; де́йствуй!

держа́ть 'to hold': держу́ де́ржит де́ржат; держи́!; -держан (in compounds)

доба́вить 'to add': доба́влю доба́вит доба́вят; доба́вь!; доба́влен; impf. **добавля́ть**

дости́гнуть (+ gen.) 'to achieve': дости́гну дости́гнет дости́гнут; дости́г дости́гла; дости́гнут; impf. **достига́ть**

дрема́ть 'to doze': дремлю́ дре́млет дре́млют

дрожа́ть 'to tremble': дрожу́ дрожи́т дрожа́т; pf. **дро́гнуть**

дуть 'to blow': ду́ю ду́ет ду́ют; pf. **ду́нуть**

дыша́ть 'to breathe': дышу́ ды́шит ды́шат

е́здить 'to travel': е́зжу е́здит е́здят; е́зди!

есть/съ- 'to eat': ем ешь ест еди́м еди́те едя́т; ешь!; съе́ден

е́хать/по- 'to travel': е́ду е́дет е́дут; поезжа́й!

жале́ть/по- 'to pity': жале́ю жале́ет жале́ют

жа́ловаться/по- (на + acc.) 'to complain (of, about)': жа́луюсь жа́луется жа́луются

жать 'to press, squeeze': жму жмёт жмут; жми!; -жат (in compounds)

ждать/подо- (+ acc./gen.) 'to wait (for)': жду ждёт ждут; ждал ждала́ жда́ло; жди!

жева́ть 'to chew': жую́ жуёт жую́т

жéртвовать/по- (+ instr.) 'to sacrifice': жéртвую жéртвует жéртвуют

жечь/с- 'to burn' (trans.): жгу жжёт жгут; жёг жгла; жги!; -жжён -жженá (in compounds)

жить 'to live': живý живёт живýт; жил жилá жи́ло

забóтиться/по- (о + prep.) 'to care about': забóчусь забóтится забóтятся

забы́ть 'to forget': забýду забýдет забýдут; (не) забýдь!; забы́т; impf. **забывáть**

завéдовать (+ instr.) 'to be in charge of': завéдую завéдует завéдуют

зави́довать/по- (+ dat.) 'to envy': зави́дую зави́дует зави́дуют

зави́сеть (от + gen.) 'to depend (on)': зави́шу зави́сит зави́сят

закры́ть 'to shut': закрóю закрóет закрóют; закрóй!; закры́т; impf. **закрывáть**

замёрзнуть 'to freeze' (intrans.): замёрзну замёрзнет замёрзнут; замёрз замёрзла; impf. **замерзáть**

замéтить 'to notice': замéчу замéтит замéтят; замéчен; impf. **замечáть**

заня́ть 'to occupy': займý займёт займýт; зáнял занялá зáняло; займи́!; зáнят занятá зáнято; impf. **занимáть**

заперéть 'to lock': запрý запрёт запрýт; зáпер заперлá зáперло; запри́!; зáперт запертá зáперто; impf. **запирáть**

запрети́ть 'to forbid': запрещý запрети́т запретя́т; запрещён запрещенá; impf. **запрещáть**

заряди́ть 'to load, charge': заряжý заряди́т заря́дят; заряжён заряженá; impf. **заряжáть**

захвати́ть 'to seize': захвачý захвáтит захвáтят; захвáчен; impf. **захвáтывать**

защити́ть (от + gen.) 'to defend (from)': защищý защити́т защитя́т; защищён защищенá; impf. **защищáть** .

заяви́ть 'to declare': заявлю́ заяви́т заяви́т; зая́влен; impf. **заявля́ть**

звать/по- 'to call': зовý зовёт зовýт; звал звалá звáло; зови́!; -зван (in compounds)

звуча́ть 'to sound': звучи́т звуча́т

знако́миться/по- (c + instr.) 'to become acquainted (with)': знако́млюсь знако́мится знако́мятся; знако́мься!

идти́ 'to go': иду́ идёт иду́т; шёл шла; иди́!

изобрести́ 'to invent': изобрету́ изобретёт изобрету́т; изобрёл изобрела́; изобретён изобретена́; impf. **изобрета́ть**

име́ть 'to have': име́ю име́ет име́ют

интересова́ться (+ instr.) 'to be interested in': интересу́юсь интересу́ется интересу́ются

иска́ть (+ acc./gen.) 'to look for': ищу́ и́щет и́щут; ищи́!

испо́льзовать 'to use' (impf. and pf.): испо́льзую испо́льзует испо́льзуют; испо́льзуй!; испо́льзован

иссле́довать 'to investigate' (impf. and pf.): иссле́дую иссле́дует иссле́дуют; иссле́дован

исче́знуть 'to disappear': исче́зну исче́знет исче́знут; исче́з исче́зла; impf. **исчеза́ть**

-каза́ть (only in compounds). -кажу́ -ка́жет -ка́жут; -кажи́!; -ка́зан; impf. **-ка́зывать**

каза́ться/по- (+ instr.) 'to seem': кажу́сь ка́жется ка́жутся

кати́ть 'to roll' (trans.): качу́ ка́тит ка́тят

ка́шлять 'to cough': ка́шляю ка́шляет ка́шляют; pf. **ка́шлянуть**

кипе́ть/вс- 'to boil' (intrans.): киплю́ (in figurative sense only) кипи́т кипя́т

класть 'to place': кладу́ кладёт кладу́т; клади́!; pf. **положи́ть**

колеба́ться/по- 'to hesitate': коле́блюсь коле́блется коле́блются

кома́ндовать (+ instr.) 'to command': кома́ндую кома́ндует кома́ндуют

корми́ть/на- 'to feed': кормлю́ ко́рмит ко́рмят; нако́рмлен

кра́сить/вы́- or **по-** 'to paint': кра́шу кра́сит кра́сят; вы́крашен

красне́ть/по- 'to blush': красне́ю красне́ет красне́ют

красть/у- 'to steal': краду́ крадёт краду́т; укра́ден

кре́пнуть/о- 'to get stronger': кре́пну кре́пнет кре́пнут; креп кре́пла

крича́ть 'to shout': кричу́ кричи́т крича́т; кричи́!; pf. **кри́кнуть**

купи́ть 'to buy': куплю́ ку́пит ку́пят; купи́!; ку́плен; impf. **покупа́ть**

ла́зить 'to climb': ла́жу ла́зит ла́зят; (не) лазь!

лгать/со- or **на-** 'to tell lies': лгу лжёт лгут; лгал, лгала́, лга́ло; (не) лги!

лежа́ть 'to lie': лежу́ лежи́т лежа́т

лезть 'to climb': ле́зу ле́зет ле́зут; лез ле́зла; лезь!

лете́ть 'to fly': лечу́ лети́т летя́т

лечь 'to lie down': ля́гу ля́жет ля́гут; лёг легла́; ляг!; impf. **ложи́ться**

лиза́ть 'to lick': лижу́ ли́жет ли́жут; pf. **лизну́ть**

лить 'to pour': лью льёт льют; лил лила́ ли́ло; лей!; -лит (in compounds)

лови́ть 'to catch': ловлю́ ло́вит ло́вят; pf. **пойма́ть**

люби́ть 'to like, love': люблю́ лю́бит лю́бят

любова́ться/по- (+ instr. or на + acc.) 'to admire': любу́юсь любу́ется любу́ются

маха́ть 'to wave': машу́ ма́шет ма́шут; pf. **махну́ть**

мести́/под- 'to sweep': мету́ метёт мету́т; мёл мела́; подметён подметена́

молча́ть 'to be silent': молчу́ молчи́т молча́т; молчи́!

мочь/с- 'to be able': могу́ мо́жет мо́гут; мог могла́

мча́ться 'to race': мчусь мчи́тся мча́тся; мчись!

мы́ться/вы́- or **по-** 'to wash' (intrans.): мо́юсь мо́ется мо́ются; мо́йся!

награди́ть (за + acc.) 'to reward (for)': награжу́ награди́т наградя́т; награждён награждена́; impf. **награжда́ть**

наде́ть 'to put on': наде́ну наде́нет наде́нут; наде́нь!; impf. **надева́ть**

наде́яться/по- (на + acc.) 'to hope (for)': наде́юсь наде́ется наде́ются

назва́ть 'to name': назову́ назовёт назову́т; назва́л назвала́ назва́ло; на́зван; impf. **называ́ть**

найти́ 'to find': найду́ найдёт найду́т; нашёл нашла́; на́йден; impf. **находи́ть**

напа́сть (на + acc.) 'to attack': нападу́ нападёт нападу́т; impf. **напада́ть**

находи́ть 'to find': нахожу́ нахо́дит нахо́дят; pf. **найти́**

находи́ться 'to be situated': нахожу́сь нахо́дится нахо́дятся

нача́ть 'to begin' (trans.): начну́ начнёт начну́т; на́чал начала́ на́чало; начни́!; на́чат начата́ на́чато; impf. **начина́ть**

нача́ться 'to begin' (intrans.): начнётся начну́тся; начался́ начала́сь; impf. **начина́ться**

ненави́деть 'to hate': ненави́жу ненави́дит ненави́дят

нести́ 'to carry': несу́ несёт несу́т; нёс несла́; неси́!

носи́ть 'to carry': ношу́ но́сит но́сят

ночева́ть/пере- 'to spend the night': ночу́ю ночу́ет ночу́ют

нра́виться/по- (+ dat.) 'to please': нра́влюсь нра́вится нра́вятся

оби́деть 'to offend': оби́жу оби́дит оби́дят; оби́жен; impf. **обижа́ть**

обня́ть 'to embrace': обниму́ обни́мет обни́мут; о́бнял обняла́ о́бняло; обними́!; impf. **обнима́ть**

обогна́ть 'to overtake, outstrip': обгоню́ обго́нит обго́нят; обогна́л обогнала́ обогна́ло; impf. **обгоня́ть**

образова́ть 'to form' (impf. and pf.): образу́ю образу́ет образу́ют; образо́ван; impf. also **образо́вывать**

обрати́ться (к + dat.) 'to turn (to)': обращу́сь обрати́тся обратя́тся; обрати́сь!; impf. **обраща́ть**

обсуди́ть 'to discuss': обсужу́ обсу́дит обсу́дят; обсуждён обсуждена́; impf. **обсужда́ть**

оде́ться 'to dress' (intrans.): оде́нусь оде́нется оде́нутся; оде́нься! impf. **одева́ться**

организова́ть 'to organize' (impf. and pf.): организу́ю организу́ет организу́ют; организо́ван

освети́ть 'to illuminate': освещу́ освети́т осветя́т; освещён освещена́; impf. **освеща́ть**

освободи́ть 'to free': освобожу́ освободи́т освободя́т; освобождён освобождена́; impf. **освобожда́ть**

оставаться 'to remain': остаю́сь остаётся остаю́тся; остава́йся!; pf. **оста́ться**

останови́ться 'to stop' (intrans.): остановлю́сь остано́вится остано́вятся; останови́сь!; impf. **остана́вливаться**

оста́ться 'to remain': оста́нусь оста́нется оста́нутся; оста́нься! impf. **оставаться**

отве́тить (на + acc.) 'to answer': отве́чу отве́тит отве́тят; отве́ть!; impf. **отвеча́ть**

откры́ть 'to open' (trans.): откро́ю откро́ет откро́ют; откро́й!; откры́т; impf. **открыва́ть**

отня́ть 'to take away': отниму́ отни́мет отни́мут; о́тнял отняла́ о́тняло; отними́!; impf. **отнима́ть**

отпере́ть 'to unlock': отопру́ отопрёт отопру́т; отопри́!; о́тпер отперла́ о́тперло; о́тперт отперта́ о́тперто; impf. **отпира́ть**

ошиби́ться 'to make a mistake': ошибу́сь ошибётся ошибу́тся; оши́бся оши́блась; impf. **ошиба́ться**

па́хнуть (+ instr.) 'to smell (of)': па́хнет па́хнут; пах па́хла

перестава́ть 'to stop' (intrans.): перестаю́ перестаёт перестаю́т; pf. **переста́ть**

переста́ть 'to stop' (intrans.): переста́ну переста́нешь переста́нут; переста́нь!; impf. **перестава́ть**

петь/с- 'to sing': пою́ поёт пою́т; пой!

печь/ис- to bake': пеку́ печёт пеку́т; пёк пекла́; испечён испечена́

писа́ть/на- 'to write': пишу́ пи́шет пи́шут; пиши́!; напи́сан

пить/вы́- 'to drink': пью пьёт пьют; пил, пила́, пи́ло; пей!; вы́пит

пла́кать 'to weep': пла́чу пла́чет пла́чут; (не) плачь!

плати́ть/за- (за + acc.) 'to pay (for)': плачу́ пла́тит пла́тят; плати́!; запла́чен

плева́ть 'to spit': плюю́ плюёт плюю́т; pf. **плю́нуть**

плыть 'to swim': плыву́ плывёт плыву́т; плыл, плыла́ плы́ло

победи́ть 'to win': победи́т победя́т; побеждён побеждена́; impf. **побежда́ть**

пове́сить 'to hang' (trans.): пове́шу пове́сит пове́сят; пове́сь!; пове́шен; impf. **ве́шать**

подве́ргнуть (+ dat.) 'to subject (to)': подве́ргну подве́ргнет подве́ргнут; подве́рг подве́ргла; подве́ргнут; impf. **подверга́ть**

подня́ть 'to lift': подниму́ подни́мет подни́мут; по́днял подняла́ по́дняло; подними́!; по́днят поднята́ по́днято; impf. **поднима́ть**

подтверди́ть 'to confirm': подтвержу́ подтверди́т подтвердя́т; подтверждён подтверждена́; impf. **подтвержда́ть**

поздра́вить (с + instr.) 'to congratulate (on)': поздра́влю поздра́вит поздра́вят; поздра́вь!; impf. **поздравля́ть**

покры́ть 'to cover': покро́ю покро́ет покро́ют; покро́й!; покры́т; impf. **покрыва́ть**

ползти́ 'to crawl': ползу́ ползёт ползу́т; полз ползла́

по́льзоваться/вос- (+ instr.) 'to use': по́льзуюсь по́льзуется по́льзуются

помо́чь (+ dat.) 'to help': помогу́ помо́жет помо́гут; помо́г помогла́; помоги́!; impf. **помога́ть**

пони́зить 'to lower': пони́жу пони́зит пони́зят; пони́жен; impf. **понижа́ть**

поня́ть 'to understand': пойму́ поймёт пойму́т; по́нял поняла́ по́няло; пойми́!; по́нят понята́ по́нято; impf. **понима́ть**

по́ртить/ис- 'to spoil': по́рчу по́ртит по́ртят; испо́рчен

посади́ть 'to plant, seat': посажу́ поса́дит поса́дят; поса́жен; impf. **сажа́ть**

посвяти́ть (+ dat.) 'to dedicate (to)': посвящу́ посвяти́т посвятя́т; посвящён посвящена́; impf. **посвяща́ть**

посети́ть 'to visit': посещу́ посети́т посетя́т; посещён посещена́; impf. **посеща́ть**

пра́вить (+ instr.) 'to rule, govern': пра́влю пра́вит пра́вят

пра́здновать/от- 'to celebrate': пра́здную пра́зднует пра́зднуют

преврати́ть (в + acc.) 'to transform (into)': превращу́ преврати́т превратя́т; превращён превращена́; impf. **превраща́ть**

предупреди́ть 'to warn': предупрежу́ предупреди́т предупредя́т; предупреждён предупреждена́; impf. **предупрежда́ть**

прекрати́ть 'to stop, curtail': прекращу́ прекрати́т прекратя́т; прекрати́!; прекращён прекращена́; impf. **прекраща́ть**

преодоле́ть 'to overcome': преодоле́ю преодоле́ет преодоле́ют; преодолён преодолена́; impf. **преодолева́ть**

прибли́зиться (к + dat.) 'to approach': прибли́жусь прибли́зится прибли́зятся; impf. **приближа́ться**

привы́кнуть (к + dat.) 'to get used (to)': привы́кну привы́кнет привы́кнут; привы́к привы́кла; impf. **привыка́ть**

пригласи́ть 'to invite': приглашу́ пригласи́т приглася́т; пригласи́!; приглашён приглашена́; pf. **приглаша́ть**

признава́ться (в + prep.) 'to confess (to)': признаю́сь признаётся признаю́тся; pf. **призна́ться**

приня́ть 'to accept': приму́ при́мет при́мут; при́нял приняла́ при́няло; прими́!; при́нят принята́ при́нято; impf. **принима́ть**

про́бовать/по- 'to test, try': про́бую про́бует про́буют; про́буй!

проси́ть/по- (+ acc./gen.) 'to request': прошу́ про́сит про́сят; проси́!

прости́ть (за + acc.) 'to forgive (for)': прощу́ прости́т простя́т; прости́!; прощён прощена́; impf. **проща́ть**

прости́ться (с + instr.) 'to say goodbye (to)': прощу́сь прости́тся простя́тся; impf. **проща́ться**

простуди́ться 'to catch cold': простужу́сь просту́дится просту́дятся; impf. **простужа́ться**

пря́тать/с- 'to hide': пря́чу пря́чет пря́чут; прячь!; спря́тан

пусти́ть 'to let go': пущу́ пу́стит пу́стят; пу́щен; impf. **пуска́ть**

ра́доваться/об- (+ dat.) 'to rejoice (at)': ра́дуюсь ра́дуется ра́дуются

разби́ть 'to smash': разобью́ разобьёт разобью́т; разбе́й! разби́т; impf. **разбива́ть**

разви́ться 'to develop' (intrans.): разовью́сь разовьётся разовью́тся; разви́лся развила́сь; impf. **развива́ться**

разде́ться 'to get undressed': разде́нусь разде́нется разде́нутся; разде́нься!; impf. **раздева́ться**

расста́ться (с + instr.) 'to part (with)': расста́нусь расста́нется расста́нутся; impf. **расстава́ться**

расти́/вы- 'to grow' (intrans.): расту́ растёт расту́т; рос росла́

рвать 'to tear': рву рвёт рвут; рвал рвала́ рва́ло

ре́зать/раз- 'to cut': ре́жу ре́жет ре́жут; режь!; разре́зан

рисова́ть/на- 'to draw': рису́ю рису́ет рису́ют; нарисо́ван

руби́ть 'to chop': рублю́ ру́бит ру́бят; -рублен (in compounds)

руководи́ть (+ instr.) 'to manage': руковожу́ руководи́т руководя́т

сади́ться 'to sit down': сажу́сь сади́тся садя́тся: сади́сь!; pf. **сесть**

свисте́ть 'to whistle': свищу́ свисти́т свистя́т; **сви́стнуть**

серди́ться/рас- 'to get angry': сержу́сь се́рдится се́рдятся; (не) серди́сь!

сесть 'to sit down': ся́ду ся́дет ся́дут; сядь!; impf. **сади́ться**

се́ять/по- 'to sow': се́ю се́ет се́ют; посе́ян

сиде́ть 'to sit': сижу́ сиди́т сидя́т; сиди́!

сказа́ть 'to say': скажу́ ска́жет ска́жут; скажи́!; ска́зан; impf. **говори́ть**

скрыть 'to conceal': скро́ю скро́ет скро́ют; скрой!; скрыт; impf. **скрыва́ть**

слать 'to send': шлю шлёт шлют; шли!

следи́ть (за + instr.) 'to track': слежу́ следи́т следя́т

сле́довать/по- (за + instr.) 'to follow': сле́дую сле́дует сле́дуют

слы́шать/у- 'to hear': слы́шу слы́шит слы́шат; услы́шан

сметь/по- 'to dare': сме́ю сме́ет сме́ют

смея́ться/по- (над + instr.) 'to laugh (at)': смею́сь смеётся смею́тся; (не) сме́йся!

смотре́ть/по- (на + acc.) 'to look (at)': смотрю́ смо́трит смо́трят; смотри́!

снять 'to take off': сниму́ сни́мет сни́мут; снял сняла́ сня́ло; сними́!; снят снята́ сня́то; impf. **снима́ть**

сове́товать/по- (+ dat.) 'to advise': сове́тую сове́тует сове́туют

согласи́ться (на + acc./с + instr.) 'to agree (to something/with someone)': соглашу́сь согласи́тся соглася́тся; impf. **соглаша́ться**

спасти́ 'to save': спасу́ спасёт спасу́т; спас спасла́; спасён спасена́; impf. **спаса́ть**

спать 'to sleep': сплю спит спят; спал спалá спáло; спи!

спроси́ть 'to ask': спрошу́ спро́сит спро́сят; спроси́!; impf. **спра́шивать**

ста́вить/по- 'to put, stand' (trans.): ста́влю ста́вит ста́вят; ставь!; поста́влен

стать 'to become': ста́ну ста́нет ста́нут; стань!; impf. **станови́ться**

стере́ть 'to erase': сотру́ сотрёт сотру́т; стёр стёрла; сотри́!; стёрт; impf. **стира́ть**

стоя́ть 'to stand' (intrans.): стою́ стои́т стоя́т; стой!

стричь/о- 'to cut (hair or nails)': стригу́ стрижёт стригу́т; стриг стри́гла; остри́жен

ступи́ть 'to step': ступлю́ сту́пит сту́пят; impf. **ступа́ть**

стуча́ть/по- (в + acc.) 'to knock (at)': стучу́ стучи́т стуча́т

суди́ть 'to judge': сужу́ су́дит су́дят

танцева́ть/с- 'to dance': танцу́ю танцу́ет танцу́ют

та́ять/рас- 'to melt' (intrans.): та́ет та́ют

темне́ть/по- 'to grow dark': темне́ет темне́ют

тере́ть 'to rub': тру трёт трут; тёр тёрла; три!

терпе́ть 'to bear, tolerate': терплю́ те́рпит те́рпят

течь 'to flow': течёт теку́т; тёк текла́

топи́ть 'to heat': топлю́ то́пит то́пят; -топлен (in compounds)

торгова́ть (+ instr.) 'to trade (in)': торгу́ю торгу́ет торгу́ют

торопи́ться/по- 'to hurry': тороплю́сь торо́пится торо́пятся; торопи́сь!

тра́тить/ис- (на + acc.) 'to expend (on)': тра́чу тра́тит тра́тят; трать!; истра́чен

тре́бовать/по- (+ gen./acc.) 'to demand': тре́бую тре́бует тре́буют

труди́ться 'to labour': тружу́сь тру́дится тру́дятся; труди́сь!

трясти́ 'to shake' (trans.): трясу́ трясёт трясу́т; тряс трясла́; pf. **тряхну́ть**

убеди́ть 'to convince': убеди́т убедя́т; убеждён убеждена́; impf. **убежда́ть**

удиви́ться (+ dat.) 'to be surprised (at)': удивлю́сь удиви́тся удивя́тся; impf. **удивля́ться**

укрепи́ть 'to strengthen': укреплю́ укрепи́т укрепя́т; укреплён укреплена́; impf. **укрепля́ть**

умере́ть 'to die': умру́ умрёт умру́т; у́мер умерла́ у́мерло; impf. **умира́ть**

уме́ть 'to know how': уме́ю уме́ет уме́ют

упа́сть 'to fall': упаду́ упадёт упаду́т; impf. **па́дать**

употреби́ть 'to use': употреблю́ употреби́т употребя́т; употреблён употреблена́; impf. **употребля́ть**

успе́ть 'to have time': успе́ю успе́ет успе́ют; impf. **успева́ть**

установи́ть 'to establish': установлю́ устано́вит устано́вят; устано́влен; impf. **устана́вливать**

уча́ствовать (в + prep.) 'to participate in': уча́ствую уча́ствует уча́ствуют

уче́сть 'to take account of': учту́ учтёт учту́т; учёл учла́; учти́!; учтён учтена́; impf. **учи́тывать**

ходи́ть 'to go': хожу́ хо́дит хо́дят; ходи́!

хоте́ть/за- 'to want': хочу́ хо́чешь хо́чет хоти́м хоти́те хотя́т

худе́ть/по- 'to lose weight': худе́ю худе́ет худе́ют

цвести́ 'to flower': цветёт цвету́т; цвёл цвела́

чеса́ть/по- 'to scratch': чешу́ че́шет че́шут

чи́стить/вы́- or **по-** 'to clean': чи́щу чи́стит чи́стят; вы́чищен/почи́щен

чу́вствовать 'to feel': чу́вствую чу́вствует чу́вствуют

шепта́ть 'to whisper': шепчу́ ше́пчет ше́пчут; pf. **шепну́ть**

шить/с- 'to sew': шью шьёт шьют; шей!

шуме́ть 'to make a noise': шуми́т шумя́т

шути́ть/по- 'to joke': шучу́ шу́тит шу́тят

эконо́мить/с- 'to economize': эконо́млю эконо́мит эконо́мят; сэконо́млен

яви́ться (+ instr. 'to be'): явлю́сь я́вится я́вятся; impf. **явля́ться**

The adverb

An adverb is a part of speech that expresses the manner, time, place, or extent of an action. It usually modifies a verb ('He is driving **fast**'), but may also modify an adjective ('a **surprisingly** apt pupil') or another adverb ('She arrived **very** early'). There are adverbs of manner ('He behaved **stupidly**'), place ('Come **here**'), time ('Do it **now**'), and extent ('It is **extremely** warm').

Formation

Many adverbs derive from adjectives by replacing the endings **-ый** and **-ий** by, respectively, **-о** and **-e**:

Adjective	Meaning	Adverb	Meaning
быстр-**ый**	quick	быстр-**о**	quickly
гла́дк-**ий**	smooth	гла́дк-**о**	smoothly
и́скренн-**ий**	sincere	и́скренн-**е**	sincerely

Note: (a) **ра́но** 'early' and **по́здно** 'late' derive, respectively, from the soft-ending adjectives **ра́нний** and **по́здний**.
(b) some adjectives in -ый/-ий which have no adverb in -о/-е form the adverb on the model **по-** + dative of adjective:

друго́й	different	по-друго́му	differently
ра́зный	various	по-ра́зному	variously
пре́жний	previous	по-пре́жнему	previously

Adjectives in -ский/-цкий and -и́ческий form adverbs in **-и**:

бра́тск-**ий**	fraternal	бра́тск-**и**	fraternally
геройческ-**ий**	heroic	геройческ-**и**	heroically

> **Note:** Adjectives of nationality and some others form their adverbs with **по-**:
> Он говори́т **по-ру́сски** 'He speaks **Russian**', Он ведёт себя́ **по-де́тски** 'He behaves **childishly**'.

Derivation of adverbs

Adverbs may derive from:

(a) nouns:

весно́й/ле́том/о́сенью/зимо́й   in spring/summer/autumn/
winter

у́тром/днём/ве́чером/но́чью   in the morning/afternoon/evening/
at night

до́ма, домо́й   at home, home(wards)

(b) preposition + long or short adjective:

в основно́м   basically
издалека́   from afar
напра́во, нале́во   to/on the right, to/on the left
сно́ва   again

(c) preposition + noun:

вме́сте   together
во́время   in time
снача́ла   (at) first

(d) numerals:

вдвоём, втроём, вчетверо́м   two, three, four together
во-пе́рвых, во-вторы́х, в-тре́тьих   firstly, secondly, thirdly
впервы́е   for the first time
одна́жды, два́жды, три́жды   once, twice, thrice

(e) possessive pronouns:

по-мо́ему, по-на́шему, по-ва́шему   in my, our, your opinion
   (**note**: **по его́/её/их мне́нию**   'in his, her, their opinion')

(f) the demonstrative pronoun **сей** 'this' + noun:

сего́дня, сейча́с   today, now

Adverbs of place

Adverbs of place can be arranged:

(a) in groups of three, the first denoting *location*, the second *direction*, and the third *source*:

(i) **Где** ваш дом? **Where** is your house?
Куда ты идёшь? **Where** are you going?
Откуда дует ветер? **From where** is the wind blowing?

(ii) Я живу **здесь** I live **here**
Идите **сюда** Come **here**
Отсюда до города недалеко It's not far **from here** to the town

(iii) Она работает **там** She works **there**
Идите **туда** Go over **there**
Оттуда до Киева час лёта **From there** to Kiev is an hour's flight

(iv) **Вдали** блестит река A river gleams **in the distance**
Она смотрит **вдаль** She looks **into the distance**
Город виден **издали** The town is visible **from afar**

(v) Он ждёт **внизу** He is waiting **downstairs**
Она спускается **вниз** She goes **downstairs**
Критика **снизу** Criticism from below (i.e. from the grass roots)

(vi) **Внутри** было темно It was dark **inside**
Дверь открывается **внутрь** The door opens **inwards**
Дверь заперта **изнутри** The door is locked **on/from the inside**

(vii) Ребёнок спит **наверху** The child is asleep **upstairs**
Она поднимается **наверх** She goes **upstairs**
сверху донизу from top to bottom

(b) in pairs, the first denoting *location*, the second *direction*:

(i) Она заперла дверь **снаружи**   She locked the door **on/from the outside**

Он вышел **наружу**   He came **outside**

(ii) Лейтенант марширует **впереди**   The lieutenant marches **in front**

Он шёл прямо **вперёд**   He was walking **straight ahead**

(iii) Я работаю **дома**   I work at **home**

Он идёт **домой**   He is going **home**

(iv) третий вагон **сзади**   the third carriage **from the back**

Назад!   Stand **back**!

(c) in pairs, one denoting *location* and *direction*, the other *origin*:

(i) Он стоял **налево** от киоска   He stood **to the left** of the kiosk

Она свернула **налево**   She turned **to the left**

Он вошёл **слева**   He entered **from the left**

(ii) Почта находится **направо** от дома   The post office is situated **to the right** of the house

Он повернул **направо**   He turned **to the right**

Они пишут **справа** налево   They write **from right** to left

Note: One pair of spatial adverbs (**всюду** 'everywhere' and **отовсюду** 'from everywhere') denotes, respectively, *location* and *origin*:

Он **всюду** побывал   He has been **everywhere**

Гости съехались **отовсюду**   Guests converged **from all sides**

Adverbs of time

(a) Adverbs of time include a number that imply frequency, often combining with a verb in the imperfective aspect (*see page 119*):

всегда́ always
иногда́ sometimes
обы́чно usually
ча́сто often

(b) Others are associated with perfective verbs: **вдруг/внеза́пно** 'suddenly', **ско́ро/вско́ре** 'soon', **сра́зу** 'at once':

Вдруг **разда́лся** крик   Suddenly a cry **rang out**
Я ско́ро **прие́ду**   I **will be there** soon
Она́ сра́зу **поняла́** э́то   She **understood** this at once

(c) **Тепе́рь** 'now' relates only to the present, while **сейча́с** 'just now, now, in a minute' can relate to past, present, or future:

Он был здесь **сейча́с**   He was here **just now**
Сейча́с она́ занята́   She is busy **at the moment**
Он **сейча́с** придёт   He will be here **in a minute**

(d) **Тогда́** 'then, at that time' is distinguished from **пото́м/зате́м** 'then, afterwards':

Тогда́ она́ была́ молода́   **Then** she was young
Отдохнём, **пото́м** порабо́таем   We'll rest, **then** do some work

(e) **До́лго** '(for) a long time' denotes a definite though unspecified period of time (Он **до́лго** жил там 'He lived there for a long time'), **надо́лго** 'for a long time' denotes a time subsequent to the completion of an action (Они́ расста́лись **надо́лго** 'They separated for a long time'), **давно́** 'for a long time' (also 'a long time ago') refers to an action or state begun in the past and not yet completed (Я **давно́** изуча́ю языки́ 'I have been learning languages for a long time') (for tense usage and **давно́ не**, *see page 120*).

(f) **Неда́вно** means 'recently':

Они́ **неда́вно** пожени́лись   They got married **recently**

(g) **Позавчера́** 'the day before yesterday', **вчера́** 'yesterday', **сего́дня** 'today', **за́втра** 'tomorrow', and **послеза́втра** 'the day after tomorrow' can combine with the names of parts of the day: **вчера́ но́чью** 'yesterday night', **сего́дня днём** 'this afternoon' **за́втра ве́чером** 'tomorrow evening', etc.

(h) **Весно́й** 'in spring', **ле́том** 'in summer', **о́сенью** 'in autumn', and **зимо́й** 'in winter' can combine with the relevant form of **про́шлый** 'last', **э́тот** 'this', and **бу́дущий** 'next', *or* with **про́шлого/э́того/бу́дущего го́да** 'of last, of this, of next year': **про́шлой весно́й** 'last spring', **э́тим ле́том** 'this summer', **о́сенью э́того го́да** 'this autumn', **зимо́й бу́дущего го́да** 'next winter'.

(i) **Ещё** means 'still' (**Вы ещё** здесь? 'Are you still here?'), **ещё не** 'not yet' (**Она́ ещё не** пришла́ 'She hasn't arrived yet'). **Ещё** 'another, an additional' (**Ещё** ча́шку? 'Another cup?') is distinguished from **друго́й** 'another, a different' (Я закажу́ **друго́е** вино́ 'I'll order another (i.e. a different) wine'). **Ещё раз** 'again' refers to a repeated action (Спрошу́ **ещё раз** 'I'll ask again'), **сно́ва** often to a resumed activity (По́сле опера́ции я **сно́ва** займу́сь аэро́бикой 'After the operation I'll take up aerobics again'), **опя́ть** 'again' often introduces a note of irritation (**Опя́ть** про́сят сда́чи! 'They're asking for change again!').

(j) **Уже́** 'already' (Он **уже́** уе́хал 'He has already left') often has no equivalent in English in indicating early implementation: Война́ начала́сь **уже́** в 1939 году́ 'The war began in (as early as) 1939'. **Уже́ не** (= бо́льше не) means 'no longer' (Она́ **уже́ не** рабо́тает здесь 'She doesn't work here any more').

(k) Many adverbial phrases are based on **пора́** 'time': **до тех пор** 'until then', **с тех пор** 'since then', **до сих пор** 'up to now', etc. **Пока́** is more emphatic than **до сих пор** (**Пока́** ничего́ не изве́стно 'So far nothing is known'). It also means 'for now, for the time being' (**Пока́** э́то всё 'That's all for now').

Adverbs of manner

(a) Many adverbs of manner in **-о** and **-е** derive from adjectives in **-ый/ -ий** and answer the question **как?** 'how?' or **каким образом?** 'in what manner?':

Он éдет **быстро**   He is driving **fast**

Она говорит **искренне**   She speaks **sincerely**

Он работает **хорошо**   He works **well**

Она идёт **медленно**   She is walking **slowly**

Он **интересно** рассказывает   He narrates in an **interesting** way

(b) Some of these function as predicative adverbs: Ему **грустно** 'He feels sad', Ей **плохо** 'She feels bad', В комнате **холодно** 'It is cold in the room', etc. They can also be used by themselves: **Весело** 'It's fun', and with verbs: Ему **стало** грустно 'He became saddened'.

(c) Some adverbs of manner, especially those in **по-**, imply similarity

Мы ещё живём **по-старому**   We are still living **in the old way**

Она одета **по-дорожному**   She is dressed **for the road**

Он **по-лисьи** хитёр   He is as cunning **as a fox**

Adverbs of degree and intensity

Most adverbs of degree qualify adjectives or other adverbs:

Он говорит **óчень** хорошо   He speaks **very** well

Она **удивительно** талантлива   She is **remarkably** talented

Сегодня **слишком** жарко   It is **too** hot today

Она **много/мало** работает   She works **hard/not very hard**

Она **совершенно** права   She is **absolutely** right

Это **крайне** интересно   That is **extremely** interesting

Он **необыкновенно** умён   He is **unusually** clever

Я **весьма** рад   I am **extremely** glad

Это **совсем** новый план   That is a **completely** new plan

Это **чрезвычайно** важно   That is **extremely** important

Indefinite adverbs in -то, -нибудь, -либо, and кое-

(a) Adverbs in **-то** (где́-то, куда́-то, ка́к-то, когда́-то, почему́-то)
denote a particular but unidentified place, manner, time, cause,
etc., mainly in the past or present:

> Он живёт где́-то в го́роде — He lives **somewhere** in the town
> Он куда́-то ушёл — He's gone off **somewhere**
> Он ка́к-то реши́л зада́чу — He solved the problem **somehow**
> Она́ когда́-то жила́ здесь — **At one time** she lived here
> Он почему́-то серди́т — **For some reason** he is angry

(b) Adverbs in **-нибудь** (где́-нибудь, куда́-нибудь, ка́к-нибудь,
когда́-нибудь, почему́-нибудь) denote a place, manner, time,
cause, etc. that is indefinite or still to be decided upon or selected.
Because of their hypothetical nature, these adverbs are found in
questions, after imperatives, in subjunctive constructions, and
where different actions, persons, things, reasons on different
occasions are referred to:

> Мы встре́тимся где́-нибудь — We will meet **somewhere**
> Поезжа́йте куда́-нибудь в воскресе́нье — Go for a drive
> **somewhere** on Sunday
> На́до ка́к-нибудь помо́чь ему́ — **Somehow or other** we must help
> him
> Вы когда́-нибудь чита́ли э́ту кни́гу? — Have you **ever** read this
> book?
> Он хо́чет, что́бы я когда́-нибудь сыгра́л с ним в ша́хматы
> He wants me to play chess with him **sometime**
> Он всегда́ почему́-нибудь опа́здывает — **For some reason or
> other** he is always late

(c) Adverbs in **-либо** are even less definite than those in **-нибудь**
(Он когда́-либо заходи́л/захо́дит? 'Did he/does he **ever** drop in?').

(d) Among the commonest indefinite adverbs in **кое-** are **ко́е-где**
(Ко́е-где встреча́ются во́лки 'Here and there one encounters
wolves'), and **ко́е-как** (Ко́е-как мы доплы́ли до бе́рега
'**Somehow or other**' (i.e. with difficulty) we reached the shore').

Negative adverbs

(a) The negative adverbs **нигде́**, **ника́к**, **никуда́**, **никогда́**, **ниоткỳда**, **ниско́лько** (like negative pronouns, *see page 78*) require the negative particle **не** before a following verb or short adjective:

> Я **нигде́ не** мог найти́ нýжную мне пласти́нку I could **not** find the record I need **anywhere**
>
> Я **ника́к не** мог узна́ть её телефо́н I could **not** find out her telephone number **at all**
>
> Она́ **никуда́ не** идёт She is **not** going **anywhere**
>
> Я **никогда́ не** пью ко́фе I **never** drink coffee
>
> Она́ **ниско́лько не** удивлена́ She is **not in the least** surprised
>
> Они́ **ниоткýда не** получа́ют посы́лок They do **not** get parcels from **anywhere**

(b) The negative adverbs may combine with negative pronouns: **Никто́ никогда́ ничего́ не** зна́ет 'No one ever knows anything'.

(c) The negative adverbs **не́где**, **не́куда**, **не́зачем**, **не́когда**, **не́откуда** denote lack of potential or (in the case of **не́зачем**) motive for carrying out an action, and combine with an infinitive:

> **Не́где** тренирова́ться **There is nowhere** to train
>
> **Не́куда** идти́ **There is nowhere** to go
>
> **Не́зачем** спо́рить **There is no point** in arguing
>
> **Не́когда** репети́ровать **There is no time** to rehearse
>
> **Не́откуда** ожида́ть по́мощи **There is nowhere** to expect help from

Note: (a) **бы́ло** and **бу́дет** are used in the past and future: **Не́где бы́ло** держа́ть кур '**There was nowhere** to keep chickens', **Не́зачем бу́дет** жа́ловаться '**There will be no point** in complaining'.

(b) The logical subject of an action appears in the *dative case*: **Им** не́где игра́ть 'They have nowhere to play', **Мне** не́когда бу́дет чита́ть 'I shall have no time to read'.

(c) The positive counterpart to **не́где**, **не́куда**, **не́откуда** involves **есть**, **бы́ло**, and **бу́дет**: **Есть** куда́ пойти́ There is somewhere to go', Нам **бы́ло** где отдыха́ть '**There was somewhere** for us to relax', Де́тям **бу́дет** где игра́ть 'The children **will have somewhere** to play'.

Comparative adverbs

(a) Comparative adverbs are formed from adverbs in **-o** or **-e** by replacing the final vowel by **-ee**. Most comparative adverbs formed in this way are identical to short-form comparative adjectives (*see also page 57*):

Она́ е́дет **быстре́е/ме́дленнее**   She is driving **faster/more slowly**
Она́ расска́зывает **интере́снее**   She narrates **in a more**
  interesting way
Он поступи́л **пра́вильнее**   He acted **more correctly**
Она́ спроси́ла **насто́йчивее**   She asked **more insistently**
Она́ отве́тила **ве́жливее**   She answered **more politely**
Я слу́шал **внима́тельнее**   I listened **more attentively**
Он писа́л **гра́мотнее**   He wrote in a **more literate** fashion

(b) Adverbs of more than two syllables have an alternative comparative in **бо́лее** 'more', e.g. **бо́лее внима́тельно** 'more attentively'. **Бо́лее** is also used to form the comparative of adverbs in **-ически**:

Они́ воева́ли **бо́лее герои́чески**   They fought **more heroically**
Они́ пра́вят страно́й **бо́лее демократи́чески**   They run the
  country **more democratically**

(c) 'Reverse' comparatives with **ме́нее** are formed from adverbs in **-о/-е** and **-и́чески** (**ме́нее ла́сково** 'less affectionately', **ме́нее физи́чески** 'less physically').

(d) Many comparative adverbs are identical with short-form comparatives that undergo consonant mutation, and some others (*see also pages 58–59*):

Она́ говори́ла **гро́мче**   She spoke **more loudly**
Самолёт летёл **вы́ше**   The aircraft was flying **higher**
Он **ча́ще** пи́шет   He writes **more frequently**
Мы разгова́ривали **ти́ше**   We were chatting **more quietly**
Она́ пришла́ **по́зже**   She arrived **later**
Она́ рабо́тает **бо́льше**   She works **harder**
Он жа́луется **ме́ньше**   He complains **less**
Он ведёт себя́ **лу́чше/ху́же**   He behaves **better/worse**

Constructions with the comparative adverb

(a) The adverb is used with:

(i) **чем** 'than':

Он живёт **да́льше** от го́рода, **чем** я   He lives further from the town **than** I do

Она́ рассказа́ла гора́здо подро́бнее, **чем** он   She narrated in much more detail **than** he did

(ii) the genitive case:

Он пришёл **ра́ньше меня́**   He arrived earlier **than** I did

(iii) **на** + accusative (quantifying a difference):

Го́род **на пять киломе́тров** бли́же   The town is **5 kilometres** nearer

(iv) **чем ... тем** 'the ... the':

чем глу́бже, **тем** лу́чше   the deeper the better

(v) **как мо́жно** 'as .. as possible':

Он отве́тил **как мо́жно** веселе́е   He answered **as** cheerfully **as** he could

(b) Many comparatives can also be used as **predicative adverbs**:

Сего́дня **холодне́е/тепле́е**   It is **colder/warmer** today
Светле́е/ темне́е   It is **lighter/darker**
Про́ще согласи́ться   It is **simpler** to agree

The superlative adverb

The superlative adverb is formed by combining a comparative adverb with **всего́** to express a comparison with things: **Бо́льше всего́** я люблю́ шокола́д 'Most of all I like chocolate' (i.e. more than anything else), and with **всех** to express a comparison with people: Я люблю́ шокола́д **бо́льше всех** 'I like chocolate more than anyone else does'. Note also the superlative adverb with **наибо́лее**: **наибо́лее** экономи́чно 'most economically'.

The preposition

(a) A preposition is a part of speech used to express the relationship of one word to another: Ча́шка **на столе́** 'The cup is **on the table**' (spatial relationship), Он дрожа́л **от хо́лода** 'He was trembling **with the cold**' (causal relationship), Она́ **из бога́той семьи́** 'She is **from a rich family**' (relationship of source or origin), etc.

(b) The word that governs the preposition may be a verb: Она́ **забо́тится** о де́тях 'She **cares** for the children', a noun: **не́нависть** к врагу́ '**hatred** for the enemy', or an adjective: Она́ **серди́та** на меня́ 'She is **angry** with me'. The word governed by the preposition is always a noun: Она́ жила́ в **Москве́** 'She lived in **Moscow**', or a pronoun: Она́ разгова́ривала с **ним** 'She conversed with **him**'.

(c) The commonest prepositions are primary, non-derivative forms (for *government of cases*, *see page 184*): **без** 'without', **в** 'in, into', **для** 'for', **до** 'as far as, until', **за** 'behind', **из** 'out of', **к** 'towards', **на** 'on, onto', **над** 'above', **о** 'about, concerning', **от** 'from', **пе́ред** 'in front of', **по** 'along', **под** 'under', **при** 'in the presence of', **с** 'with, down from', **у** 'at', **че́рез** 'across'.

(d) Other prepositions derive:

(i) from adverbs: **близ** 'near', **вме́сто** 'instead of', **вокру́г** 'around', **ми́мо** 'past', **накану́не** 'on the eve of', **о́коло** 'close to', **про́тив** 'opposite, against', **сквозь** 'through', **согла́сно** 'according to', **среди́** 'among'.

> **Note:** Some derivatives involve primary prepositions: **вме́сте с** 'together with', **незави́симо от** 'independent of', **ря́дом с** next to'.

(ii) from nouns, combining either with *one* primary preposition: **ввиду́** 'in view of', **во вре́мя** 'during', **в тече́ние** 'in the course of', or with *two* primaries: **в связи́ с** 'in connection with', **по отноше́нию к** 'in relation to'.

> **Note:** Some prepositions derive from gerunds: **благодаря́** 'thanks to', **несмотря́ на** 'despite', **спустя́** 'after', **су́дя по** 'judging by'.

Government of cases

(a) Most prepositions take one case only. This may be:

 (i) the prepositional: **при** 'in the presence of'

 (ii) the instrumental: **между** 'between', **над** 'above', **перед** 'in front of'

 (iii) the accusative: **сквозь** 'through', **спустя** 'after', **через** 'through'

 (iv) the genitive: **без** 'without', **близ** 'near to', **ввиду** 'in view of', **вдоль** 'along(side)', **вместо** 'instead of', **во время** 'during', **вокруг** 'around', **в течение** 'during the course of', **для** 'for', **до** 'as far as', **из** 'out of', **из-за** 'from behind', **из-под** 'from under', **кроме** 'except for', **мимо** 'past', **накануне** 'on the eve of', **около** 'close to', **от** 'from', **после** 'after', **против** 'opposite, against', **среди** 'among', **у** 'at'

 (v) the dative: **благодаря** 'thanks to', **к** 'towards', **согласно** 'according to'

(b) Five prepositions take two cases (the accusative and one other):

 (i) **в** + prepositional 'in', + accusative 'into'

 (ii) **на** + prepositional 'on', + accusative 'onto'

 (iii) **о** + prepositional 'about, concerning', + accusative 'against'

 (iv) **за** + instrumental 'behind' (position), + accusative 'behind' (direction)

 (v) **под** + instrumental 'under' (position), + accusative 'under' (direction)

(c) Two prepositions take three cases each (the accusative and two others):

 (i) **по** + dative 'along', + accusative 'up to and including', + prepositional 'after'

 (ii) **с** + instrumental 'with', + genitive 'down from', + accusative 'approximately'

I Prepositions that take the prepositional case

The preposition в + prepositional case

В + prepositional case means 'in, inside' and is used:

(a) with containers: **в коро́бке** 'in the box'

(b) with most buildings, places: **в аэропорту́** 'at the airport', **в университе́те** 'at the university'

(c) with certain parts of buildings: **в ва́нной** 'in the bathroom'

(d) with certain parts of theatres: **в парте́ре** 'in the stalls'

(e) with continents: **в А́фрике** 'in Africa', **в А́зии** 'in Asia'

(f) with geographical features: **в пусты́не** 'in the desert', **в степи́** 'in the steppe', **в тайге́** 'in the taiga'

(g) with countries: **в Росси́и** 'in Russia'

(h) with mountain ranges that have plural names: **в А́льпах** 'in the Alps'

(i) with towns and cities: **в Москве́** 'in Moscow', **в Пари́же** 'in Paris'

(j) with city regions: **в Отра́дном** 'in Otradnoe'

(k) with parts of towns: **в при́городе** 'in the suburbs'

(l) with vehicles: Мы сиде́ли **в маши́не** 'We were sitting in the car', Он спал **в авто́бусе** 'He slept in the bus'

(m) with clothes, etc.: Он **в га́лстуке** 'He is wearing a tie'. Она́ **в очка́х** 'She is wearing glasses' (cf. Она́ **но́сит** очки́ 'She wears glasses')

Spatial expressions with в or на

A number of nouns combine in the prepositional case with *either* в *or* на (frequently with a different meaning; *see also page 191*):

Самолёт **в во́здухе**   The aircraft is in the air

Я сиде́л **в глубине́** за́ла   I sat at the back of the hall

Они́ игра́ют **во дворе́**   They are playing in the yard

В Се́верном мо́ре во́дится треска́   Cod is found in the North Sea

Я держу́ кни́гу **в рука́х**   I hold a book in my hands

в све́те неда́вних собы́тий   in the light of recent events

Он рабо́тает **в ша́хте**   He works down the mine

> **Note:** Ме́сто 'place' combines with certain adjectives and pronouns: в друго́м ме́сте 'somewhere else', в одно́м ме́сте 'in the same place', в краси́вом ме́сте 'in a lovely spot'.

Meanings of state or condition

The dependent noun in prepositional phrases with в can denote state, condition, position, or form:

Он **в отча́янии**   He is in despair

Всё **в поря́дке**   Everything is in order

Она́ **в ку́рсе де́ла**   She is in the picture

Маши́на полома́лась **в пути́**   The car broke down en route

Он вы́бежал **в па́нике**   He ran out in a panic

Она́ **в хоро́шем настрое́нии**   She is in a good mood

Мы бы́ли у них **в гостя́х**   We were paying them a visit

Expressions of time with в + prepositional case

The preposition **в** is used

(a) with the prepositional case of **месяц** 'month' and the names of months:

в прошлом/в этом/в будущем месяце   last/this/next month
в январе, в феврале, в марте   in January, February, March
в октябре прошлого года   last October
в ноябре этого года   this November
в декабре будущего года   next December

(b) with the prepositional case (singular and plural) of **год** 'year' and the names of particular years:

в прошлом/в этом/в будущем году   last/this/next year
Она родилась в 1986 году   She was born in 1986
в двухтысячном году   in the year 2,000
в две тысячи десятом году   in 2,010
в сороковых годах XX (двадцатого) века   in the 1940s

(c) with the prepositional case of **век/столетие** 'century' and **тысячелетие** 'millennium':

в прошлом/в этом/в будущем веке   last/this/next century
Я родился в XX (двадцатом) веке   I was born in the 20th century
Какова будет жизнь в третьем тысячелетии?   What will life be like in the third millennium?

(d) with the prepositional case of **начало** 'beginning', **середина** 'middle', **конец** 'end', of **прошлое** 'the past', **настоящее** 'the present', **будущее** 'the future', and of words denoting stages in a life:

в конце фильма   at the end of the film
в прошлом/в настоящем/в будущем   in the past/present/future
в детстве/в молодости/в старости   in childhood/youth/old age
в каком возрасте?   at what age?

(e) with intervals (**антра́кт** 'interval', **переры́в** 'break'):

В антра́кте мы е́ли моро́женое   In the interval we ate ice-cream
В переры́ве они́ обе́дали   At break they had lunch

(f) in asking 'at what time?' and in some expressions involving the time of day:

в кото́ром часу́? (= во ско́лько)?   at what time?
во второ́м часу́   just after one
в полови́не пе́рвого   at half-past twelve

Other uses of в + prepositional case

В + prepositional case is used:
(a) after words that denote accusation, confession, certainty, refusal:

Её **обвини́ли в шантаже́**   She was accused of blackmail
Он **призна́лся в уби́йстве**   He confessed to murder
Я **уве́рен в э́том**   I am sure of this
Ей **отказа́ли в ви́зе**   She was refused a visa.

(b) in phrases such as **де́ло в том, что** 'the fact is that', **беда́ в том, что** 'the trouble is that', etc.

(c) in phrases denoting extent or degree: **в како́й-то ме́ре** 'in some measure', **в вы́сшей сте́пени** 'to the highest degree'.

! **Note:** В is spelt **во** in во Владивосто́ке 'in Vladivostok', во всём 'in everything', во вся́ком слу́чае 'in any case', во вто́рник 'on Tuesday', во второ́й полови́не дня 'in the afternoon', во Вьетна́ме 'in Vietnam', во дворе́ 'in the yard', во мне 'in me', во мно́гом 'in many ways', во рту 'in the mouth', во ско́лько? 'at what time?', во фло́те 'in the navy', во Фра́нции 'in France'.

The preposition на + prepositional case

Spatial meanings

На + prepositional case means 'on, on top of, on the surface of': **на кры́ше** 'on the roof', **на полу́** 'on the floor', **на стене́** 'on the wall', **на столе́** 'on the table'.

It is also used (*see also* **в** + prepositional case, *page 185*):

(a) with the names of certain places: **на вокза́ле** 'at the station, railway terminus', **на да́че** 'at the country cottage', **на заво́де** 'at the factory', **на по́чте** 'at the post office', **на почта́мте** 'at the main post office', **на скла́де** 'at the warehouse', **на ста́нции** 'at the station', **на фа́брике** 'at the factory'

(b) with certain parts of a ship: **на корме́** 'in the stern', **на носу́** 'in the prow', **на па́лубе** 'on the deck'

(c) with certain parts of a university: **на ка́федре** хи́мии 'in the chemistry department', **на** филологи́ческом **факульте́те** 'in the faculty of philology'

(d) with certain parts of buildings (including theatres): **на крыльце́** 'in the porch', **на чердаке́** 'in the attic', **на второ́м этаже́** 'on the first floor'; **на балко́не** 'in the balcony', **на галёрке/райке́** 'in the gallery/the gods', **на я́русе** 'in the circle'

(e) with points of the compass: **на се́вере** 'in the north', **на ю́ге** 'in the south', **на восто́ке** 'in the east', **на за́паде** 'in the west', **на ю́го-восто́ке** 'in the south-east', **на се́веро-восто́ке** 'in the north-east', **на се́веро-за́паде** 'in the north-west', **на ю́го-за́паде** 'in the south-west'

(f) with the names of islands, peninsulas, archipelagoes: **на Аля́ске** 'in Alaska', **на Гава́йях** 'in Hawaii', **на Камча́тке** 'on Kamchatka', **на Кана́рах** 'in the Canaries', **на Ки́пре** 'in Cyprus', **на Ку́бе** 'in Cuba', **на Кури́лах** 'in the Kuriles', **на Ма́льте** 'in Malta'

(g) with mountain ranges that have singular names: **на Алта́е** 'in the Altai', **на Кавка́зе** 'in the Caucasus', **на Пами́ре** 'in the Pamirs', **на Ура́ле** 'in the Urals'

(h) with **Украи́на** 'Ukraine': **на Украи́не** 'in Ukraine' (в Украи́не 'in Ukraine' is also found since the country's independence)

(i) with certain city regions: **на Арба́те** 'in the Arbat'

(j) with certain parts of a town: **на окра́ине** 'on the outskirts', **на у́лице** 'in a street', **на пло́щади** 'in a square', **на ры́нке** 'at a market'

(k) with the names of sports arenas: **на ба́зе** 'at a base', **на катке́** 'at a rink', **на ко́рте** 'on a court', **на стадио́не** 'at a stadium', **на своём по́ле** 'at home' (cf. в гостя́х 'away')

(l) with the names of events: **на заседа́нии** 'at a session, meeting', **на конце́рте** 'at a concert', **на ма́тче** 'at a match', **на о́пере** 'at an opera', **на пье́се** 'at a play', **на похорона́х** 'at a funeral', **на сва́дьбе** 'at a wedding', **на собра́нии** 'at a meeting', **на уро́ке** 'at a lesson'

(m) miscellaneous: **на куро́рте** 'at a health resort', **на орби́те** 'in orbit', **на расстоя́нии** 'at a distance', **на ро́дине** 'in the homeland'

Spatial expressions with на or в + prepositional case (usually with different meanings, *see page 186*)

Я сижу́ **на све́жем во́здухе**   I sit in the fresh air
на глубине́ трёх ме́тров   at a depth of three metres
На дворе́ о́сень   It is autumn outside
Мы отдыха́ли **на Чёрном мо́ре**   We holidayed on the Black Sea
Она́ сиде́ла с Ма́шей **на рука́х**   She sat with Masha in her arms
ни за что **на све́те**   not for anything in the world
Он рабо́тает **на ша́хте**   He works at the mine

> **!** **Note:** На combines with the prepositional case of ме́сто to denote motionlessness (стоя́ть **на ме́сте** 'to stand still'), possession (Ты сиди́шь **на моём ме́сте** 'You are sitting in my place'), previous location (Маши́ны стоя́ли **на пре́жнем ме́сте** 'The cars were parked where they were before'), conduct (**на ва́шем ме́сте** 'if I were you'), priority (**На тре́тьем ме́сте** – экономи́ческие усло́вия 'In third place are economic conditions').

Other uses of на + prepositional case

На also combines with the prepositional case of nouns that denote:

(a) transport: éхать **на по́езде** (or по́ездом) 'to travel by train' (also éхать **на ли́фте** 'to take a lift', лете́ть **на самолёте** 'to go by plane', éхать **на велосипе́де** 'to go by bicycle'). Note that в is also used with 'being inside' some vehicles (**В маши́не** éхало тро́е 'There were three passengers travelling in the car'), though not with ships, thus: плыть **на парохо́де** 'to go by steamer'

(b) support: ката́ться **на конька́х** 'to skate', ходи́ть **на лы́жах** 'to ski'

(c) state, condition: Он **на пе́нсии** 'He has retired', **на ра́нней ста́дии** 'at an early stage', Он **на вое́нной слу́жбе** 'He is on military service'

(d) climatic features: сиде́ть **на со́лнце** 'to sit in the sun'

(e) language: он говори́т **на двух языка́х** 'he speaks two languages'

(f) time: **на про́шлой неде́ле** 'last week'

Verbs that take на + prepositional case

Among verbs that take на + prepositional case are игра́ть 'to play' (игра́ть **на скри́пке** 'to play the violin'), жени́ться 'to marry' (of a man: Он жени́лся **на мое́й сестре́** 'He married my sister').

The preposition о + prepositional case

О + prepositional case denotes

(a) the object of thought processes ('about, concerning, of'): ду́мать о 'to think about', напомина́ть/напо́мнить о 'to remind of', мечта́ о 'a dream of', по́мнить/вс- о 'to remember about', упомина́ть/упомяну́ть о 'to mention'

(b) the object of requests: про́сьба о деньга́х 'a request for money', призы́в о по́мощи 'an appeal for help'

(c) the object of concern: забо́та о дере́вьях 'concern for trees', забо́титься о де́тях 'to care for the children'

> **Note:** (a) the preposition о also takes the accusative case, in the meaning 'against', *see page 204*.
>
> (b) о is spelt об before words starting with а, э, и, о, у, and обо in the phrases обо всём/обо всех 'about everything/about everyone', обо мне 'about me'.

The preposition по + prepositional case

По + prepositional case combines mainly with verbal nouns in the meaning 'on, after', and is characteristic of official styles:

по оконча́нии университе́та   *on graduating*
по получе́нии ви́зы   *on receipt of the visa*
по его́ сме́рти   *on his death*
По прибы́тии в го́род он взял такси́   *On arrival in the town, he took a taxi*

> **Note:** По also takes the dative case in the meaning 'along' (*see page 213*) and the accusative in the meaning 'up to and including' (*see page 204*).

The preposition при + prepositional case

При + prepositional case has the following meanings:

(a) 'attached to (an organization)': **при университе́те** есть
поликли́ника 'there is a polyclinic attached to the university'

(b) 'in the presence of': Она́ сказа́ла э́то **при свиде́телях** 'She said
that in the presence of witnesses'; **при ла́мпе** 'by lamplight'

(c) 'during the lifetime of': **при отце́/при жи́зни отца́** 'in father's
(life)time'

(d) 'under a social/political system, a ruler': **при социали́зме**
'under socialism', **при Хрущёве** 'under Khrushchev, in
Khrushchev's time'

(e) 'proximity': **при впаде́нии** Во́лги в Ка́спий 'where the Volga
joins the Caspian'

(f) 'on, during, at' (mainly with verbal nouns and with words
denoting perception – **звук** 'sound', **вид** 'sight', **мысль** 'thought'):
при взлёте 'on, during take-off', **при ви́де** кро́ви 'at the sight of
blood', **при зву́ке** звонка́ 'at the sound of the bell', **при мы́сли** о
неуда́че 'at the thought of failure'

(g) 'at (an opportunity)': **при пе́рвой/при ка́ждой возмо́жности** 'at
the first/at every opportunity'

(h) 'in (circumstances)': **При каки́х обстоя́тельствах** его́
при́няли в институ́т? 'In what circumstances was he accepted for
the institute?'

(i) 'at (a temperature)': **при ста гра́дусах** (**при температу́ре** в сто
гра́дусов) 'at 100 degrees'

(j) 'despite': **при всём жела́нии** 'with the best will in the world'

Prepositions that take the instrumental case

The preposition за + instrumental case

За takes the instrumental case of nouns and pronouns when it means:

(a) 'behind, beyond, on the other side of': **за до́мом** 'behind the house'. Common phrases include **за́ го́родом** 'out of town, in the country', **за грани́цей** 'abroad', **за две́рью** 'outside the door', **за окно́м** 'outside the window', **за рулём** 'at the wheel', **за столо́м** 'at the table' (also **за за́втраком** 'at breakfast', **за обе́дом** 'at lunch', **за у́жином** 'at supper', **за ча́ем** 'at tea'), **за угло́м** 'round the corner'.

> **!** Note: **За́мужем** means 'married' (of a woman): Она́ за́мужем за Ива́ном 'She is married to Ivan'.

(b) 'after, in succession (in space and time)': Ученики́ повторя́ли **за мной** 'The pupils were repeating after me', **час за ча́сом** 'hour after hour'

(c) pursuit, supervision: **охо́титься за** (ти́грами) 'to hunt (to capture) tigers' (cf. охо́титься **на** ти́гров 'to hunt [to kill] tigers'), **гна́ться/по- за** 'to chase after', **сле́довать/по- за** 'to follow', **смотре́ть за** (детьми́) 'to look after (the children)'

Котёнок наблюда́ет **за кро́ликом**   The kitten is observing the rabbit

Я слежу́ **за разви́тием** собы́тий   I follow the development of events

(d) 'fetching, obtaining, for' (also figurative):

Он идёт **за водо́й**   He is going for water

Она́ зашла́ **за подру́гой**   She called for her friend

Мы стоя́ли в о́череди **за хле́бом**   We stood in a queue for bread

Он пришёл **за сове́том**   He has come for advice

Он обрати́лся к ней **за подде́ржкой**   He turned to her for support

> **!** Note: **За** also takes the accusative case, *see pages 200–201*.

The preposition мéжду + instrumental case

Мéжду + instrumental case means 'between', in both space and time: **Мéжду домáми** есть дорóга 'There is a road between the houses', **мéжду пóчтой и бáнком** 'between the post office and the bank', **мéжду нáми** 'between ourselves', **мéжду революциями** 1905 и 1917 годóв 'between the revolutions of 1905 and 1917', **мéжду зáвтраком и обéдом** 'between breakfast and lunch'.

> **!** Note: Мéжду takes the genitive plural in certain set phrases, e.g., читáть мéжду строк 'to read between the lines'.

The preposition над + instrumental case

Над + instrumental case means 'over, above': Самолёты летéли **над гóродом** 'The aircraft were flying over the town', **Над рекóй** сооружён мост 'A bridge has been constructed over the river', **над головóй** 'overhead'. It is also used in contexts of dominance, work, and mockery:

победа **над врагóм**   victory over the enemy
суд **над убийцей**   the trial of the murderer
Он рабóтает **над проéктом**   He is working on the project
Онá ломáла себé гóлову **над проблéмой**   She was racking her brains over the problem
Егó коллéги **смеялись над ним**   His colleagues laughed at him

> **!** Note: Над is spelt **нáдо** before **мной**: **нáдо мной** 'over me'.

The preposition пéред + instrumental case

(a) **Пéред** means 'in front of': **Пéред дóмом** растёт рябúна 'In front of the house grows a rowan tree' (note figurative use: **Пéред нáми** большáя задáча 'We are faced with a sizeable task').

(b) It also means 'just before' in time: **пéред едóй** 'before meals', **пéред сном** 'before going to bed', **пéред отъéздом** 'before departure'.

> **!** Note: Пéред is spelt **пéредо** before **мной**; e.g. Он извинúлся **пéредо мной** 'He apologized to me'.

The prepositional под + instrumental case

Под + instrumental case means 'under':

под де́ревом *under a tree*
Он рабо́тает **под землёй** *He is working underground*

> **!** **Note:** (a) Он идёт **под дождём** 'He is walking in the rain'.
> (b) The meaning 'proximity to a town': Она́ живёт **под Москво́й** 'She lives near Moscow'.
> (c) Figurative use: **под аре́стом** 'under arrest', быть **под угро́зой** 'to be under threat'.
> (d) **Под** is spelt **пóдо** before **мной**: **пóдо мной** 'under me'.

The preposition с + instrumental case

(a) **С** + instrumental case means 'with, together with':

Я рабо́тал там **с бра́том** *I worked there with my brother*
Она́ гуля́ет **с сы́ном** *She is strolling with her son*

> **!** **Note:** It also combines with **вме́сте** 'together': Она́ пришла́ **вме́сте с отцо́м** 'She came together with her father'.

(b) Some contexts imply joint involvement:

Он попроща́лся **с на́ми** *He said goodbye to us*
Она́ согласи́лась **со мной** *She agreed with me*

(c) **С** can also denote 'holding', 'accompanied by':

Я сиде́л **с карандашо́м** в руке́ *I sat with a pencil in my hand*
бли́нчики **с варе́ньем** *pancakes with jam*

> **!** **Note:** The instrumental case *without* a preposition (*see page 37*) is used in *functional* meanings: Я пишу́ **ру́чкой** 'I am writing with a pen'.

(d) It also denotes a concomitant feeling or feature:

Она́ чита́ла **с интере́сом** *She read with interest*
Он говори́т **с акце́нтом** *He speaks with an accent*

> **!** **Note:** **С** is spelt **со** in the phrases **со вре́менем** 'in the course of time', **со все́ми** 'with everyone', **со мной** 'with me', **со столо́м** 'with a table', etc. It also takes the accusative and genitive cases, *see pages 184, 210*.

I Prepositions that take the accusative case

The preposition в + accusative case

B + accusative case is used to denote **direction** to/into in the following contexts:

(a) the locations referred to in the section on **в** + the prepositional case (*see pages 185–186*):

Я éду **в аэропóрт**   I am driving to the airport

Он попáл **в университéт**   He got into the university

Самолёт поднялся **в вóздух**   The plane rose into the air

Ветврáч взял котёнка **в рýки**   The vet took the kitten in his hands

Позвони **в Москвý**   Ring Moscow

(b) vehicles:

Онá сéла **в автóбус**   She got into the bus

(c) states or conditions:

Он пришёл **в отчáяние**   He despaired

Онá привелá всё **в порядок**   She put everything in order

Я ввёл егó **в курс дéла**   I put him in the picture

Онá отпрáвилась **в путь**   She set off on her way

Он впал **в пáнику**   He panicked

Онá привелá меня **в хорóшее настроéние**   She put me in a good mood

Я идý к ним **в гóсти**   I am going to pay them a visit

Temporal meanings of в + accusative case

B + accusative case is used

(a) in telling the time (*see pages 94–95*);

(b) with the accusative case of **days** (**в пе́рвый день** войны́ 'on the first day of the war', **в бу́дни** 'on working **days**', **в выходны́е дни** 'on days off'), and **days of the week**:

в сре́ду, в четве́рг   on Wednesday, on Thursday
в э́ту пя́тницу, в про́шлую суббо́ту   this Friday, last Saturday
в бу́дущее воскресе́нье   next Sunday

(c) with **parts of days, when qualified by pronouns or adjectives**:

в э́то у́тро, в э́тот ве́чер   that morning, that evening
в бе́лые но́чи   on white nights

(d) with **seasons of the year, weeks, months, years, when qualified by pronouns, adjectives, or пе́рвый 'first'** (for **на** + other ordinals, *see page 203*):

в ту зи́му   that winter
в пе́рвые неде́ли о́сени   in the first weeks of autumn
в ле́тние ме́сяцы   in the summer months
в послевое́нные го́ды   in the post-war years

(e) with **general time words**:

в а́томный век   in the atomic age
Мы живём в истори́ческое вре́мя   We live in an historic time
во вре́мя уро́ка   during the lesson
в тече́ние десяти́ мину́т   in the course of ten minutes

! Note: **В тече́ние** is used with times and activities, **во вре́мя** only with activities.

(f) with **ages**:

Он жени́лся в 18 лет   He married at the age of 18

(g) to denote **recurrence**:

3.000 рубле́й в ме́сяц   3,000 roubles a month

(h) to denote **the state of the weather**:

В плохýю погóду он сидúт дóма   In bad weather he stays in

(i) to denote **the time taken to perform an action**:

Онá вы́здоровела в пять недéль   She recovered in 5 weeks

(j) in combination with **cardinal or ordinal numerals** + **раз**:

во вторóй раз   for the second time
в пять раз бóльше   five times bigger/more

Other uses of в + accusative case

В + accusative case is also used
(a) to denote the object of:

(i) **aiming, wounding, knocking**: стрелять **в цель** 'to shoot at the target', Он рáнен **в гóлову** 'He is wounded in the head', стучáть **в дверь** 'to knock at the door'
(ii) playing a game: игрáть **в футбóл** 'to play football'
(iii) belief: Онá вéрит **в Бóга** 'She believes in God'

(b) to denote '**looking through/in**': Я смотрю́ **в окнó** 'I look through the window', Я смотрю́ **в зéркало** 'I look in the mirror';

(c) to denote **reaction, purpose, representation**, etc.: **в обмéн** на квартúру 'in exchange for an apartment', **в отвéт** на письмó 'in answer to a letter', получúть браслéт **в подáрок** 'to receive a bracelet as a present', приём **в честь** делегáции 'a reception in honour of the delegation'

The preposition за + **accusative case**

За + accusative case is used to denote:

(a) **direction** to the locations referred to in the section on **за** + instrumental case (*see page 194*): Мы поéхали **зá город** 'We drove out of town' (cf. Мы живём зá городом 'We live out of town'), Он сел **за стол** 'He sat down at the table', Онú éздили **за грани́цу** 'They went abroad'.

> **!** Note: Онá вы́шла зáмуж **за Ивáна** 'She married Ivan' (cf. Онá зáмужем за Ивáном 'She is married to Ivan').

(b) **excess**:

Сегóдня морóз **за три́дцать** грáдусов   There are over thirty degrees of frost today

Бы́ло **зá полночь**   It was past midnight

Ему́ **за сóрок**   He is over forty

(c) **contact, seizure**:

Он взял её **зá руку**   He took her by the hand

Он схвати́лся **зá голову**   He clutched his head

(d) **responsibility, proxy**:

Он отвечáет **за мáльчиков**   He is responsible for the boys

Я рад **за тебя́**   I am glad for you

Онá бои́тся **за сы́на**   She is afraid for her son

(e) **the object of struggle**:

Они́ борóлись **за социали́зм**   They struggled for socialism

(f) **'tackling'**:

Он приня́лся/взя́лся **за осуществлéние плáна**   He set to work on implementing the plan

(g) **recompense and retribution**:

Она́ заплати́ла **за биле́ты**   She paid for the tickets

Меда́ль **за отва́гу**   A medal for courage

Его́ суди́ли **за кра́жу**   He was tried for theft

Спаси́бо **за ва́шу по́мощь**   Thank you for your help

Он наказа́л нас **за оши́бку**   He punished us for our mistake

Он критикова́л меня́ **за мои́ взгля́ды**   He criticized me for my
   views

(h) **temporal meanings**:

(i) **'over a period'**:

За 10 лет он то́лько два ра́за был в теа́тре   In ten years he only
   visited the theatre twice

За э́тот год он повзросле́л   Over that year he matured

including the time taken to perform an action:

Она́ реши́ла кроссво́рд **за 20 мину́т**   She did the crossword in
   20 minutes

Он написа́л запи́ску **за полчаса́**   He took half an hour to write
   the note

(ii) the time by which one event precedes another:

Он прие́хал в аэропо́рт **за час** до вы́лета   He arrived at the
   airport an hour before take-off

Он у́мер **за неде́лю** до Па́схи   He died a week before Easter

Я заказа́л биле́ты **за пять неде́ль**   I ordered the tickets five
   weeks in advance

The preposition на + accusative case

Spatial meanings of на + accusative case

In spatial terms, the preposition **на** + accusative case means 'onto' (Поста́вь таре́лку **на стол** 'Put the plate on(to) the table'), and is also used to denote direction to the locations referred to in the section on **на** + prepositional case (*see pages 189–190*):

Она́ е́дет **на вокза́л/на да́чу/на заво́д/на по́чту**   She is driving to the station/to the dacha/to the factory/to the post office

Он ле́зет **на черда́к**   He is climbing up into the attic

Он подня́лся **на шесто́й эта́ж**   He went up to the fifth floor

Она́ поступи́ла **на филфа́к/на ка́федру фи́зики**   She joined the faculty of philology/the physics department

Они́ отпра́вились **на Ку́бу/на Ура́л**   They set off for Cuba/for the Urals

Она́ вы́шла **на у́лицу**   She came out onto the street

Я подвёз сестру́ **на Арба́т**   I gave my sister a lift to the Arbat

Directional meanings involving boarding transport, state, language, etc. (for equivalents with на + prepositional case, *see page 191*)

Они́ се́ли **на самолёт**   They boarded the plane

Он поступи́л **на вое́нную слу́жбу**   He joined up

Она́ ушла́ **на пе́нсию**   She retired

Она́ перевела́ рома́н **на ру́сский язы́к**   She translated the novel into Russian

> **!** **Note:** Other constructions of a semi-directional nature include зака́з **на (пла́тье)** 'an order for (a dress)', охо́титься **на (медве́дя)** 'to hunt (a bear)', жа́ловаться/по- **на** 'to complain of', производи́ть/произвести́ впечатле́ние **на** 'to make an impression on', обраща́ть/обрати́ть внима́ние **на** 'to pay attention to', влия́ть/по- **на** 'to influence', мо́да **на (америка́низмы)** 'fashion for (Americanisms)', о́чередь **на (кварти́ру)** 'a waiting list for (an apartment)'.

Temporal expressions with на + accusative case

The preposition **на** appears in the phrase **на слéдующий день** 'the next day' and in phrases that combine a time word with ordinals (apart from пéрвый 'first', *see page 198*): **на трéтий год** 'in the third year', and also denotes:

(a) festivals: **на Пáсху** 'at Easter', **на Рождествó** 'at Christmas'

(b) scheduling for a particular time: Собрáние назнáчено **на срéду** 'The meeting is scheduled for Wednesday'

(c) a time subsequent to the completion of an action: Он вы́шел **на пять минýт** He has gone out for 5 minutes

Meanings of extent

Он **на три гóда** стáрше меня́   He is 3 years older than me

Населéние увеличилось **на миллиóн**   The population has increased by a million

Он прóсит мáрок **на 70 рублéй**   He asks for 70 roubles' worth of stamps

Часы́ спешáт **на семь минýт**   The watch is 7 minutes fast

Он сдал экзáмены **на пятёрки**   He passed the exams with top marks

На + accusative case can also denote (a) projection over distance: бег **на 5.000 мéтров** 'a 5,000-metre race'; (b) the object of feelings such as anger: Онá зла **на меня́** 'She is angry with me'; (c) direction to an event or activity: Он вы́бежал **на тренирóвку** 'He ran out to the training session'; (d) expenditure: трáтить дéньги **на пустяки** 'to spend money on trifles'; (e) authorization: рецéпт **на таблéтки** 'a prescription for tablets'; (f) entitlement: прáво **на óтдых** 'the right to relaxation'; (g) similarity: Он похóж **на отцá** 'He is like his father'; (h) exchange: обмéн фýнтов стéрлингов **на рубли** 'exchange of pounds sterling for roubles'; (i) reaction: реáкция **на температýру** 'reaction to the temperature'.

The preposition о + accusative case

The preposition о + accusative case denotes collision, friction, contact:

Он ударился ногой **о стул**   He banged his leg on a chair
Она споткнулась **о камень**   She tripped over a stone
Она облокотилась **о перила**   She leant against the railings

It also takes the prepositional case, *see page 192*.

The preposition по + accusative case

(a) The preposition **по** + accusative case denotes 'up to and including' (i) in space (вода **по щиколотку** 'water up to the ankles') (ii) in time (**по сентябрь** 'up to and including September') (iii) figuratively (занят **по горло** 'up to one's eyes in work').

(b) It is also used in distributive meaning with numerals above 'one': Мы выпили **по две чашки/по пять чашек** 'We drank two cups/ five cups each (for the distributive dative with 'one', *see page 213*). It is also used with сторона 'side': **по ту сторону** 'on the other side'.

По also takes the dative and prepositional cases, *see pages 213, 192*.

The preposition под + accusative case

(a) The preposition **под** + accusative case is used to denote direction to the locations and states referred to in the section on **под** + instrumental case (*see page 196*):

Мы сели **под дерево**   We sat down under a tree
Я попал **под дождь**   I got caught in the rain
ставить **под угрозу**   to place under threat

(b) It can also denote (i) accompaniment': Они танцуют **под оркестр** 'They are dancing to an orchestra' (ii) towards a certain time: Он вернулся **под вечер** 'He returned towards evening', Она встала **под утро** 'She got up in the early hours', **под Новый год** 'on New Year's Eve'.

The preposition **сквозь** + **accusative case**

Сквозь means 'through' (involving difficulty of passage):

Он пробира́лся **сквозь толпу́**   He was making his way through the crowd

Он смотре́л **сквозь щель**   He was peering through a crack

The preposition **спустя́** + **accusative case**

Спустя́ means 'after' (with time words):

Он прие́хал **спустя́ неде́лю** (ог **неде́лю спустя́**)   He arrived a week later

The preposition **че́рез** + **accusative case**

Че́рез means:

(a) 'across, over, via' in spatial contexts:

Он перебежа́л **че́рез доро́гу**/перепры́гнул **че́рез забо́р**   He ran across the road/jumped over the fence

Мы е́хали **че́рез Хе́льсинки**   We travelled via Helsinki

мост **че́рез ре́ку**   a bridge across a river

(b) 'further on': **че́рез пять киломе́тров** 'five kilometres further on', 'through (a medium)':

Мы говори́ли **че́рез перево́дчика**   We spoke through an interpreter

and can denote intervals: .

печа́тать **че́рез два интерва́ла**   to type double spacing

(c) 'in, later, at intervals' with time words:

Он верну́лся **че́рез пять мину́т**   He returned five minutes later

Он вернётся **че́рез пять мину́т**   He will return in five minutes

че́рез ка́ждые три часа́   every three hours

I Prepositions that take the genitive case

Без 'without, in the absence of': **без биле́та** 'without a ticket', **скуча́ть без дру́га** 'to miss one's friend'.

Близ 'near': **близ до́ма** 'near the house'.

Вме́сто 'instead of': **вме́сто отве́та** 'instead of an answer'.

Вокру́г 'around, in connection with': **вокру́г фонта́на** 'around the fountain', **вокру́г э́той те́мы** 'in connection with this subject'.

Для denotes

(a) 'meant for': Э́тот пода́рок **для тебя́** 'This gift is for you'

(b) relationship: Э́то поле́зно/вре́дно **для здоро́вья** 'This is good/bad for the health'

(c) comparative meanings: Тепло́ **для ноября́** 'It's warm for November'.

The preposition до + genitive case

До + genitive case denotes

(a) 'to, up to' a point in space or time:

> Отсю́да **до забо́ра** три ме́тра   It is 3 metres from here to the fence
>
> с понеде́льника **до среды́**   from Monday to Wednesday

(b) 'before' or 'until':

> **до перестро́йки**   before perestroika
>
> Она́ отложи́ла всё **до ве́чера**   She postponed everything until evening

(c) 'as far as':

> Он дое́хал **до угла́**   He drove as far as the corner

(d) 'to' in some phrases of extent:

> Она́ промо́кла **до косте́й**   She got soaked to the skin
>
> довести́ **до слёз**   to reduce to tears

The preposition из + genitive case

Из + genitive case denotes:

(a) emergence or withdrawal from the types of location and state referred to in the section on **в** + prepositional case, *see pages 185–186*:

> Он верну́лся **из го́рода/из о́тпуска/из госте́й** He returned from the town/from holiday/from a visit

(b) composition, source, and selection from a larger number:

> Рома́н состои́т **из двух часте́й** The novel consists of two parts
> у́жин **из пяти́ блюд** a five-course dinner
> Они́ постро́или дом **из ка́мня** They built the house of stone
> Он оди́н **из мои́х лу́чших друзе́й** He is one of my best friends
> Он стреля́ет **из ружья́** He fires a shot-gun

(c) the feeling that motivates an action:

> Он солга́л **из стра́ха** He lied out of fear
> Она́ отказа́лась **из упря́мства** She refused out of stubbornness

The preposition из-за + genitive case

Из-за + genitive case denotes

(a) withdrawal from the types of location referred to in the section on **за** + instrumental, *see page 194*:

> Он встал **из-за стола́** He got up from the table
> Она́ верну́лась **из-за грани́цы** She returned from abroad
> **Из-за угла́** вы́шел мой друг My friend came round the corner

(b) the cause of an undesirable consequence:

> По́езд опозда́л **из-за тума́на** The train was late because of the fog

The preposition из-под + genitive case

Из-под + genitive case denotes

(a) 'from under', withdrawal from the types of location referred to in the section on **под** + instrumental, *see page 196*:

Ребёнок вы́полз **из-под стола́**   The child crawled out from under the table

(b) the former content of a container:

ба́нка **из-под варе́нья**   a jam-jar

Ми́мо + genitive case means 'past':

Он прошёл **ми́мо до́ма**   He walked past the house

Накану́не + genitive case means 'on the eve of':

накану́не пра́здника   on the eve of the festival

The preposition о́коло + genitive case

Óколо + genitive case means:

(a) 'close to, near':

Он жил **о́коло по́чты**   He lived close to the post office

(b) 'about, approximately':

Биле́т сто́ит **о́коло сорока́ рубле́й**   The ticket costs about 40 roubles

Он лёг **о́коло полу́ночи**   He went to bed at about midnight

Я ве́шу **о́коло восьми́десяти килогра́ммов**   I weigh about 80 kilograms

The preposition от + genitive case

От + genitive case denotes:

(a) withdrawal from the types of location referred to in the section on **у** + genitive case, *see page 211*:

Я отошёл **от окна**   I moved away from the window

(b) the initial point of a distance between two points:

От стола до стены 4 метра   It is 4 metres from the table to the wall

(c) from/away from a person:

Я получил пакет **от Ильи**   I received a package from Ilya
Она ушла **от мужа**   She left her husband

(d) physical cause or the cause of an involuntary reaction:

Он умер **от рака**   He died of cancer
Он дрожит **от страха**   He trembles with fear

(e) the object of defence:

защищать **от холода**   to protect against the cold
лекарство **от кашля**   cough medicine

The preposition против + genitive case

Против + genitive case means

(a) 'opposite':

Он сел **против гостя**   He sat down opposite his guest

(b) 'against':

плыть **против течения**   to swim against the current

The preposition с + genitive case

С + genitive case means:

(a) 'from/off/from on top of/from the surface of':

Он снял ка́рту **со стены́**   He took the map off the wall
Он встал **со сту́ла**   He got up from the chair

(b) withdrawal from the locations referred to in the section on на + prepositional case, *see pages 189–190*:

Они́ верну́лись **с заво́да**   They returned from the factory
Мы е́хали **с восто́ка на за́пад**   We travelled from east to west
Она́ прилете́ла **с Ки́пра**   She has flown in from Cyprus
Я возвраща́лся **с уро́ка**   I was returning from the lesson

> **❗ Note:** с горы́ 'downhill', переводи́ть с ру́сского на по́льский 'to translate from Russian into Polish'.

(c) 'since' (a point in past time), 'from' (a point in present or future time'), 'from ... (to)' :

Он здесь **с про́шлого го́да**   He has been here since last year
с ча́су до двух   from one (o'clock) to two
начина́я **с понеде́льника**   with effect from Monday

С also takes the accusative and instrumental cases, *see pages 184, 196*.

The preposition среди́ + genitive case

Среди́ + genitive case means

(a) 'in the middle of':

среди́ ле́са/толпы́/но́чи   in the middle of the forest/the crowd/ the night

(b) 'among':

пе́рвый **среди́ ра́вных**   the first among equals

The preposition у + genitive case

У + genitive case denotes:

(a) 'at, close by' an object or place:

Он стоя́л **у окна́/у две́ри/у стола́**   He stood at the window/at the door/by the table

Мы отдыха́ли **у мо́ря**   We holidayed by the sea

(b) 'at/at someone's place':

Он был **у врача́**   He was at the doctor's

Я отдыха́л **у бра́та на да́че**   I relaxed at my brother's dacha

Он живёт **у роди́телей**   He lives at his parents' house

(c) possession:

У неё была́ маши́на/**не́** было маши́ны   She had/didn't have a car

У него́ хоро́ший вкус   He has good taste

(d) the person from whom something is borrowed, learnt, requested, bought, etc.:

Он занима́ет **у меня́** де́ньги   He borrows money from me

Я беру́ **у него́** уро́ки му́зыки   I take music lessons from him

Она́ попроси́ла **у меня́** каранда́ш   She asked me for a pencil

Я спроси́л доро́гу **у милиционе́ра**   I asked a policeman the way

У них мо́жно мно́гому научи́ться   One can learn a lot from them

Я узна́л об э́том **у свое́й сестры́**   I heard about it from my sister

Я купи́л дом **у дру́га**   I bought a house from my friend

(e) a person experiencing some event, emotion, condition:

У Ма́ши родила́сь дочь   Masha gave birth to a daughter

У меня́ боли́т голова́   I have a headache

Prepositions that take the dative case

The preposition к + dative case

К + dative case denotes:

(a) 'towards' an object:

Она побежала **к машине**   She ran towards the car

(b) contact, connection, addition:

Он прислонился **к забору**   He leant against the fence
Она пришила пуговицу **к рубашке**   She sewed a button onto the shirt
к трём прибавить два   add three and two

(c) 'to/to see' a person:

Она ходила **к врачу**   She went to see the doctor

(d) attitude to someone or something:

интерес **к истории**   interest in history
Она относится **ко мне** иначе   She treats me differently
Он способен **к музыке**   He is good at music

(d) goal:

Я готов **к отъезду**   I am ready for departure
стремиться **к счастью**   to strive for happiness
переход **к рыночной экономике**   transition to a market economy

(e) emotional reaction:

к счастью   fortunately
к сожалению   unfortunately
к нашему удивлению   to our surprise

(f) 'by' in time:

к вечеру   by evening
к тому времени   by then

The preposition по + dative case

По + dative case denotes:

(a) 'over the surface of, along, up, down', etc.:

Он бежáл **по бéрегу**   He was running along the shore

Он спускáлся **по лéстнице**   He was coming down the stairs

Нас вози́ли **по всей Индии**   They drove us all over India

(b) a number of destinations:

Я ходи́л **по магази́нам**   I went shopping

(c) 'along lines of communication':

**по рáдио/по телеви́зору/по пóчте/по фáксу/по телефóну/по
моб**и́**льнику/по электрóнной пóчте**   on the radio/on
television/by mail/by fax/by phone/on a mobile/by email

(d) 'in accordance with':

по плáну   according to plan

(e) recurrent points in time:

по утрáм/по вечерáм/по ночáм/по четвергáм   in the mornings/
in the evenings/nights/on Thursdays

(f) distributive meanings (singular dependent nouns only):

Дéвочки получи́ли **по я́блоку**   The girls received an apple each

(g) criteria for judgement:

Он сýдит о погóде **по облакáм**   He judges the weather by the
clouds

(h) the sphere of activity to which the dominant word relates:

чемпиóн **по тéннису**   tennis champion

(i) order of priority:

трéтья **по длинé** рекá   the third longest river

(j) cause:

по рáзным причи́нам   for various reasons

По also takes the accusative and prepositional cases, *see pages
204, 192.*

The conjunction

A conjunction is a part of speech that links words, phrases, or clauses. Conjunctions subdivide into:

(a) **Co-ordinating** conjunctions. These include **и** 'and', **но** 'but', **тóже/ тáкже** 'also', **или** 'or', **однáко** 'however', etc. They are used to join words, phrases, and clauses of equal status: молодóй **и** энергичный 'young and energetic', Он хотéл помóчь, **но** не мог 'He wanted to help, but couldn't'.

(b) **Correlative** conjunctions, which constitute pairs of the same conjunction; **и ... , и** 'both ... and', **или ... , или** 'either ... or', **ни ... , ни** 'neither ... nor'.

(c) **Subordinating** conjunctions. These include **что** 'that' (explanatory conjunction), **чтóбы** 'in order to' (conjunction of purpose'), **потомý что** 'because' (causal conjunction), **пóсле тогó**(,)**, как** 'after', **прéжде** (,)**чем** 'before' (conjunctions of time), **éсли** 'if' (conditional conjunction), **хотя** 'although' (concessive conjunction), **как** 'as', **как бýдто** 'as if' (comparative conjunctions). Subordinating conjunctions are used to link main clauses with subordinate clauses: Он встал, **чтóбы** закрыть окнó 'He got up to shut the window'.

Co-ordinating conjunctions

The conjunction и

(a) The conjunction **и** 'and' is used to link like parts of speech (e.g. two verbs, two adjectives, two adverbs):

Дéти **бéгают и прыгают**	The children run and jump
Он **молодóй и сильный**	He is young and strong
Самолёт летéл **быстро и высокó**	The aircraft flew fast and high

(b) It also links compatible phrases. A comma precedes **и** if the subjects of the two clauses are different:

Идёт дождь, **и** я сижу дома   It is raining, and I am staying in

The conjunction **a**

The conjunction **a** 'and, but':

(a) makes a statement via a negative:

Это не дом, **а** дача   That is not a house, but a dacha
Сегодня не холодно, **а** тепло   Today it is not cold, but warm
Он не пишет, **а** читает   He is not writing, but reading

(b) links clauses that contrast without conflicting (the same parts of speech usually appear on either side of the conjunction):

Он читает, **а** она пишет   He is reading and she is writing
Собака белая, **а** кошка чёрная   The dog is white and the cat is black
Он ездит быстро, **а** она ездит медленно   He drives fast and she drives slowly

(c) in dialogue, often appears at the beginning of a sentence

– Пойдём в кино!   'Let's go to the cinema!'
– **А** у тебя есть билеты?   'And have you got tickets?'

(d) combines with **также** 'also', in conveying supplementary information (in the meaning кроме того 'apart from that'):

Он изучает немецкий, **а также** испанский   He is learning German, and also Spanish

! **Note: Тоже** 'also' is, by contrast, used to identify with the subject of a sentence, someone already referred to: – Он изучает немецкий 'He is learning German' – Я тоже 'So am I'.

The conjunction но

The conjunction **но** 'but' introduces a note of antithesis or illogicality, often linking clauses that express incompatible ideas:

Он мо́лод, **но** о́пытен   He is young but experienced

> **Note:** The meaning of **но** is often close to that of **одна́ко** 'however' and **зато́** 'on the other hand': Я тебе́ писа́л, **одна́ко** ты не отве́тил 'I wrote to you, but you didn't reply', Он опозда́л, **зато́** принёс хоро́шие но́вости 'He was late, but brought good news to make up for it'.

The conjunction и́ли

The conjunction **и́ли** 'or' offers alternatives:

Хо́чешь чай **и́ли** ко́фе?   Do you want tea or coffee?

I Correlative conjunctions

(a) The conjunction **и ... , и** 'both ... and' is more emphatic than **и**:

Она́ спосо́бна **и к хи́мии, и к фи́зике**   She is good both at chemistry and physics

(b) The conjunction **ни ... , ни** means 'neither ... nor' and combines with не, нет, or нельзя́:

Она́ **не** уме́ет **ни** петь, **ни** танцева́ть   She can neither sing nor dance

У него́ **нет ни** друзе́й, **ни** колле́г   He has neither friends nor colleagues

Здесь **нельзя́ ни** есть, **ни** пить   Here you can neither eat nor drink

(c) The conjunction **и́ли ... , и́ли** (ли́бо ... ли́бо) means 'either ... or':

И́ли я зайду́, **и́ли** позвоню́   I'll either drop by or I'll ring

I Subordinating conjunctions

The explanatory conjunction что

The conjunction **что** 'that' is used with the verbs знать 'to know', сказа́ть 'to say', ду́мать 'to think', and some other words:

Я знал, **что** он помо́жет   I knew he would help

Она́ сказа́ла, **что** она́ гото́ва   She said she was ready

Мы ду́мали, **что** он заболе́л   We thought he had fallen ill

! **Note:** (a) the retention in reported speech of the tense used in direct speech.
(b) the frequent omission in English of the conjunction 'that' (but *not* of **что** in Russian).
(c) **бу́дто** or **бу́дто бы** may be used instead of **что** to express an element of doubt or uncertainty: Он говори́т, **бу́дто (бы)** ничего́ не знал 'He alleges that he knew nothing'.

The conjunction of purpose чтобы

The conjunction **что́бы** + past tense is used

(a) after words that denote desire, request, necessity, demand, etc.:

Я хочу́, **что́бы** он ушёл   I want him to go away

Он попроси́л, **что́бы** ему́ принесли́ меню́   He asked to be brought the menu

Необходи́мо, **что́бы** все молча́ли   It is essential for everyone to be silent

(b) to denote the purpose of an action:

Он дал мне бу́лку, **что́бы** я не голода́л   He gave me a roll, so that I shouldn't starve

Он купи́л компа́кт-диск-прои́грыватель, **что́бы** все слу́шали му́зыку   He bought a CD-player, so that everyone could listen to music

! **Note:** If the subject of the two clauses is the same, the infinitive is used: Она́ вста́ла, что́бы **встре́тить** гостей 'She got up to welcome the guests'.

Conjunctions of cause

(a) The commonest of the causal conjunctions is **потому́ что**
'because':

Он оде́лся потепле́е, **потому́ что** то́лько что вы́пал снег   He
  dressed more warmly because it had just snowed

The main clause usually precedes the **потому́ что** clause. Other
conjunctions of cause either precede or follow the main clause:
благодаря́ тому́(,) **что** 'thanks to' (implying a favourable
consequence), **из-за того́**(,) **что** 'because of' (implying an
unfavourable consequence'), and **оттого́**(,) **что** 'through'
(implying an unintended consequence):

Она́ сдала́ экза́мен, **благодаря́ тому́ что** повтори́ла
  про́йденное   She passed the exam thanks to having revised
  the course work
Из-за того́ что он пло́хо подгото́вился, он провали́лся на
  экза́мене   Through preparing badly, he failed the examination
Я простуди́лся, **оттого́ что** выходи́л без пальто́   I caught a
  cold by going out without a coat

(b) The conjunction **так как** 'since' can follow or precede the
main clause:

Он снял пальто́, **так как** ему́ бы́ло жа́рко   He took off his
  coat, since he was hot
Так как ему́ бы́ло жа́рко, он снял пальто́   Since he was hot,
  he took off his coat

Conjunctions of time

(a) Many conjunctions of time can combine with a 'logical' *future* tense, unlike their English counterparts: когда́ он **придёт** 'when he arrives', как то́лько он **начнёт** 'as soon as he begins', пре́жде чем вы **умо́етесь** 'before you wash', etc. (*see also* 129).

(b) The conjunction **когда́** 'when, while' combines with a verb in the imperfective aspect to denote a habitual action or an action in progress, and with a verb in the perfective aspect to denote a completed action. **Как то́лько** 'as soon as' and **по́сле того́ (,) как** 'after' are also used in the context of a completed action:

Когда́ мы слу́шали (impf.) ра́дио, пришли́ на́ши друзья́
While we were listening to the radio our friends arrived

Когда́ зако́нчилась (pf.) переда́ча, я вы́ключил телеви́зор
When the programme finished I switched off the television

Как то́лько он прочита́л (pf.) письмо́, он разорва́л его́   As soon as he had read the letter he tore it up

По́сле того́ как он накача́л (pf.) ши́ны, мы пое́хали да́льше
After he had pumped up the tyres we drove on

(c) Other conjunctions of time include **пре́жде (,) чем** 'before', **пока́** 'while', **пока́ не** 'until', **с тех пор(,) как** 'since':

Пре́жде чем она́ перевела́ фра́зу, она́ спра́вилась в словаре́

Before she translated the phrase she consulted the dictionary

Пока́ шёл дождь, я сиде́л до́ма   While it was raining I stayed in

Я подожду́, **пока́ он не** придёт   I will wait until he comes

С тех пор как он прие́хал, он всё вре́мя жа́луется на пого́ду

He has been complaining about the weather ever since he arrived

> **Note:** (i) **До того́(,) как** 'before' can replace **пре́жде (,)чем**.
> (ii) **Пе́ред тем как** means 'just before'.
> (iii) **Пре́жде(,) чем** can be followed by the infinitive if the subject of both clauses is the same (**Пре́жде чем** перевести́ ... 'Before translating ...').

The conditional conjunction **éсли**

(a) The conjunction **éсли** 'if' is used with finite verbs in any tense (past, present, future) when applied to real situations:

Éсли ты вы́учил уро́ки, мо́жешь смотре́ть телеви́зор   If you have done your homework you can watch TV

(b) Unlike English 'if', **éсли** can take a 'logical' future:

Éсли он забу́дет, я напо́мню ему́   'If he forgets I'll remind him'

(c) The infinitive may be used when there is no grammatical subject:

Éсли вы́ключить свет, мо́жно показа́ть фильм   If the light is turned off the film can be shown

(d) **Éсли бы** + past tense is used where an action is possible only if certain (currently non-existent) conditions are met:

Éсли бы у меня́ была́ иго́лка, я приши́л бы пу́говицу   If I had a needle I would sew on the button

! Note: (i) 'if' is rendered as **ли** (never **éсли**) in an indirect question: Я не зна́ю, пойду́ **ли** я 'I don't know if I'll go'.
(ii) for further information on conditional constructions with **éсли**, *see page 134.*

Concessive conjunctions

Concessive conjunctions (e.g. **хотя́** 'although', **несмотря́ на то**(,) **что** 'despite the fact that') express incongruity, describe situations that run counter to existing circumstances:

Он вас при́мет, **хотя́** он о́чень за́нят   He will see you, although he is very busy

Они́ пошли́, **несмотря́ на то что** шёл дождь   They set out despite the fact that it was raining

The conjunctions как and как бу́дто (бы)

(a) The conjunction **как** is used with comparative meaning:

бе́лый, **как** снег   as white as snow

Ва́ше се́рдце рабо́тает, **как** часы́   Your heart is running like clockwork

(b) **Как** also means 'as, in the capacity of':

Я говорю́ с тобо́й **как** друг   I speak to you as a friend

(c) It is also used with verbs of perception, and introduces clauses:

Я слы́шу, **как** она́ поёт   I hear her singing

Я слу́шаю, **как** игра́ет орке́стр   I listen to an orchestra playing

Мы смо́трим, **как** он рабо́тает   We watch him working

(d) **Как бу́дто (бы)** may imply variance with reality:

Он сиди́т с закры́тыми глаза́ми, **как бу́дто (бы)** спит   He sits with his eyes closed, as if he were asleep

Word order

I Word order in Russian and English

(1) Russian word order is quite often the same as English:

Ива́н стра́стно люби́л кни́ги   Ivan passionately loved books
Я хоте́л написа́ть ему́ письмо́   I wanted to write him a letter
Он защити́л диссерта́цию   He defended his dissertation

(2) In many cases, however, word order *differs* in the two languages:

Вчера́ в Москве́ откры́лась вы́ставка совреме́нного
иску́сства   An exhibition of modern art opened in Moscow
yesterday

What factors determine this contrast?

'New' and 'given' information in Russian sentences

(a) The most important feature of Russian word order is that the
most essential information, the 'new' information, the reason
why a statement is being made at all, appears *at or near the end
of the sentence*, while 'given' information (information that is
already known) appears at or near the beginning. English, by
contrast, tends to maintain the order: subject + verb + object *or*
circumstantial detail.

(b) Sometimes the two principles of word order coincide, in
which case both languages adopt the same word order. This
happens in the first three sentences quoted above. In each of them
the essential, 'new', information, appears at the end of the
sentence ('loved books', 'to write him a letter', 'defended his
dissertation').

(c) In the fourth sentence above, however, the exhibition of
modern art (вы́ставка совреме́нного иску́сства) is the essential
'new' information, the reason why the statement is being made in
the first place, and thus it appears in final position. The English
equivalent adheres to the pattern: subject + verb +
circumstantial detail.

What is 'given' information?

(a) 'Given' information is information that is known (or presumed to be known) to the reader or speaker, or information that has already been referred to, or that is incidental to the event being described and less essential than the event itself. 'Given' information is never the point of the utterance. Thus, the sentence:

Де́вочка **загора́ет на со́лнце**   The girl is sun-bathing

implies that the girl ('given' information) has already been mentioned, or that she is known to the speaker or to the speaker and addressee. The 'new' information (that she is sun-bathing), the reason why the statement is being made, appears in final position.

(b) Adverbs or adverbial expressions of time or space are another type of 'given' information. These are usually of secondary importance to the event itself, which counts as 'new' information and appears in final position:

Сего́дня по пе́рвой програ́мме **бу́дет передава́ться конце́рт**
    A concert will be televised on channel one today

4 октября́ 1957 го́да **был запу́щен пе́рвый иску́сственный спу́тник Земли́**   On 4 October 1957 the first artificial Earth satellite was launched

(However, in answering a different question: 'When was the first earth satellite launched', the date would be 'new' information [since it is the reason why the question is being asked], and would appear in final position: Пе́рвый иску́сственный спу́тник Земли́ был запу́щен 4 октября́ 1957 го́да. For other examples of adverbs or adverbial modifiers in final position, *see pages 227, 228*.)

In the rest of this chapter the 'new' information will appear in **bold** print, the 'given' information in regular print.

Two differences between Russian and English

(a) Russian is a highly inflected language. One effect of this is that wherever an inflected form appears in a sentence, its ending will convey its grammatical function. As a consequence of this, word order can be much freer in Russian than in English (where only strict word sequence can ensure understanding). Thus, the Russian sentence:

Óльга **поцелова́ла малю́тку**   *Olga kissed the baby*

which answers the question Что сде́лала Óльга? 'What did Olga do?', has the same meaning (but with a different emphasis) as:

Малю́тку поцелова́ла **Óльга**   *It was Olga who kissed the baby*

which answers the question Кто поцелова́л малю́тку? 'Who kissed the baby?' In either case, differing word order notwithstanding, the noun endings show that Óльга 'Olga' is in the nominative case and is the agent of the action and that малю́тку is in the accusative case (of малю́тка 'baby') and the object of the action.

(b) Russian has neither a definite nor an indefinite article. Thus, маши́на means 'a car' or 'the car'. In English, 'a car' implies that the vehicle is being referred to for the first time, while 'the car' implies that it has already been mentioned. Russian renders this distinction by word order. Thus, in:

Пе́ред до́мом стои́т **маши́на**   *A car is parked in front of the house*

маши́на 'a car', as 'new' information, appears in final position, while in:

Маши́на стои́т **пе́ред до́мом**   *The car is parked in front of the house*

маши́на 'the car', as 'given' information, appears at the beginning of the sentence. 'In front of the house' is 'new' information (since the purpose of the statement is to say *where* the car is parked), and therefore appears in final position.

Statements as answers to hypothetical questions

(a) The relationship between 'given' information (which comes at or near the beginning of the sentence) and 'new' information (which comes at or near the end of the sentence) can be clarified by considering utterances as answers to questions.

(b) Thus, the answer to the question Что идёт в Ма́лом теа́тре? 'What is on at the Maly Theatre?' might be:

В Ма́лом теа́тре идёт пье́са <<Бу́ря>>   "The Tempest" is on at
    the Maly Theatre

where Ма́лый теа́тр is 'given' information and appears first, and <<Бу́ря>> is 'new' information and appears in final position.

(c) If, however, the questioner knows that "The Tempest" is on at a local theatre, but is not sure at which one (and so asks Где идёт пье́са <<Бу́ря>>? 'Where is "The Tempest" on?'), then "The Tempest" is 'given' information and appears at the beginning of the sentence, while 'The Maly Theatre' is 'new' information and appears in final position:

Пье́са <<Бу́ря>> идёт **в Ма́лом теа́тре**   "The Tempest" is on at
    the Maly Theatre

(d) Similarly, the statement:

На ка́федре храня́тся **архи́вы**   Archives are kept in the
    department

answers the question: Что храни́тся на ка́федре? 'What is kept in the department?', while:

Архи́вы храня́тся **на ка́федре**   The archives are kept in the
    department

answers the question Где храня́тся архи́вы? 'Where are the archives kept?'

The role of context

Word order is often determined by context, for example:

Опера́ция прошла́ успе́шно. Опери́ровал **профе́ссор Ильи́н**
The operation was successful. **Professor Il'in** was operating

Here, опери́ровал 'was operating' is 'given' information (since the operation has been mentioned in the first sentence), and Professor Il'in is 'new' information and therefore in final position. Similarly:

Вы смотре́ли <<Алекса́ндра Не́вского>>? Му́зыку к фи́льму написа́л **Серге́й Проко́фьев**   Have you seen "Alexander Nevsky"? Sergei Prokofiev composed the music to the film

Here, Му́зыку к фи́льму is 'given' information (since the film has already been mentioned), and thus appears at the beginning of the sentence, while Серге́й Проко́фьев is new information (since the point of the statement is to say *who* composed the music), and appears in final position.

Adverbial modifiers of time and place as given information

(a) Where adverbial modifiers of time and place are of less importance to the speaker than the event being described, they constitute background information and precede both the verb and 'new' information, which appears in final position (*see also pages 222–225, 228*):

В лесу́ разда́лся **вы́стрел**   In the forest a shot rang out
На са́ммите реша́лись **ва́жные вопро́сы**   Important issues were being resolved at the summit
Вчера́ начался́ **конгре́сс**   A congress began yesterday
Наконе́ц наступи́ла **весна́**   At last spring came

(b) An adverbial modifier of time precedes one of place:

За́втра в Ки́еве откро́ется **вы́ставка**   An exhibition will open in Kiev tomorrow

Adverbial modifiers of manner

These usually appear before the verb (however, *see pages 223–225, 228* for examples where they follow the verb, as 'new' information):

Он **быстро** переоде́лся   *He changed quickly*
Она́ **хорошо́** говори́т по-ру́сски   *She speaks Russian well*

The order verb + subject

(a) The word order verb + subject occurs in contexts where the components are so inseparably linked that the whole sentence is 'new'. This occurs in sentences consisting only of two elements (relating to the weather, occurrences, states or processes, existence, non-existence, beginning, concluding, etc.):

Шёл снег   *It was snowing*
Произошёл несча́стный слу́чай   *An accident occurred*
Идёт уро́к   *A lesson is in progress*
Игра́л орке́стр   *An orchestra was playing*
Быту́ет мне́ние   *An opinion is current*
Зако́нчилась война́   *The war ended*
Начина́ется уче́бный год   *The academic year begins*

(b) However, the principle whereby 'given' precedes 'new' information overrides other considerations. For example, the answer to the question: Когда́ начина́ется уче́бный год? 'When does the academic year begin?' would be Уче́бный год ['given' information] начина́ется **1 сентября́** ['new' information, since the *date* is the point of asking the question] 'The academic year begins on 1 September'.

! **Note:** the order verb + subject may also appear in questions introduced by an interrogative (*see also page 229*): Куда́ идёт э́тот авто́бус? *Where is this bus going to?*

Word-order variants in simple sentences

(1) Word order as in English

(a) The performer of the action is the only 'given' information; all else is 'new'. The word order is **subject** + **verb** + **object**:

Мой брат **читáет ромáн**   My brother is reading a novel

(b) The action or state is 'given' information. The place, cause, time, etc. of the action or state are 'new' information. The word order is **subject** + **verb** + **adverb**:

Это случи́лось **рáнней весно́й**   It happened in early spring

(2) Word order differs from English

(a) The action or state is known ['given' information]. The performer is 'new' information. The word order is **object** + **verb** + **subject**:

Фотогрáфии сдéлал **я**   It was I who took the photographs

(b) The place/time of an event are 'given' information. The event itself is 'new' information. Word order is **adverb** + **verb** + **subject**:

Весно́й **прово́дится фестивáль**   A festival is held in the spring

(c) The object is known ['given' information]. The action or state is 'new'. The word order is **object** + **subject** + **verb** (+ **adverb**):

Маши́ну **они́ купи́ли вчерá**   They bought the car yesterday

(d) The object and subject are known ['given' information]. The verb is 'new'. The word order is **object** + **subject** + **verb**:

Дом мы уже́ **про́дали**   We have already sold the house

Word order in interrogative sentences

Either (a) the order is the same as in a statement, with a sharp rise in intonation on the stressed syllable:

Вы уве́рены в э́том?   Are you sure of that?

> ! **Note:** If the sentence begins with an interrogative pronoun or adverb, the interrogative word bears the stress and rising intonation. In such cases, the verb precedes or (less usually) follows a subject noun: Где нахо́дится като́к? *or* Где като́к нахо́дится? 'Where is the skating rink?' but always *follows* a subject pronoun: Что вы де́лаете? 'What are you doing?'

or (b) the 'operative' element (the word or phrase that constitutes the questioned item) appears in initial position, followed by ли:

Реа́лен ли полёт на Марс?   Is flight to Mars feasible?
Все ли номера́ заброни́рованы?   Are all the rooms booked?

or (c) the speech is reported (ли follows the operative word):

Я не по́мню, **завёл** ли он часы́   I don't remember if he wound the clock

Word order in the reporting of direct speech

Either (a) The subject + the speech verb + a colon precede the speech (which is in quotation marks):

Он сказа́л: <<Почему́ ты опозда́л?>>   He said, "Why are you late?"

or (b) The speech (which is in quotation marks + a comma + a dash) precedes the speech verb + subject:

<<Ещё ра́но>>, – отве́тил Ва́ня.   "It's early yet,"   answered Vanya

or (c) The speech is interrupted by the speech verb + subject:

<<Ты не по́мнишь, – спроси́ла Ма́ша, – как его́ зову́т?>>

"Do you remember," asked Masha, "what his name is?"

Word order and reading Russian

(a) Word order is one of the main barriers to comprehension in reading Russian. Faced with a difficult passage, it is important to identify the subject and then the verb. In most cases only one element can be the grammatical subject. Thus, in the following extract: На 32 языка́х говори́т с ми́ром радиоста́нция <<*Го́лос Росси́и*>> ... , only *радиоста́нция* 'radio station', as a nominative singular, is capable of being the subject, and говори́т 'speaks' the verb. The sentence translates: 'The radio station "The Voice of Russia" speaks to the world in 32 languages'.

(b) Similarly, in the following, only *америка́нцы* 'Americans', as a nominative plural, can be the subject, and составля́ют the verb: Бо́льшую часть Интерне́т-аудито́рии составля́ют америка́нцы 'Americans make up the greater part of the Internet audience'.

(c) If there is no nominative subject, the construction is impersonal. It should never be assumed that the first word in the sentence is the subject. Thus, in: Переда́чи из Москвы́ принима́ют в далёких стра́нах, переда́чи is the **object** of third-person plural impersonal принима́ют (it could not be its subject). The sentence translates: 'Broadcasts from Moscow are received [literally 'they receive broadcasts from Moscow'] in distant countries'.

(d) Another type of impersonal construction involves **мо́жно** 'one may', **ва́жно** 'it is important', **жаль** 'it is a pity', etc. In the following sentence there is no subject. The key to a correct translation lies in **мо́жно** and its dependent infinitive **знако́миться** 'to become acquainted': Но тепе́рь с информа́цией <<Го́лоса Росси́и>> мо́жно знако́миться в любо́е вре́мя су́ток 'But now one can become acquainted with the information broadcast by "Voice of Russia" at any time of the day or night.'

(e) Care should be taken with constructions in which grammatical information (e.g. the object accusative) appears between a participle and the noun it qualifies: Ра́дио до́лго ещё бу́дет ми́рно сосе́дствовать с **набира́ющим** *си́лу* **конкуре́нтом** 'For a long time yet radio will peacefully coexist with its competitor, which is gathering momentum [literally 'with its gathering momentum competitor']'.

Punctuation

I The comma

Commas are used in Russian:

(a) to **separate two or more adjectives** qualifying the same noun, **two or more adverbial modifiers**, **verbs**, **nouns**, etc.:

краси́вая, молода́я же́нщина   a beautiful young woman

Я иска́л его́ **в до́ме, в саду́, на у́лице**   I looked for him in the house, in the garden, in the street

Он заходи́л **у́тром, ве́чером, но́чью**   He would drop in in the morning, in the evening, at night

Мы **пе́ли, танцева́ли, игра́ли**   We sang, danced, played

(b) to mark off words **standing in apposition or parenthesis**:

Са́ша, мой оте́ц, встал   Sasha, my father, got up

Он, **коне́чно, прав**   He is, of course, right

(c) to mark off **participial and gerundial phrases**:

Ма́льчик, **чита́ющий кни́гу**, сдаёт за́втра экза́мен   The boy reading a book is taking an exam tomorrow

Она́ сиде́ла, **чита́я кни́гу**   She sat reading a book

(d) after **exclamations** and **forms of address**:

Да, я зна́ю/**Нет**, я не зна́ю   Yes, I know/No, I don't know

Здра́вствуйте, колле́ги!   Hello, colleagues!

Эй, кто там?   Hey, who's there?

(e) between clauses **linked by most conjunctions** (*see pages 214–221*):

Со́лнце све́тит, **но** хо́лодно   The sun is shining but it's cold

Доса́дно, **что** он опозда́л   It's a nuisance that he arrived late

(f) to mark off **relative clauses**:

Де́вочка, **кото́рая** сдала́ экза́мен, поступи́ла в университе́т

The girl who passed the exam has gone to university

(h) in **comparisons**:

Лу́чше по́здно, **чем** никогда́   Better late than never

The colon

The colon is used to introduce:

(a) **an enumeration**:

Нам нужны́ специали́сты: **бухга́лтеры, юри́сты, врачи́** We need specialists: accountants, lawyers, doctors

(b) **an explanation**:

Он не рабо́тает: **заболе́л** He's off work: he's fallen ill

(c) **direct speech or a quotation** (*see also page 229*):

Он сказа́л: <<**Я рад вас ви́деть**>> He said, "I'm glad to see you"

The semi-colon

The semi-colon is used to **separate a series of extensive clauses**:

Он исполня́л все обя́занности учи́теля: **вёл уро́ки хи́мии и фи́зики; проверя́л со́тни тетра́дей; помога́л отстаю́щим ученика́м** He carried out all the duties of a teacher: took chemistry and physics lessons; marked hundreds of exercise books; helped pupils who were falling behind

The dash

The dash is used

(a) in the meaning '**to be**', separating subject and predicate nouns:

Кремль – центр Москвы́ The centre of Moscow is the Kremlin

(b) to **replace a word that is 'understood'**:

Он лю́бит её, а она́ – его́ He loves her, and she loves him

(c) to render **direct speech** (*see also page 229*):

<<**Как ты постаре́л!**>>, – сказа́ла она́ "How you've aged!", she said

Glossary of grammatical terms

NB: Items in **bold** type refer the user to a separate entry in the glossary.

Accusative: In Russian, the **case** used to express the **direct object** of a **transitive verb**; also, the case used after certain prepositions.

Active: In an active **clause**, the **subject** of the verb performs the action, e.g. '*Sam* (subject) *identified* (verb) *the suspect*' (as opposed to the passive construction 'the suspect was identified by Sam', where *the suspect* is the subject but is not doing the identifying). Cf. **Passive**.

Adjectival noun: An adjective that functions as a noun, e.g. 'the *empties*' (= empty bottles), '*mobile*' (= mobile phone), 'the *Greens*' (= environmentalists), Russian *столóвая* 'dining room', *морóженое* 'ice cream'.

Adjective: A word that describes a **noun** or **pronoun**, giving information about its shape, colour, size, etc., e.g. *triangular, red, large, beautiful* in 'a *triangular* sign', 'the *red* dress', 'it is *large*', 'they are *beautiful*'.

Adverb: A word expressing the manner, frequency, time, place, or extent of an action, e.g. *slowly* and *often* in 'Sue walked *slowly*', 'He *often* stumbled'. Adverbs can also **modify** clauses, e.g. 'Sue *probably* went home', **adjectives**, e.g. 'Sue is *very* tall', and other adverbs, e.g. 'Sue left *extremely* early'.

Affirmative: An affirmative **sentence** or **clause** is a positive statement that explicitly asserts a state of affairs, e.g. *The taxi is waiting*. Cf. **Negative**.

Agree: Words are said to agree when they are put in the correct form in relation to another word. In Standard English and in Russian, a singular noun or pronoun has to have a singular verb, e.g. '*he goes*' (Russian *он идёт*), and a plural noun or pronoun has to have a plural verb, e.g. '*they go*' (Russian *они идýт*). **Demonstratives** also agree in **number** with the **nouns** they modify, e.g. '*this table*' (Russian *этот стол*), '*these tables*' (Russian *эти столы*). In Russian, adjectives, pronouns, and most declined numerals are in the same **case** as the noun they modify, and adjectives, nouns, and verbs have the same **gender** and **number**.

Animate accusative rule: A convention in Russian, whereby in some contexts the form of the accusative is identical with that of the genitive case. This applies **(a)** to masculine singular animate nouns: *Я вúжу мáльчика* 'I see the boy', **(b)** to all plural animate nouns: *Я вúжу мáльчиков/дéвочек/живóтных* 'I see the boys/girls/animals', **(c)** to pronouns, adjectives, and participles that agree with the nouns listed under (a) and (b): *Я знáю этих нóвых учителéй* 'I know these new teachers', and **(d)** to the numerals *одúн, два/две, три, четы́ре,* and to *óба/óбе* (also all the collective numerals, see p. 89): *Она пригласила трёх подруг* 'She invited three friends', *Он смотрел на обоих братьев* 'He was looking at both brothers'.

Animate noun: A noun denoting a living being, e.g. *captain*, *elephant* (Russian *капитан*, *слон*).

Antecedent: An earlier word, phrase, or clause to which another word (especially a following **relative pronoun**) refers back, e.g. 'The man (whom) I know' (Russian *Человек*, *которого я знаю*).

Article: see **Definite article**, **Indefinite article**.

Aspect: A grammatical category of the verb that expresses the nature of an action or process, viewing it either as continuous or habitual (imperfective aspect), or as completed (perfective aspect). Cf. **Submeanings of the aspects**.

Attributive adjective: An **adjective** placed in front of the noun it modifies, e.g. *empty* in 'the *empty* house' (Russian *пустой дом*). Cf. **Predicative adjective**.

Auxiliary verb: In English, a verb which functions together with another verb to form a particular **tense** of the other verb, or to form the **passive**, a question, a **negative**, or an **imperative**. In Russian, the future of the verb *быть* 'to be' combines, as an auxiliary verb, with the infinitive of imperfective verbs to form the future of those verbs, e.g. *Я буду работать* 'I will work', while the past and future tenses and the conditional mood of *быть* combine with the short forms of perfective passive participles to express past, future, and conditional meanings,

e.g. *он был назначен* 'he was appointed', *он будет назначен* 'he will be appointed', *он был бы назначен* 'he would be/would have been appointed'.

Case: In Russian, the form of a noun, pronoun, adjective, or numeral that shows its function within the **clause** (e.g. whether it is the **subject** or **object**). Russian has six cases (**nominative**, **accusative**, **genitive**, **dative**, **instrumental**, and **prepositional**).

Clause: A sentence, or part of a sentence, consisting of a **subject** and a **verb**, e.g. *Mike snores*, or a structure containing **participles** or **infinitives** (with no subject), e.g. 'While *waiting* for a bus, I fell asleep' or 'I asked her *to call a taxi*'.

Collective: A term applied to nouns that denote a group of beings or objects, e.g. *herd* (Russian *стадо*), *clientele* (Russian *клиентура*), *luggage* (Russian *багаж*). In Russian, there are also collective numerals (for the numbers from two to ten), which denote a group of individuals, e.g. *двое* ('two'), *трое* ('three'), *десятеро* ('ten'), or combine with **plural-only nouns**.

Comparative: The form of an **adjective** or **adverb** used when comparing one thing with another, to express a greater degree of a quality, e.g. *cheaper, more expensive, more accurately* in 'this book is *cheaper*', 'a *more expensive* holiday ', 'he described it *more accurately*'. Cf. **Superlative**.

Compound: A word or phrase created by putting two or more existing forms together. In English and Russian, compounds are sometimes written as one word, sometimes as two, and sometimes hyphenated, e.g. *motorway* (Russian *автострада*), *good-humoured* (Russian *добродушный*), *drawing board* (Russian *чертёжная доска*), *bow tie* (Russian *галстук-бабочка*).

Conditional: A verb form which expresses what *would* happen, or *would have* happened, if something else (had) occurred. English normally uses *if* with a form of the **auxiliary verb** *would* to express this notion: *If I won the lottery ... I would buy a car. / If I had won... I would have bought....* Russian uses the particle *бы*: *Я поехал бы, если бы было время* 'I *would* have gone if there had been time'.

Conjugate: To list the different forms or **inflections** of a verb as they vary according to tense, number, person, or voice, e.g. the verb 'to read' is conjugated in the present tense as follows: (I) *read*, (you) *read*, (he/she/it) *reads*, (we) *read*, (you) *read*, (they) *read*. Cf. the equivalent Russian conjugation of *читать*: (я) *читаю*, (ты) *читаешь*, (он/она/оно) *читает*, (мы) *читаем*, (вы) *читаете*, (они) *читают*.

Conjugation: In inflected languages, a class to which a verb is assigned according to how it is **conjugated**. In Russian, *читать* belongs to the first (or -е) conjugation and *говорить* belongs to the second (or -и/-я) conjugation.

Conjunction: A word whose function is to join single words, **clauses**, or **phrases**. Co-ordinating conjunctions (notably *and* and *or*) join words, clauses, or phrases, e.g. 'John *and* Mary', 'I'll go to the cinema *or* meet my friend for dinner'. Subordinating

conjunctions (e.g. *that, because, while*) join clauses, e.g. 'I think *that* he is wrong', 'They left *because* it was late', 'I'll push *while* you lift'. Correlative conjunctions consist of words corresponding to each other and regularly used together, e.g. *both ... and, either ... or.*

Consonant: A speech sound that is produced with some restriction on the flow of air, e.g. *b, ch, r*. It can be combined with a **vowel** to form a **syllable**.

Consonant mutation: The change in a consonant when it occurs adjacent to another sound.

Continuous: A verb form indicating that an action or process is ongoing, e.g. 'He *is waiting*', 'She *was laughing*'. Also known as *progressive*.

Dative: In Russian, the **case** used to express the **indirect object** of a **verb**; also, the case used after certain prepositions and certain verbs.

Declension: In inflected languages, the class to which a noun is assigned according to how it is **declined**. Russian has three declensions. The first affects masculine nouns (except for those ending in *-a* or *-я*) and neuter nouns, the second feminine nouns (except for those ending in a soft sign), and the third feminine soft-sign nouns.

Decline: To list the different forms or **inflections** of a noun, adjective, pronoun, or numeral as they vary according to **case**. In English, only pronouns can really be said to decline, e.g. *he, him*.

Definite article: In English, the word *the*, which introduces a noun phrase and implies that the thing mentioned has already been mentioned or is common knowledge, e.g. 'the book on the table'. Russian has no definite article, but achieves the same effect through word order (with the thing which has already been mentioned in first position in the sentence, e.g. *Кни́га* на столе́ 'The book is on the table'), or by using words such as *э́тот* 'this'. Cf. **Indefinite article**.

Delimitation: A process by which the meaning of an adjective is limited to a particular sphere, e.g. Страна́ бога́та *ле́сом* 'The country is rich in forest'.

Demonstrative: A word indicating the person or thing referred to, e.g. *this*, *that*, *these*, *those* in 'this book' (Russian *э́та* кни́га), 'that house' (Russian *тот* дом), 'these books' (Russian *э́ти* кни́ги), 'those people' (Russian *те* лю́ди).

Direct object: A word or phrase **governed** by a verb, e.g. *dogs* in 'She loves *dogs*' (Russian Она́ лю́бит *соба́к*). In an **active** sentence, the person or thing affected by the action is the direct object. In Russian, the direct object is usually expressed by the accusative case. Cf. **Indirect object**.

Direct speech: In direct speech, the speaker's words or thoughts are presented unchanged, using quotation marks, e.g. '"*The shops are still open*," said Jill'. Russian uses « » or a dash to show direct speech. Cf. **Indirect speech**.

Emphatic pronoun: The pronouns *myself*, *himself*, *themselves*, etc., used for emphasis or to personalize,

e.g. 'I did it *myself*'. Russian uses *сам*: Я *сам* сде́лал э́то.

Ending: A letter or letters added to the stem of a word when it is declined or conjugated, e.g. (in English) dog*s*, laugh*ed*, (in Russian) вод*а́* 'water', на стол*е́* 'on the table', зелёны*ми* (instrumental plural) 'green', пиш*у́* 'I write', писа́*ла* 'she was writing').

Feminine: see **Gender**.

Finite: A verb form which has a specific **tense**, **number**, and **person**, e.g. *rings* in 'She *rings* the doctor' (Russian Она́ *звони́т* врачу́). Here, *rings/звони́т* is the third-person singular present tense of the verb *to ring/звони́ть*. A **clause** with a finite verb is called a finite clause. Cf. **Non-finite**.

Fleeting vowel: A vowel (*e*, *ё*, or *o*) that appears in some forms of a Russian word, but not in others, e.g. *e* in *бо́лен* (masculine short form of *больно́й* 'sick'), *ё* in *сестёр* (genitive plural of *сестра́* 'sister'), *o* in *сон* 'sleep' (genitive singular *сна*), *разобью́* (first-person singular of *разби́ть* 'to smash').

Future: The future **tense** is used when the time of the event described has not yet happened. English uses the auxiliary verbs *shall* and *will*, the present continuous, and *going to*, to express this notion: '*I shall meet* you in the restaurant', '*They will be* pleased', '*We're leaving* at six', '*I'm going to buy* a new car'. To express **imperfective** future meaning, Russian uses the future tense of *быть* + imperfective infinitive, e.g. Я *бу́ду рабо́тать*, 'I *shall work*' or 'I *shall be working*'. To express **perfective** future meaning, Russian uses conjugated forms of the perfective verb, e.g. Я спрошу 'I *shall ask*'. Cf. **Aspect**.

Gender: In some languages, nouns and pronouns are divided into grammatical classes called genders. The gender of a noun or pronoun can affect the form of words such as verbs or adjectives that accompany them and may need to **agree** with them in gender. Russian has three genders, **masculine**, **feminine**, and **neuter**. The gender of a Russian noun can usually be identified from its ending: nouns ending in a consonant or *-й* are masculine (e.g. *стул* 'chair', *край* 'edge'); most nouns ending in *-а* or *-я* are feminine (e.g. *яма* 'hole', *шея* 'neck'), and nouns ending in *-о* or *-е* are neuter (e.g. *окно* 'window', *море* 'sea'). Gender in Russian applies in the singular only. Plural nouns and pronouns do not exhibit gender.

Genitive: In Russian, the **case** used to express possession; also, the case used after most cardinal numerals and after **indefinite numerals**, certain prepositions, and certain verbs.

Gerund: In English, a verb form in *-ing* that functions like a noun, e.g. *running* in 'She loves *running*' (cf. the Russian use of the **infinitive** in this meaning: Она любит *бегать*). By contrast, the Russian gerund is a verbal adverb that replaces a clause. The imperfective gerund usually ends in *-я* (e.g. Он стоит, *куря* 'He stands, *smoking*'), the perfective in *-в* (e.g. *Поужинав*, он встал 'Having dined, he got up').

Govern: A word requiring a noun or pronoun to be in a particular **case** is said to govern the noun or pronoun (e.g. the Russian verb *владеть* 'to

own' governs the instrumental case, and the preposition *через* 'across' governs the accusative case).

Hard consonant: A consonant that appears at the end of a word (e.g. final *-т* in *нет* 'no'), or is followed by *а, ы, о, у*, or (rarely) *э* (e.g. *г* and *т* in *газета* 'newspaper', *н* in *чёрный* 'black', *л* and *в* in *слово* 'word', *д* and *м* in *дума* 'duma'). Exceptions are the consonants ч and щ which are always soft even if at the end of a word or followed by the above-listed vowels, and ж, ц, and ш which are always hard. Cf. **Soft consonant**.

Historic present: Use of the present tense in order to make the description of a past event more vivid, e.g. 'Suddenly he *breaks* into a run'.

Imperative: The form of the verb used to express a command, e.g. *come* in '*Come* here!'

Imperfective: see **Aspect**.

Impersonal construction: A construction in which an action or state does not involve a specific person or thing as the grammatical subject, e.g. *Стемнело* 'It grew dark', *Как тебя зовут?* 'What is your name?'

Inanimate noun: A noun denoting a non-living thing, e.g. *hall, happiness* (Russian *зал, счастье*).

Indeclinable: A term applied to a noun, pronoun, or adjective that has no **inflections**. In English, the pronoun *you* is indeclinable (whereas *I, he, she*, and *they* change to *me, him, her*, and *them* in the object case, e.g. the dog bit *me/you/him/her/them*). In Russian, many **loanwords** are indeclinable (e.g. *такси* 'taxi', *беж* 'beige'), as are the possessive pronouns *его*, 'his/its', *её* 'her(s)/its', *их* 'their(s)'.

Indefinite adverb: An adverb that does not refer to any place, time, manner, etc. in particular, e.g. *somewhere*, *sometime*, *somehow* (Russian *где-то*, *когда-то*, *как-то*).

Indefinite article: In English, the word *a/an*, which introduces a noun phrase and implies that the thing mentioned is non-specific, e.g. 'she bought *a* book'. Russian has no indefinite article, but achieves the same effect through word order (with an object mentioned for the first time appearing at the end of the sentence, e.g. На столе лежит *карта* '*A* map is lying on the table'). Cf. **Definite article**.

Indefinite numeral: In Russian, a numeral that denotes an indefinite quantity, e.g. *много* 'much, many', *несколько* 'several'.

Indefinite pronoun: A pronoun that does not refer to any person or thing in particular, e.g. *someone* (Russian *кто-то*), *something* (Russian *что-то*), *anyone* (Russian *кто-нибудь*), *anything* (Russian *что-нибудь*).

Indicative: The form of a verb used to express a simple statement of fact, when an event is considered to be definitely taking place or to have taken place, e.g. 'He *is asleep*' (Russian Он *спит*), 'He *fell asleep*' (Russian Он *заснул*). Cf. **Subjunctive**.

Indirect object: A word or phrase referring to the person who receives the **direct object**, e.g. *the driver* in the sentences 'She gave the ticket to *the driver*' or 'She gave *the driver* the ticket'. In Russian, the indirect object is usually expressed by the dative case, e.g. Она подарила часы *сыну* 'She gave the watch *to her son*'. Cf. **Direct object**.

Indirect speech: In indirect speech, the speaker's words or thoughts are reported in a subordinate clause using a reporting verb. In English a change of tense and person is needed, e.g. 'He said "*I want* a drink"' (direct speech) becomes 'He said *he wanted* a drink'. In Russian, only the person changes, not the tense, e.g. Он сказал: «*Я голоден*» 'He said "I'm hungry"' becomes Он сказал, что *он голоден* 'He said that *he was* hungry'.

Infinitive: The basic form of the verb, e.g. *laugh, damage, be*. It is not bound to a particular subject or tense and in English is often preceded by *to* or by another verb, e.g. 'I want *to see* her', 'She came *to see* me', 'Let me *see*'. Russian infinitives end in *-ть*, *-ти*, or *-чь* (e.g. *писать* 'to write', *вести* 'to lead', *мочь* 'to be able').

Inflection: A change in the form of a word (usually the ending), to express tense, gender, number, or case, etc., e.g. the English plural ending *-s* in 'cars' or the past tense inflection *-ed* in 'I visit*ed* my uncle'. Russian is a highly-inflected language in which nouns, pronouns, adjectives, and numerals decline, and verbs conjugate. Cf. **Case, Conjugate, Conjugation, Declension**, and **Decline**.

Instrumental: In Russian, the **case** used to express the means by which something is done; also, the case used after certain prepositions and certain verbs.

Interrogative adverb: An adverb used to ask questions, e.g. *how* in 'How are you?' (Russian *Как* вы поживáете?) or *when* in 'When will they arrive?' (Russian *Когдá* они приéдут?).

Interrogative pronoun: A pronoun used to ask questions, e.g. *which* in 'Which do you want?' (Russian *Какóй* вы хотúте?).

Intonation: The use of the pitch of the voice to convey meaning, e.g. *Well? Did you ask her?* (rising intonation) and *Well! I've never been so insulted!* (falling intonation). Different languages have different intonation patterns.

Intransitive verb: A verb not taking a **direct object**, e.g. *slept* in 'He *slept* soundly' (Russian Он крéпко *спал*), and *read* in 'He can't *read*' (Russian Он не умéет *читáть*). Cf. **Transitive verb**.

Invariable: another term for **indeclinable** (when referring to nouns, adjectives, and pronouns). Adverbs and gerunds are also invariable in Russian.

Irregular verb: In English, a verb such as *sing* whose **inflections** do not follow one of the usual **conjugation** patterns of the language (past *sang* by contrast with the usual past tense suffix -ed, e.g. *walked*). In Russian, the only truly irregular verbs are *бежáть* 'to run', *дать* 'to give', *есть* 'to eat', and *хотéть* 'to want'. Cf. **Regular verb**.

Loanword: A word borrowed from another language, e.g. Russian *кóфе* 'coffee'.

Locative case: A term used as an alternative to the prepositional case

to describe prepositional phrases that denote location and are introduced by *в* 'in' or *на* 'on': *в дóме* 'in the house', *на столé* 'on the table'. Some nouns have special locative forms in stressed *у*, *ю*, or *и*: *в лесý* 'in the forest', *на краю́* 'on the edge', *на дверú* 'on the door'.

Main clause: In a **sentence** with more than one **clause**, the clause which is not **subordinate** to any of the others is known as the main clause, e.g. *Peter stopped* in 'When it got too dark to see where he was going, *Peter stopped*'. A main clause can stand alone as a sentence. Cf. **Subordinate clause**.

Masculine: see **Gender**.

Mobile stress: A feature of some Russian words whereby the stressed syllable changes in one or more forms of the word's declension or conjugation etc. Stress may move from the stem onto the ending, e.g. *стол* 'table', genitive singular *столá*; *слóво* 'word', nominative plural *словá*; *печь* 'stove', locative singular *печú*; masculine short form *дóрог* 'is dear', feminine *дорогá*; *пять* 'five', genitive *пятú*. It may also move from the ending onto the stem, e.g. *рекá* 'river', accusative singular *рéку*; *окнó* 'window', nominative plural *óкна*. In conjugation, stress shift occurs only from the ending onto the stem, e.g. *пишý* 'I write', *пúшет* 'he writes'.

Modify: A word or phrase modifies another word or phrase when it provides additional information about it. Modifying expressions include **adjectives**, e.g. *slow* in 'A slow train', and **adverbs**, e.g. *slowly* in 'The train moved *slowly*'.

Negative: A negative **sentence** or **clause** asserts that something is not the case, using a negative **particle**, e.g. 'The taxi is *not* waiting'. Similarly, a negative **adverb** (*nowhere, never*) or negative **pronoun** (*nobody, nothing*). Cf. **Affirmative**.

Neuter: see **Gender**.

Nominative: In Russian, the **case** used to express the **subject** of a clause.

Non-finite: A term applied to a verb form which has no specific **tense**, **number**, or **person**, e.g. *waiting* in 'While *waiting* for a bus, Peter read the paper'. Russian uses a **gerund** in such contexts, e.g. *Ожидая* автобуса, Пи́тер чита́л газе́ту. Cf. **Finite**.

Noun: A word that identifies a person, e.g. *milkman, girl, uncle*, a physical object, e.g. *cup, book, building*, or an abstract notion, e.g. *beauty, health, unpleasantness*.

Noun phrase: A group of words including a noun, which functions in a sentence as subject, object, or prepositional object.

Number: A grammatical classification whereby a word is either **singular** or **plural**.

Numeral: A word expressing a number. Members of the series of numbers *one, two*, etc. are referred to as cardinal numbers or cardinal numerals. Members of the series *first, second*, etc. are referred to as ordinal numbers or ordinal numerals. Russian also has a series of collective numerals, e.g. *двóе* in *двóе* дете́й 'two children', *трóе* in *трóе* са́нок 'three sledges'.

Object: see **Direct object**, **Indirect object**.

Oblique cases: All **cases** other than the **nominative**.

Participle: In English, a word formed from a verb and used as an adjective or as a noun, or to form compound verb forms. The English present participle ends in *-ing*, e.g. '*Thinking* I was late, I hurried'(Russian uses a **gerund** in such contexts: *Ду́мая*, что я опа́здываю, я торопи́лся), and the past participle ends in *-ed*, e.g. 'I have *finished*' (Russian uses a **finite verb** in such contexts: Я ко́нчил). Russian has four participles, present active, past active, present passive, and past passive, which either replace **relative clauses**, e.g. Дéвочка, *читáющая/читáвшая/ прочитáвшая* кни́гу 'the girl *who is reading/who was reading/who has read* the book', мото́р, *прове́ренный* меха́никами 'an engine *which has been checked* by the mechanics', or (using the short form of the past passive participle) function as **predicates**, e.g. Дом *про́дан* 'The house *has been sold*'.

Particle: In Russian, a word or a part of a word that invests other words or phrases with expressive nuances of meaning, e.g. *Не* я оши́бся! 'I'm *not* the one who got it wrong!', *Ну*, проголода́лся же я! 'Am I hungry!'

Partitive genitive: The genitive case used to denote a part, as opposed to the whole, of a substance, e.g. мно́го *молока́* 'a lot of milk', кусо́к *мя́са* 'a piece of meat'. Some nouns have special partitive genitive forms in *-у* or *-ю*: таре́лка су́пу 'a plate of soup', Хо́чешь ча́ю? 'Would you like some tea?'

Part of speech: Any of the classes into which words are categorized for grammatical purposes. The main ones are **Noun**, **Adjective**, **Pronoun**, **Verb**, **Adverb**, **Preposition**, and **Conjunction**.

Passive: The form of the **clause** used when the individual referred to by the **subject** undergoes (rather than performs) the action, e.g. '*The soldier was nominated* for an award' (Russian *Солдáт был предстáвлен к нагрáде*). Cf. **Active**.

Past: The past **tense** is used when the time of the event described precedes the time of utterance, e.g. 'Peter *lived* in London'. Cf. **Present**.

Perfect: A verb form indicating an action or process seen as completed, e.g. 'She *has paid* the bill'. In Russian this is rendered by a perfective past form of the verb, e.g. *Онá оплатúла счёт*.

Perfective: see **Aspect**.

Person: Person forms are the grammatical forms (especially **pronouns**) that refer to or agree with the speaker and other individuals addressed or mentioned, e.g. *I, we* (first-person pronouns, Russian *я, мы*), *you* (second-person pronoun, Russian *ты, вы*), *he, she, it, they* (third-person pronouns, Russian *он, онá, онú*).

Personal pronoun: A **pronoun** that refers to a person or to people known to the speaker, e.g. *I, he, she, it, they* (Russian *я, он, онá, онó, онú*).

Phrase: A group of words that function together in a **clause**, e.g. *The courier* is a (noun) phrase within the clause '*The courier* will go there'.

Plural: A word or form referring to more than one person or object, e.g. *children, books, we, are*. Cf. **Singular**.

Plural-only noun: A noun that has the form of a plural but can refer to a singular object or a number of like objects, e.g. *сáнки* 'sledge, sledges'.

Possessive: A pronoun indicating possession, e.g. Russian *мой* 'my, mine', *твой* 'your, yours', *егó* 'his, its', *её* 'her, hers, its', *наш* 'our, ours', *ваш* 'your, yours', *их* 'their, theirs'. Possessives are used both adjectivally (e.g. *наш дом* 'our house') and pronominally (e.g. *Этот дом – наш* 'This house is ours').

Predicate: The part of a clause that states something about the **subject**, e.g. *closed the door softly* in 'Mary *closed the door softly*', or *went home* in 'We *went home*'. Cf. **Subject**.

Predicative adjective: An **adjective** that appears in a separate **phrase** from the noun it modifies, often following the verb 'to be', e.g. *empty* in 'The house was *empty*'. Russian often uses a short-form adjective in such contexts: Дом был *пуст*. Cf. **Attributive adjective**.

Predicative adverb: In Russian, an adverb that is used as a predicate, e.g. *Вéсело* 'It's fun', Емý *грýстно* 'He feels sad'.

Prefix: An element that is added to the beginning of a word to change its meaning or grammatical form, e.g. *mis-* and *re-* in '*mis*understand', '*re*consider', Russian *при-* in *при*бáвить 'to add' and *от-* in *от*платúть 'to pay back'. Cf. **Suffix**.

Preposition: A word governing and usually preceding a noun or pronoun, expressing its relationship to another word in the sentence e.g. 'She arrived *after* dinner', 'What did you do it *for*?'. This relationship can be spatial, e.g. 'The book is *on* the table' (Russian Кни́га *на* столе́), temporal, e.g. 'He arrived *in* March' (Russian Он прие́хал *в* ма́рте), causal, e.g. 'She blushed *with* shame' (Russian Она́ покрасне́ла *от* стыда́), etc. A Russian preposition governs one of the **oblique cases**.

Prepositional: In Russian, the **case** used after certain prepositions, mainly to express location.

Present: The present **tense** is used when the time of the event described includes the time of utterance, e.g. *lives* in 'Peter *lives* in London'. Cf. **Past**.

Progressive: another term for **Continuous**.

Pronoun: A word that substitutes for a noun or noun phrase, e.g. *them* in 'Children don't like *them*' (instead of 'Children don't like *vegetables*'). Cf. Russian Де́ти не лю́бят *их* (instead of *овоще́й*).

Reflexive pronoun: A pronoun that is the object of the verb, but refers back to the subject of the clause in denoting the same individual, e.g. *herself* in: 'She blamed *herself*'. Russian uses the declinable reflexive pronoun *себя́* in such contexts, e.g. Он смо́трит на *себя́* 'He looks at *himself*', Он купи́л *себе́* мотоци́кл, 'He bought *himself* a motorcycle', Она́ дово́льна *собо́й* 'She is pleased with *herself*'. Cf. also **Reflexive verb**.

Reflexive verb: In Russian, a verb that ends in the reflexive ending -ся/-сь, e.g. Он одева́ется 'He dresses (*himself*)', Я мо́юсь 'I wash (*myself*)'.

Regular verb: A verb such as *laugh* whose **inflections** follow one of the usual **conjugation** patterns. In English, this involves (among other things) forming the **past tense** by adding -*ed* to the infinitive, e.g. laugh*ed* in 'They *laughed* at me'. Cf. **Irregular verb**.

Relative clause: A clause that is introduced by a **relative pronoun**.

Relative pronoun: A pronoun (*who, whose, which,* or *that*) used to introduce a subordinate clause and referring back to a person or thing in the preceding clause, e.g. 'Peter lost the book *that/which* he bought', 'The man *who* is waiting is my brother', or 'Have you met the man *whose* sister got married?' Russian uses the relevant forms of *кото́рый*.

Reported speech: another term for **Indirect speech**.

Sentence: A structure with at least one **finite** verb, and consisting of one or more **clauses**, e.g. 'John laughed', 'John sat down and waited', 'While waiting for the bus, John saw an accident'.

Singular: A word or form referring to just one person or thing, e.g. *child, book, I, is*. Cf. **Plural**.

Soft consonant: In Russian, a consonant followed by a soft sign (e.g. *m* in *мать*), or by the vowels *я, е, и, ё,* or *ю* (e.g. *n* in *пять, н* in *не́бо, n* in *пи́во, л* in *лёд, m* in *утю́г*). The consonants *ч* and *щ* are always pronounced soft, while *ж, ц,* and *ш* are always pronounced hard. Cf. **Hard consonant**.

Spelling rules: In Russian, the following rules:

(a) *ы* is replaced by *и* after г, к, х, ж, ч, ш, and щ.

(b) unstressed *о* is replaced by *е* after ж, ч, ш, щ, and ц.

(c) *ю* and *я* are replaced by *у* and *а* after г, к, х, ж, ч, ш, and щ.

(d) the preposition *о* 'about, concerning' is spelt *об* before words beginning *а*, *э*, *и*, *о*, and *у*, and *обо* before *мне* and *всём/всех*: *обо мне* 'about me', *обо всём* 'about everything', *обо всех* 'about everyone'.

Stem: The base form or root of the word to which **endings**, **prefixes**, and **suffixes** may be added, e.g. *box* in *boxes*, *consider* in 'reconsider' and *understand* in 'understanding'. Cf. Russian книг- in книга 'book', говор- in говори́ть 'to speak', and -ход in восхо́д 'rising', студе́нт- in студе́нтка 'female student'.

Stress: The **syllable** of a word receiving relatively greater force or emphasis than the other(s) is said to receive stress or to be the stressed syllable, e.g. *wíndow*, *ка́рта* 'map', (stressed on the first syllable), *dedúction*, *доро́га* 'road' (stressed medially), *suppóse*, *страна́* 'country'(stressed on the final syllable).

Subject: The part of the **clause** referring to the individual of whom or the object of which the **predicate** is asserted, e.g. *Anna* in: 'Anna closed the door' or *The picture* in 'The picture hangs on the wall'. In Russian, the subject usually appears in the nominative case, e.g. *А́нна*

закры́ла дверь, *Карти́на* виси́т на стене́. Cf. **Predicate**.

Subjunctive: The form of the verb used in some languages when no claim is being made that the action or event actually takes (or took) place. The subjunctive is not often used in English, but can still be seen in expressions like *if I were you*. In Russian, the subjunctive is the structure used when an action is desired. It is formed using *что́бы* + past tense, e.g. Она́ хо́чет, *что́бы я уше́л* ('She wants me *to go away*'). Cf. **Indicative**.

Subordinate clause: A clause that cannot normally stand alone without a **main clause** and is usually introduced by a **conjunction**, e.g. *when it rang* in 'She answered the phone *when it rang*', or *because he is ill* in 'He is not at work *because he is ill*'. Cf. **Main clause**.

Submeanings of the aspects: Aspectual meanings other than those that denote continuous or habitual action or process (imperfective), and those that denote completion (perfective). Submeanings describe intermittent action or process (imperfective *поба́ливает* 'hurts on and off'), inception (perfective *запла́кать* 'to burst into tears'), and short duration (perfective *поспа́ть* 'to have a nap'). Cf. **Aspect**.

Suffix: An element that is added to the end of a word or **stem** to change its meaning or grammatical form, e.g. *-ing* and *-ness* in 'understand*ing*', 'kind*ness*', Russian *-ка* in студе́нт*ка* 'female student', *-ина* in глуби*на́* 'depth'. Cf. **Prefix**.

Superlative: The form of an **adjective** or **adverb** used when comparing one thing with another to express the greatest degree of a quality, e.g. *cheapest* (Russian *са́мый деше́вый*), *most beautiful* (Russian *са́мый краси́вый*), *least desirable* (Russian *наиме́нее жела́тельный*). Cf. **Comparative**.

Syllable: A unit of pronunciation that is normally less than a word but greater than a single sound, e.g. *abracadabra* has five syllables: *a-bra-ca-da-bra*, as does Russian *путеводи́тель* ('guide'): *пу-те-во-ди́-тель*.

Tense: The relationship between the time of utterance and the time of an event described in the clause is expressed by verb tense forms or **inflections**, e.g. 'Anna *waits*' (present tense, Russian *А́нна ждёт*), Anna *waited*' (past tense, Russian *А́нна ждала́*).

Transitive verb: A verb taking a **direct object**, e.g. *read* in 'She *was reading* a book' (Russian *Она́ чита́ла кни́гу*). Cf. **Intransitive verb**.

Verb: A word that expresses an action, process, or state of affairs, e.g. 'He *closed* the door' (Russian *Он закры́л дверь*), 'She *laughs*' (Russian *Она́ смеётся*), 'They *were* at home' (Russian *Они́ бы́ли до́ма*).

Verbal noun: In Russian, a noun derived from a verb stem and describing the action of the verb from which it derives, e.g. *разви́тие* 'development', *приготовле́ние* 'preparation', *обрабо́тка* 'processing'.

Verbs of motion: In Russian, a series of fourteen pairs of imperfective verbs that denote various types of motion, one in each pair (the 'unidirectional') describing movement in one direction (*Он идёт домо́й* 'He is on his way home'), the other (the 'multidirectional') describing movement in general (*Она́ хо́дит бы́стро* 'She walks fast'), movement in various directions (*Он хо́дит взад и вперёд* 'He is walking up and down'), or habitual movement (*Я ча́сто хожу́ в кино́* 'I often go to the cinema').

Voiced and voiceless consonants: Consonants pronounced, respectively, with and without vibration of the vocal cords. In Russian, the voiceless consonants are к, п, с, т, ф, х, ц, ч, ш, and щ. The other consonants are voiced.

Vocative: In Russian, the form of a noun used in addressing someone. The nominative case usually fulfils this function: *Серге́й Па́влович!* 'Sergei Pavlovich!', but some truncated forms are used in colloquial Russian, e.g. *мам!* 'Mum!', *Вань!* 'Vanya!' *Бо́же* in *Бо́же мой!* 'My God!' is a relic of the former vocative case (the nominative form being *Бог*).

Vowel: A basic speech sound that is produced by the unrestricted flow of air, e.g. *a* in h*a*t, *ee* in f*ee*t, or *ow* in h*ow*. A vowel forms the nucleus of a **syllable**. Cf. **Consonant**.

Index of subjects

Index of Russian words

Note: The word index lists items of particular grammatical significance: prepositions, adverbs of time, indefinite pronouns and adverbs, conjunctions, verbs of motion, verbs that illustrate particular patterns of conjugation, nouns with irregular plurals, numerals, and others. The index is designed to interact with the subject index in affording easy access to all parts of the grammar.

The Russian alphabet

Capital letters	Lower-case letters	Letter names
А	а	а
Б	б	бэ
В	в	вэ
Г	г	гэ
Д	д	дэ
Е	е	е
Ё	ё	ё
Ж	ж	жэ
З	з	зэ
И	и	и
Й	й	и кра́ткое
К	к	ка
Л	л	эль
М	м	эм
Н	н	эн
О	о	о
П	п	пэ
Р	р	эр
С	с	эс
Т	т	тэ
У	у	у
Ф	ф	эф
Х	х	ха
Ц	ц	цэ
Ч	ч	че
Ш	ш	ша
Щ	щ	ща
Ъ	ъ	твёрдый знак
Ы	ы	ы
Ь	ь	мя́гкий знак
Э	э	э
Ю	ю	ю
Я	я	я